Note for Librarians: a cataloguing record for this book that includes Dewey Decimal
Classification and US Library of Congress numbers is available from the Library and
Archives of Canada. The complete cataloguing record can be obtained from their online
database at:
www.collectionscanada.ca/amicus/index-e.html
ISBN 1-4120-4332-8
Printed in Victoria, BC, Canada

# TRAFFORD

*Offices in Canada, USA, Ireland, UK and Spain*
This book was published *on-demand* in cooperation with Trafford Publishing. On-demand
publishing is a unique process and service of making a book available for retail sale to the
public taking advantage of on-demand manufacturing and Internet marketing. On-demand
publishing includes promotions, retail sales, manufacturing, order fulfilment, accounting and
collecting royalties on behalf of the author.
**Book sales for North America and international:**
Trafford Publishing, 6E–2333 Government St.,
Victoria, BC V8T 4P4 CANADA
phone 250 383 6864 (toll-free 1 888 232 4444)
fax 250 383 6804; email to orders@trafford.com
**Book sales in Europe:**
Trafford Publishing (UK) Ltd., Enterprise House, Wistaston Road Business Centre,
Wistaston Road, Crewe, Cheshire CW2 7RP UNITED KINGDOM
phone 01270 251 396 (local rate 0845 230 9601)
facsimile 01270 254 983; orders.uk@trafford.com
**Order online at:**
www.trafford.com/robots/04-2139.html

10 9 8 7 6 5 4 3 2 1

If you read as much as the cover, you already know this book is about the stock market and trading. However, the operative word of this book's content is Plan. Let me tell you why.

Years of mentoring traders of different levels of experience, from the beginners to those with several years under their belt, showed me a huge gap in trading education. This gap is an absence of a clear plan. Traders make money when they know what they are doing. Traders fail when they shoot darts. The problem is many think they know what they are doing, when in reality they have merely learnt odd pieces. Those pieces never click together because they are not integrated into a master plan. In a strange way many successful traders admit that they started with no such plan and realized its necessity much later – after suffering plenty of unnecessary grief and losses. Painful to admit and I am no exception.

Had we all started with a master idea of what we are going to do, the rate of survival would be much higher in the markets. And survival of the learning curve is a necessary condition for moving to prosperity.

Can you make a living and prosper trading the markets? Of course, you can – many did and continue doing it, why not you? However, if you are looking for a sure-fire "get-rich-quick" scheme – close this book and put it back on the shelf. If you want to know how I, after many years of my own trading and consulting hundreds of other traders, would have started now – then this book is for you. If you want to know how to plan your action and act according to your plan - this book is for you. If you want to maximize your chances to become a winner in the greatest game ever invented, avoid the mistakes made by legions – this book is for you.

Still interested? Turn the page.

# Contents

# Acknowledgements

I wish to thank my two closest team members, Vic Jung and Nestor Suarez. They together, with the Reality Trader room members, make each day seriously fun and never seem like a day at the office.

Special thanks are extended as well to my trading peers, namely Alan Farley, Bo Yoder, Stephen Sherwood, Chris Schumacher, Chuck Collins and Daryl Guppy, who shared their reminiscences of their early trading days and details of their trading plans. Thanks to Jeff Tappan whose systematic approach to planning helps me outline the vision of Reality Trader as a leader in trading education field and define the necessary steps to make it reality.

To those new traders I have spoken to who are just commencing their journey in the trading world, thank you for your truthful insights into why and how you have started trading as your new career. Discussions of the challenges you face helped me reinforce the best approach to trading education.

The community of traders that I work with continues to inspire me and I, too, learn from the market every day. Thank you for creating a welcome home at Reality Trader.

To Steve Demarest and the MBTrading team, thank you for continuing to work to create the best trading tools in the industry.

To Dan Mirkin and the entire team that worked to create IntelliScan, the best scanning software out there, thank you for your dedication and hard work.

And finally, my thanks to my family who encouraged me when I started trading and continues to do so today.

# Preface

This book provides help to potential traders, guiding them through the stages of setting up trading as a business in a comprehensive way.

During the past decade, the number of people interested in trading financial markets increased dramatically. Technology improvements opened access to active trading for the public, and interest across North America and throughout the world exploded. The hot market of 1998 to early 2000 fuelled this interest. Trading presented, for many, a sparkling dream of life without pressure of an office environment, without reporting to a boss and without a rigid schedule. Unfortunately, for too many this dream turned out to be just that. The failure rate in trading turned out to be enormous. Seemingly easy, it hid many traps and presented many dangers that destroyed the hopes and dreams of most beginning traders. Granted, trading like any other self-governed endeavor is not suitable for all. Yet, this rate of failure seems unnecessarily high.

My own experience, coupled with the experience of hundreds of traders I taught over the years, led me to realize that education in this field lacked one hugely important aspect that was common in practically all other fields of activity. It lacked STRUCTURE and let me illustrate what I mean by this.

Here is what my own road has been like and I will just outline it briefly here (the entire story is described in detail in my first book *Techniques of Tape Reading*, McGraw Hill, 2003.)

I started learning trading by reading a couple of books, picked from the sea of material available then. I did my first trade having read half way through the first book. I went into some websites and listened to some traders. Were those books I started with the right ones? Was the material on those websites thorough and logical? Did those traders I talked to, know what they were doing? How would I know all that?

I had no standard to measure against. My limited knowledge would not allow me to understand even what I was looking for. I simply plunged into this profession having no slightest idea how to proceed. Several hard losses forced me to adapt and read more, starting to trade more carefully and applying tight risk control. It took two years to turn my trading around, and at the end of second year, I was at the brink of failure, with just 25% of my original account left.

Was my way unique, uncharacteristic for the trading profession? By no means. Time-and-time again I see the same experience with other traders. They come into trading, they pick up tidbits of information, and they start trading. Reality hits fast enough. Realizing that their knowledge is not enough they start looking for the right path through education. Do they find any real structure, any idea where to start, and then how to proceed? Generally no.

One would think that after 10 years since a broad interest in active trading appeared, that such a structure had to be in place. Yet, go to any trading forum and ask the question "How do I begin?" I hear this question asked frequently and invariably the answer is "start watching the markets, start paper trading, trade small shares, read these two books, observe patterns, collect experience and lose until you learn how to stop losing." You will hear numerous accounts of traders succeeding only after an initial failure and often after multiple failures. These trader's accounts are cited as proof that this is the only way to learn. What is wrong with this picture? Let us see.

# Before We Start

## Trading Education

### Practice vs. Theory

Can you imagine similar advice given to someone starting to learn how to fly planes? Just crash some and if you survive you will learn how to do it. Do you want to become a surgeon? Start performing surgeries and learn from your experience. An engineer, build a bridge or two, see if they hold. With each bridge breaking, you will get more experience and your next one will be even better. Does this seem ridiculous to you? However, this is exactly what happens in trading.

How is it even possible that trading is so vastly different from other professions approach to learning? The answer is simple. In all the examples above you would put other people at risk by learning through experience. Thus, your learning must be structured in such a way that you are allowed to learn while minimizing risk to others. Not so in trading. Nobody but you and your family gets hurt when you fail. You do not kill your passengers as with a pilot's mistake; you do not hurt your patient as with a surgeon's mistake; cars do not tumble down from the bridge as with an engineer's mistake. Thus, nobody regulates the way trading is learned and taught.

Do not get me wrong. I am not for regulation of this profession. In my firm opinion, educating traders should remain a self-regulated industry. Let us look at another example. There is one more field of activity very similar to trading, including harm to others when poor decisions are made. I am talking about business, about entrepreneurship. Just as with trading, it is a highly personalized and individualized endeavor. Yet, there is a structure available in business education. There are logical steps, there are business schools, there is a realization that you need to study some theory before you take the plunge. An entrepreneur creates a business plan and adjusts it according to experience and conditions.

I see no reason why trading should be any different. The only explanation of this divergence is the relative novelty of the very phenomenon of the broad public access to the trading field. It is high time to try to put the structure in place.

### Making Educated Choices

Many books and courses aimed at educating traders tend to teach a particular approach or trading method. It is natural that authors share their experiences and findings. However, for the beginning trader this carries a certain danger. Not being aware of all of the choices he has, he takes for granted the author's word that a particular method described is the right way to trade. It very well could be, but there is no single right way to trade. There are choices, and many of them are valid. Your choice should be made with consideration for many aspects that are individual to you. Before a trader forms his approach, he should see what is available to him and go over all of the alternatives. Without this approach, a trader is likely to stick with something that is not a good fit to his personal circumstances, his type of personality or his objectives. I have seen natural born scalpers trying to swing trade; and I have seen great analytics trying to apply their skills in lightning fast scalping. It led them nowhere until they realized that they had adopted a trading style that was not suited to them.

## From the Forest to the Trees

Observing scores of traders I have worked with, and reviewing my own way, I see one more aspect where the process of studying trading is deviating from the norm.

Let us look at analogies we cited before once again. When studying for the medical profession, do you become familiar with the olfactory nerve, optic nerve, occulomotor nerve etc., and then presented with the concept of the nervous system as a whole? Just how much does the sentence "The trigeminal nerve is responsible for sensory enervation of the face and motor enervation to muscles of mastication" help you in the early stages of learning? Studying to become an engineer, you do not study different ways of steel reinforcement in a concrete structure before you get familiar with the very concept of how the concrete works under the load.

Let us see how it happens in trading. A trader new to the field starts with picking certain indicators or technical studies. Sometimes a trader starts with certain setups. He runs into those almost randomly, hearing or reading about them here and there. He tries to apply them in practice and they do not work for him. Is there something wrong with those setups or indicators? Not necessarily. Our trader could run into a situation where the same setups work for someone but will not work for him. How come, he asks? How is it possible that the same thing works for one person and does not work for another?

The answer is there is no conceptual framework behind our trader's attempt. Unlike those he tries to mimic (providing they know what they are doing), he has never worked out the more general things for him - his trading philosophy, his basic understanding of how the market works, what his edge is, what are the signs of movements he can read and exploit. Not having all this background, he misses many of the distinctions that tell something valuable to more experienced traders.

To cite another analogy, it is like seeing someone cooking meat and trying to do the same, but with no knowledge of different kinds of meat and different ways to prepare it. The meat cooked by your mentor could be a delicious T-bone steak. Now, imagine that you know nothing about meat. You buy a turkey and try to do the same. You do not know that there is beef, pork, chicken, turkey, and wild game or lamb steaks. You do not know about different cuts and you do not know about different ways to marinate them, to apply different rubs or sauces. Would you reasonably expect your meal to be as delicious as what you sampled, or even edible at all for that matter?

Yet this is exactly what is done in trading when a trader tries to form his trading style without forming his trading philosophy first. The proverbial cart is put before the horse. I have met traders that have spent a couple of years learning the profession and never formed their own trading philosophy. They did not know what kind of traders they were. They did not realize what their setups were based on. They were blind pilots flying their planes without the knowledge of plane behavior or weather patterns. They were surgeons trying to perform surgery on particular parts of the body without knowing what the body consists of and how different parts and organs interact. They had not learned the system because they tried to learn it limb by limb, never asking how the entire system works.

The problem with this approach is traders make their choices regarding what and how they trade before they learned about all the choices and have studied them. They have no clear understanding of consequences of their choices before they studied the whole system. No wonder their choices are often either wrong or not suitable for their purposes and their personality.

I always start my mentoring with a request to the mentored that they present me with their own questions. When I hear the questions, I usually try to go to the bigger picture to see whether they comprehend it and need to just home in on particular details. More often than not, (in fact in the majority of cases), I find out that there is no real big picture for them and their particular questions are just another attempt to "get down this one more element that is lacking." This is a great illusion many have: they always feel that there is some last thing that is left to learn, and when they do, things will click together. They will not succeed if there is no trading philosophy behind the whole approach.

## Keeping an Eye on the Whole Picture

Now, let us see what happens with many traders as they go deeper into the learning process. They learn trading element by element. As with any complex system consisting of many components, it is important to see how they are inter-connected. It is a frequent occurrence that traders do not grasp this inter-connection. Plenty of these links, that are obvious for experienced traders, get lost for someone who studies trading in a linear manner.

Volume is an important element of reading stock movement and volume is an important element of risk evaluation. Risk evaluation will impact the size of your trade. Sizing of your trade is a subject of your money management. Your money management is connected to the timeframe you pick for your trades. The timeframe will directly impact your risk evaluation procedure.

While this is just a small part of what is happening in a trader's brain in the decision-making process, it all happens in a matter of seconds sometimes. How do you study all these inter-connections, seemingly so enormously complex? Is there even a way to learn them other than years of painful experience? Not to dismiss the role of experience, but there sure is.

We learn from the way we were taught from our early years. There is major topic I and it's broken down by subtopics I.1, I.2 etc. Those subtopics were broken down further by additional levels, for example I.1.1, I.1.2 etc. While this is a good way to get things organized, it is not really a good way to see the connection between the topics. When you were at VI.4.5, were you really able to make a connection with what you learned in III.7.6? Chances are it was hard to do. Even if you were told about this connection, you had to go back and reread III.7.6 to see the connection. Yet effective trading does require a clear understanding of all the mutual impacts and inter-connections, and it requires you to keep the whole picture in mind. Clearly, there is a problem with this linear approach and there is a need in teaching trading in a way that preserves all the links in the trader's mind.

## What Does this All Come to?

Let us return to the analogy we discussed earlier – studying business. This is a good analogy as business is the closest endeavor to trading in many regards. All business courses, their entire structure lead the students through the logical steps of forming their business plan. The role of business planning is enormous. As Dr. Walter S. Good wrote in his book *Building a Dream*, "The business planning process focuses on the future. It enables you to relate what you wish to achieve to what your business concept or idea can deliver. It entails working your way through each of… steps in a logical and sequential way".

What this book is aiming to achieve is to take you through the entire process of forming your **trading plan**. Instead of being a blind pilot you will be able to clearly see where to go and why. It will present you with the choices you need to make and help you make those choices. It will make sure that there are no gaps in your trading education. Whatever comes your way is not going to be something totally unforeseen. There will be a good foundation for your practical trading, and your trading plan will guide you through what you encounter in the markets.

By no means is your trading plan intended to remain the same over the years. It is going to be a live, changing guide that you adjust as your experience grows. The more you learn about the markets and about yourself, the closer your trading plan reflects your financial achievements and abilities. Your trading plan will change under the impact of two major factors. One of them is your own experience, your self-discovery. As you learn more about yourself, your personal preferences, comfort zones, risk tolerance and other sides of your personality, you adjust your trading plan to reflect these realizations. Another factor is the changing market. Your trading plan will include elements that consider how the markets act, and your behavior is going to adjust to factor in those changes. It can happen in the longer term basis as you recognize major trend change or even on a daily basis as you see the market switching form trend to range, narrowing, breaking out, calming down or going ballistic.

# How Is This Book Structured?

In light of all that is said above, let us see how we achieve setting goals and overcoming the obstacles I have described.

## Theory Comes First

There will not be the traditional advice to start trading before your final plan of action and trading plan are in place. Neither will there be advice to only observe the market and learn from it.

We will go over everything you need to learn. You will be shown all the elements of trading. Your choices are going to be described in a clear manner. There will be descriptions of all of the choices and their consequences. Having read this book and materials it refers to, you will have a clear understanding of what you are up against and what you need to do in order to achieve your goals without suffering huge losses. You will learn how the body works before you are to perform your first surgery.

Similar to forming a business plan, you will be taken through the stages, through the questions to answer, through the forms to fill out. They will converge, shaping up as a complete, thorough plan of action.

## Finding Your Way Through the Maze

This book is not suggesting any particular approach or trading method as superior to others. Rather, it helps you see how they fit your particular circumstances, objectives and personality and presents you with alternatives. It describes your options in a way that makes it possible for you to see what fits.

## Starting From the Forest, Going Down to the Trees

This book will start you out with a discussion of the big picture. Before you start learning each of the elements, you will be shown what they form when they are put together. Our horse is going to be in front of our cart at all times.

We are then going to break down the whole by its elements, as is customary with all complex systems. As your trading plan develops it is going to include more and more elements, yet they are going to remain within the framework of the big picture. You will make your choices consciously, seeing how they impact other elements of your trading plan and what they are linked to.

Many of the elements that you need to study and master will appear in different parts of the book. In this sense, the book is moving in a circular motion, returning to the discussed matter on a deeper level or from a different standpoint. You will see the discussion of risk control in *Trading Philosophy*, *Trading Psychology*, *Creating Your Trading System* and *Practical Trading* parts every time from a different angle and on another level of depth. Studying this way, you will understand the role of each element in the bigger picture and inter-dependence of the elements.

## Keeping the Whole Picture in Mind

Earlier we discussed the problem with a linear approach to studying. Fortunately, there is a different approach offering an easier way to present the big picture and see all of the links between the elements. This approach is known by the name of 'mind mapping' and was originated in the late 1960s by Tony Buzan. As the Buzan Center website puts it, *Similar to a road map, a Mind Map will:*

- Give you an overview of a large subject/area.

- Enable you to plan routes/make choices and let you know where you are going and where you have been.

- Gather and hold large amounts of data for you.

- Encourage problem solving by showing you new creative pathways.

- Enable you to be extremely efficient.

- Be enjoyable to look at, read, muse over and remember.

- Attract and hold your eye/brain.

- Let you see the whole picture *and* the details at the same time.

Many find this graphic technique to be extremely powerful for planning and studying purposes. It enables you to see the connections between elements in a very easy, visual way. The graphic representation of this kind solves many problems we face when studying complex material. Unlike usual decision trees, it allows you to create an image of the material without prioritizing it. This is very useful in cases where there are elements of equal importance; where there are elements not following each other in a sequential way but rather composing the whole; and, finally, in cases where those elements consist of sub-elements so the whole picture becomes quite complex. This technique with involvement of images, curved lines and different fonts engages the right half of your brain. This engagement is known to wake up creative thinking and positively impact memory. Presentation of the material in this way makes it much easier to memorize it and remember it by a single glance at the mind map.

The technique itself is very simple. The main topic, the subject of research or a problem to be solved is placed at the centre of the map in a form of image. The elements, or ideas that your main topic could be broken down into, are drawn in a form of branches with key words printed on them. Sub elements, in turn, branch out from main branches. A map drawn in this way creates radial hierarchy. The use of colors and images helps organize and memorizing the whole subject with all its details and links. Constructing your mindmap can be done manually or with software.

In order to achieve the purposes of this book, the stages to go through and elements to learn will be presented in this way. Below is a mind map of everything that has been said up to this point, so you can see for yourself how this technique is powerful and facilitates understanding.

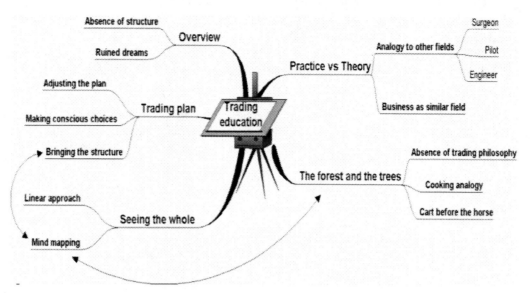

*This mind map and the rest in this book are created with software ConceptDraw MINDMAP Pro by Computer Systems Odessa.*

## What this Book is and is Not

This book is not intended to teach you everything there is to know about trading. No single book can do that. There are many resources out there that do a great job from their respective point of view. I have no intention of repeating here everything that is mentioned in those books. Rather, I want to provide you with a framework for all the resources you are going to need. This book is intended to be your gateway into the world of trading, to help you find your way in the sea of information and to sift through it, taking what you need and being aware of what else is out there. It will also help you understand what you need and make sure that nothing significant is missed by you.

By no means is this book intended to teach you "the best and only" approach to trading or a "Holy Grail Trading System". Just the opposite – it will show you why such a system cannot exist and why you should run away when you are promised one. It is a workbook, and not a map to the secret location of a Get-Rich-Magic-Button. Reading samples of trading plans and traders' interviews, you will be amazed by the huge differences in their trading approaches. This fact is going to emphasize once again that the best approach to trading is the one that works for you.

## How to Use this Book

The entire content of this book is inter-linked by a **Mind Map** that grows as the book moves forward. Review it to preserve a feeling of the big picture as you advance into the material. As new elements are added, track the arrows between them to see their inter-connections and mutual impacts.

Each part consists of several subtopics. It contains a **Mind Map** of the part content so you can see the material in its entirety. The elements of the part or subtopic content are described and then analyzed. When a subtopic is complicated enough or presents certain choices to make, it has its own mind map.

There are sections named **Traders Talk**, which are interviews with traders of different levels of experience and various approaches to trading. They will help you understand the real challenges traders face. You will be able to see how others deal with those challenges and shape up their trading style. Those interviews tie together many subjects discussed in the book. You will become fascinated by the fact that traders with different timeframes and methods are so uniform in many aspects of their general approach and philosophy. I encourage you to return to the interviews after reading through the entire book, as each next part will make you see new sides and levels in what traders say about their experiences and discoveries. Reading interviews will also help you shape up your own trading plan.

There are '**Useful Tips**' marked by a symbol in the text. They supply additional information that is going to be of use to you as you go deeper into the practical details.

Each part also contains a section named '**You Asked**.' I have compiled questions from real mentoring sessions and conversations with traders. They answer many of the questions that I receive most often. This is an invaluable resource allowing you to find solutions for many typical problems. If others asked those questions often, chances are you will too.

Each part ends with '**Resources'** which is supplementary information of useful websites. The world of trading internet resources is vast and your searches will give you plenty of materials to look at. Be picky though, as many of them are opinionated. I have tried to cite resources that I personally use or have become familiar with. There are also references to books listed in a '**Recommended Reading**' list. They are marked by **RR##,** where the ## matches the book's number in the list. This list is located at the end of this workbook with brief comments on each book's content so you can easily pick up the ones related to the topic of your interest. Links to both, resources and books from the recommended reading list, also appear at www.realitytrader.com/masterplan for your convenience.

Transitions from one part to another are covered in '**Trading Plan Forms**'. Those elements that need to be included in your trading plan contain the snapshots of the form you will need to fill in. The forms themselves can be down loaded from the website:

www.realitytrader.com/masterplan

Each form on the website contains a reference to the pages related to it. You can also get help and receive answers to your questions using the e-mail form at www.realitytrader.com. As you fill in the forms and combine them, your trading plan begins to shape up. Some elements of the trading plan are fixed, while most are varied, i.e., they are specific from one trader to another. The fixed elements will be entered into trading plan forms as text. You can find different wording for those elements that best matches your personality, or you can include more of what is discussed in the according parts of the book in your trading plan if that helps you better remember the context of the particular part of the plan. However, do not change their meaning – this is the wisdom created by generations of traders. Varied elements contain the beginning of the statement and lines to fill in. All the material you read in the book either helps you define your choices or directs you to additional resources that will help you study the necessary field.

Do not take the forms as dogma. You might feel a need to add some elements or exclude others. The trading plan samples cited at the end of the book will show you how traders approach their trading plans. Those samples are from real plans, with exclusion of elements that authors wanted to keep private. The only corrections made by me are slight adjustments to keep the uniformity within the book context such as inclusion of the headers provided in the forms in this book, and insignificant change of order – again, to keep things uniform for the reader's convenience.

Following the study plan outlined in this book, you are going to get a better understanding of the potential for your trading success and requirements for you to meet in order to achieve this success.

## Resources

www.realitytrader.com/masterplan
http://www.mind-map.com
http://www.realitytrader.com/mindmap.asp

## Recommended Reading

RR16

# Mastering Trading Skills

There are five major parts you are going to go through in order to master this profession.

The first part is your **Trading Philosophy**. This is a general overview of your approach. At this stage, you are going to choose your general outlook which defines what kind of trader you are and how you see the markets. The choices made at this point are going to impact everything you learn and do in your trading.

The second part is your **Trading Psychology**. This element is going to shape up your mindset in a way that suits your needs as a trader and arm you with an arsenal of methods to control your actions. It will also help you better understand the psychology of other market participants so you can use their action to your advantage.

The third part is **Creating a Trading System**. This is where you get down to choosing your method of reading the market, timeframes in which you trade, particular trading vehicles and signals for your entries and exits. Various choices are described for you allowing you to determine which approach suits you best.

The fourth part is **Trading Tools**. What do you use to place your orders, to see the movement of the market, scan for your trades, monitor your positions – all of these are topics in this part. You will be shown how to pick the tools that best suit your chosen trading method.

The fifth part is finally, **Practical Trading**. This is where you get your toes wet – slowly and carefully. This part will show you how to start your trading minimizing your risk and shortening your learning curve. It will also go over the way in which you monitor your performance and make necessary corrections.

The order of these parts is chosen in a fashion that allows you to move systematically. It does not make sense to try to create your trading system before you define your trading philosophy. There is no point in choosing your tools before you determine the details of your trading system. The book will take you deeper into details; the choice of each of those details will be governed by the choices made at more general stages, and in turn is going to govern the choices of the next stage.

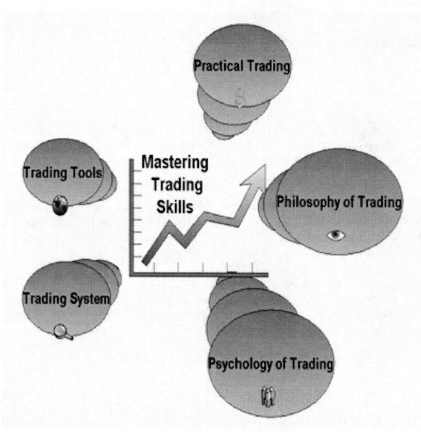

*Mind Map for Mastering Trading Skills*

# Trading Plan

At this point you are ready to start composing your Trading Plan. Understandably, you have not studied much yet – however, if you bought this book, you know what you want to achieve, and this is what we can formulate at this point.

Your trading plan starts with a **Vision Statement**, which is a description of your ideal perception of what you want to become as a trader. It should be brief and easy to read and remember. It lays out your big goal to achieve. It answers the major question: What do you want from trading?

An example of such a statement could be, for instance:

*I plan to become a full time trader. Trading is going to provide my primary income. I plan to achieve financial independence combined with a lifestyle of freedom.*

Another example:

*I plan to make trading my supplementary source of income. I intend to achieve a better lifestyle through the confidence of a financially sound environment.*

One of my students provided me with his somewhat extravagant and very interesting vision statement that I cite here with his permission:

*I am an eternal student studying human beings. I plan to use trading as a tool to learn more about human behavior and about myself. I am going to use my skills in this area to grant myself financial independence.*

## Trading Plan Form: Vision Statement

What do you want to achieve in trading? What do you want to become?

The next form in your trading plan contains your **financial commitments and objectives**. It describes your goals in monetary terms. Formulate here what you expect in monetary terms. Following the book material will help you realize how realistic your expectations are. Try to be reasonable at this stage, but do not undercut your dreams. The best way to approach this process, in my opinion, is to define your goal and check it against the reality. If in the course of further studying you decide that the original goal is not achievable, correct it to what appears to be realistic and see if you still think it is worth pursuing. If so, you did a good job keeping your expectations reasonable yet still worthwhile for you. If not, then the only financial commitment you made is the price of this book, and believe me, it is much less that what one can lose going into markets without appropriate preparations.

It is almost impossible to assign exact numbers to find out typical returns for traders. There is practically speaking, no 'typical' amount in this area. There are traders that make 1-2% of their trading capital each day; there are traders that make 20% of their capital over the course of a year; and then, there are traders that fail. One thing is certain: plan on a reasonable timeframe to achieve your objectives. The interviews with traders appearing in the book will assist you in calculating what is reasonable in this regard.

There are also operating expenses that you will need to budget for during the first period of your learning curve. Consider them, too, in this form. You will need certain tools for your trading. Most likely, you cannot figure them out at this moment. Simply skip it and return to it as you advance through the book and define your tools and their pricing.

## Trading Plan Form: My Financial Commitments and Objectives

My trading capital is going to be  $_____

My goal is to make $_____ a year, or _____ % of my trading capital. I plan to achieve this goal within _____ months/years.

I plan to limit my expenses to _____ a month. Those are:

- charting software  _____

- scanning software _____

- books _____

_____

_____

_____

- subscription to services: _____

_____

_____

# *Traders Talk - Patience Rogers*

*Trades sporadically using a broker since 2000, full time trading since 2004. Mostly scalping NASDAQ stocks with rare overnight holds. 44 years old, British Columbia, Canada*

My learning curve was very much built on painful experiences. I was starting from a position of complete neophyte, unfamiliar with how the business worked, with terminology or tools of the trade.

My previous career required me to immediately jump into unrelated business fields, evaluate them under time constraints, select best practices, develop project plans and execute with an expectation of a high rate of success. All of my job assignments required me to make immediate decisions based on limited information under pressure. I thought my learning curve in trading would be like learning any other new business area for me. I was wrong.

My first exposure to trading equities was from learning about company fundamentals from my family. I 'found' charting and technical indicators about four years ago and enjoyed learning the various techniques and approaches. Do I now pay attention to any of these three approaches with trading? The answer is 'no'. Most of the time I have no idea what the name of the company is, what its p/e ratio is, or if the Bollinger bands are narrowing, I just trade the symbol and what I see setting up.

Over the past 7 months, I have been humbled by my mistakes. I would have avoided a significant percentage of them if I were exposed to a structured, disciplined trading approach. After my first months trading, I evaluated my performance and saw I was heading down a slippery slope. I had to stop and accept that I did not know what I needed to know, nor was I following any plan. I accelerated my learning curve by mentoring with an experienced, reputable trader for a period of a month. This mentoring experience accelerated my understanding to the point where I gained confidence, mainly because I was now following a trading plan and could grasp the 'big picture'. The subsequent months following the implementation of a trading plan have been spent gaining experience and actually enjoying the mental challenges trading provides.

I would say I became consistent, on a day-to-day basis, by my fifth month of trading. My account is progressing upward, although some days I experience drawdowns and accept this part of the business.

I did not know what was considered to be 'small' shares when I started. In the earliest days, I traded 1,000 share lots. That did not last long. I quickly found my risk tolerance to be around 500 shares and I rarely deviate upward. Just my comfort level. I do however, trade small lot shares of 100 when I want to experiment or refine a particular trading skill, such as seeing how well I trade when faced with low volume, thinly traded shares. I like to discover new trading techniques, practice them until I can execute them cleanly and then decide whether this is an approach I want to incorporate into my trading plan.

The question about initial losses makes every trader pause, remember and reflect on one or more hurtful experiences. I suspect I lost more than many in learning about trading. I made a decision early on that losses were the tuition cost for a rapid ramp-up in my trading education. Unfortunately, my own bugaboo was not keeping a stop loss because mentally I felt I knew what a stock was going to do.

My wake-up came one day when my mentor made a comment to me that instantly made me grow up and approach trading as a profession. Today, I allow a loss of approximately .15 – .25 cents on a trade that fails a setup.

I have a trading plan, tailored to my personal trading tastes and tolerances. When I first started out trading, I was looking for metrics or measurements, or a plan, which I could follow. I am a highly structured individual by nature and was flustered without a defined approach to trading. My plan developed itself in month 2 to 3, and I refine it iteratively as time goes on. Once I had my plan in place, I was released from responding emotionally to trading and fell into a structured, methodical behavior resulting in increased consistency in my trades.

I do not have a defined trading philosophy per se. I do have a set of unwritten beliefs. They are:

Trade when you are mentally alert and have time to dedicate yourself to the task. Do not become distracted or half-heartedly trade. You are asking to learn a lesson.

It is all about you. Do not trade someone else's style. You will fail if you do not develop and refine your own edge.

Do not go back to the trough too many times. Know when to be satisfied with the trades you have done in the day and stop even if it is 10:30 in the morning.

Be absolutely clear in your mind why you are entering a trade and when to exit it.

If you do not know, ask. What you do not know will kill your account.

At the exact moment when your head is resting on your arms because the stock is not moving as anticipated, you will experience sheer terror when it unexpectedly runs one way or another and blasts your brain into action. At this point, you react within your setup discipline and act accordingly.

Reviewing my method of reading the market, I can summarize it as the following: I read the tape of a stock and mentally consolidate its movements in my mind. I do not know how to describe it other than I watch the flow of the trend.

I am risk intolerant. Scalping provides me with my cleanest trading and highest success ratio. I am in, out and gone on to the next trade.

As a total newbie, I just looked for stocks going up, increasing volume and I bought when the buyers were buying and sold when the buyers were buying. I avoided shorting stocks because I was internally torn over this type of trading. My mentor was kind enough to persevere with me and helped me to get past my own mental block about shorting. Now I toggle between going long on a stock on the way up and short on the way down if there is a large enough range. Occasionally I will trade one stock for that particular trading day using this approach.

I do not believe I have ever been an aggressive trader. I started off instinctively avoiding certain stock setups that do not suit my personality, such as trading the 'hot' stock of the day which has huge spreads. I shake my head and walk away from them. I suspect it is because my brain has become hard-wired to avoid overly aggressive approaches and to follow safe practices.

I continue to learn risk management on a daily basis. One of the fears I dealt with when starting trading was that by pursuing, what may be my true calling, I would end up putting my family in the poorhouse. I think I used a large amount of emotional energy fearing what might happen if I could not manage my risk. I learnt that education and experience helped me face this fear and manage stress about risk. Starting to trade full time in late spring 2004 was probably not the most opportune time to start my new career. However, I doubt there is ever a good or bad time, as you still have to gain experience and educate yourself at any point as a trader. Trading, for the most part, is not stressful once you remove the emotional uncertainties and follow your plan. The more disciplined I become in choosing to enter a trade, or not, helps reinforce good risk controls.

As a single mother with four dependents, earning a living by trading, I regard risk control as the single most important element to ensuring I remain in the business and provide for my family.

I am also intent on being a trader for the long haul and in order to do this, I need to manage risk with my trading capital ensuring I do not erode it. If I continue on and become a mature trader, I expect that at the point in time when I want to retire, I will be in a profession which lends itself well to part-time employment, working from home and flexible work days for as long as I wish to continue working.

Every morning when I sit down at my computer to start working, I approach the day mentally saying "I know nothing", and wonder what I will learn today.

When I started my apprenticeship in trading, I looked for excellence in trading to emulate. I had a few years exposure to sporadically reading financial websites and watching CNBC in order to learn about long term investments for my retirement account and to keep current with market conditions. I looked around at what was available and had a choice of attending an on-line trading 'university' course, sitting in a hotel conference room with others new to trading or joining an online trading room. I settled on the latter as the most expedient, convenient educational route.

I tried the swing trading first but found the fit for me with overnight trades was not well suited to my comfort level. I then switched to day trading and found a community of individuals, honestly posting their trade wins and losses and educating its members as trades were made throughout the day. It is here I found a mentor who spent a month patiently working with me through each trade I made and answered my constant, novice questions, shaping me, making me think and internalize what he was teaching me. During this month, I read numerous trading books, prepared my student notes, questions for the next day to ask my mentor and studied as if I were back at university cramming for exams. I deliberately placed myself into the student's mindset for learning new concepts.

I would have to say as a trading novice, I feel fortunate to be affiliated with the others in the trading room. I particularly enjoy observing the support and acknowledgement of members who experience personal success or achievement in learning to trade, using different approaches tailored to their particular style.

To summarize, I made a conscious decision to leave a 26-year career that offered me an increasing workload, escalating stress, a constant need to survive downsizing or outsourcing, an electronic leash by means of work provided cell phones and home workstation which make me always accessible to my employer. I knew that I would be expected to accommodate even greater job demands while watching job security disappear into thin air. I finally realized my work and family life had blurred and I knew my hours would never be scaled back.

Trading is a career where I feel I am in control of my environment. I am self-sufficient, independent and autonomous from the dictates of others. I look forward to my new job each morning, I know I have better control of my life and I am highly motivated because I am experiencing personal success, albeit modestly, and a sense of achievement every day.

It really is true that if you do what you enjoy, it is not work.

# Part I: Trading Philosophy

# Questions, Questions

Most traders start their career without a defined approach to many aspects of trading. Those that survive, work out their general approach over a course of years, coming to a certain set of paradigms often caused by painful experience and observation. It is a commonly accepted way of learning in trading. It seems logical; how to come to certain ways of looking at matters without prior experience and knowledge? However, in practice this usually leads to situations where a trader simply walks without a map. Not only does he not match his actions to some set of standards, he does not even know what those standards are, or what his map should consist of. My firm opinion is that a trader should think of his approach in terms of the big picture before he even starts trading. It is not a problem to adjust his trading approach and change it later on; it is a normal process of a paradigm shift. As he encounters the reality of the market and the reality of his own personality, he should and will adjust. However, there should be something to adjust in the first place. I see this approach as putting together an aerial map before walking the ground. Sure, you are going to make plenty of adjustments to your preliminary map and put many additional details on it. Maybe you will even have to change major parts of your map as you see the real landscape. However, walking the grounds without such a map would be much more dangerous and counterproductive.

In the course of designing one's trading philosophy, one should answer the following set of questions:

- What is the moving force behind price changes?
- What is the market's reality?
- Is there certainty in the markets?
- What is the loss? Is it avoidable?
- How do I approach the risk?
- What is it that constitutes the difference between gambling and trading?
- What am I going to trade in terms of market movement?
- How aggressive am I going to be?

In this part of the book we are going to go over these concepts. As you think of them and form your take, you shape up the "shell" that is going to define your entire trading approach. Some of these questions do not have definitive answers; you will have to listen to yourself and find out what rings true for you. Remember that trading is a highly individualized endeavor; there is no right or wrong approach. Each trader has his own truth. You can no more tell someone that trading breakouts is better than to trade pullbacks than you can tell someone to run a restaurant instead of a gas station. At the same time, some of these questions have been answered by the trading community over the last couple of thousand years. With these, our purpose will be to understand those answers and to incorporate them in our trading plan.

# What is it that Moves a Market?

There are two distinctive approaches to this matter: **fundamental** and **technical**. We will discuss psychological traits necessary for each approach in the *Trading Psychology* part in greater details. The *Creating Your Trading System* part is going to show you how to build your system based on this choice, and the *Trading Tools* part will show you what to use to make your trading decisions. At this point it is important to decide which approach appeals to you.

From the point of view of a **fundamental** approach, **value** dictates the price. This approach discards all the movements between the current price level and the price that matches value as a fundamental trader sees these movements as just noise. Essentially this approach looks at the company's "story" and dictates buying the stock that is priced below its real value. The idea of such a method is that eventually the market will recognize real value and the price will become "fair". Timing of entry is not too important with this approach; the only reason for closing the trade before the target is reached is a change of a story that impact that fair value. Obviously, this method requires great patience as it could take the market months and even years to take the price where a trader thinks it should be. Most often a fundamental approach leads a trader into long term trades. It also involves a good deal of endurance as the price can and often will fluctuate. If this approach becomes your trading style, your research is going to involve the data concerning the company and its industry.

From the point of view of a **technical** approach, it is **perceived value** that dictates the price. It means that a trader is not too concerned about the fair value of a stock. Rather, he is concerned with how the majority of market participants perceive this fair value. The main idea of this approach is since buying and selling impacts the price then the players' perception is a moving factor. It does not matter whether their perception is right or wrong. The important thing is this perception makes the price change when the players act on their perception. In other words, **such a trader trades not a stock itself but other players**. His decisions are based on the psychology of other traders as he can read it. For such a trader it does not really matter whether a $20 stock should cost $100. What does matter for him is whether most of the other traders believe in this target – and if he sees a signs that they do, he is going to trade on their actions to exploit their buying. Trading this way, a trader attempts to read the intentions of other participants by utilizing certain methods of reading the market that we are going to discuss in the part *Creating Your Trading System*.

The choice between these two approaches affects practically every aspect of your trading: **timeframe**, **method of reading**, **method of risk control** – all the factors that will be detailed in the *Creating Your Trading System* part. At this point, let us establish those interconnections.

This matter is closely tied to a **timeframe** in which a trader wants to operate. A fundamental approach usually leads to a longer timeframe, while a technical approach can be done in any of them, including scalping in a matter of minutes or even seconds. Continuing this line of thought, a stock is likely to arrive sooner or later at your target – providing your reasoning is correct. Now, let us see what happens in a shorter timeframe. If a company announces good news in the morning, a big new order for instance, the price goes up. After certain movements, it stalls and retreats. Obviously the news has not changed during this time. What has happened is players start participating, entering and exiting, taking profits, taking stops, managing their trades and affecting the price. This is what we meant by noise from the standpoint of a fundamental trader; for him it is just meaningless action. However, for someone trading in a short timeframe being armed with methods of reading such movements, this is quite exploitable action. In discussing selection of your timeframe in the *Creating Your Trading System* part, we are going to revisit this matter from another angle.

Let us see how the **method of reading** is impacted by this choice. Being a fundamental trader, you are going to read the market using according tools. The subject of your interest is a company's state of affairs, sector and industry development and general market climate. As far as a market participant's perception is concerned, you are going to simply wait for the market to recognize the value that you see in a company – or prove you wrong. Being a technical trader, you are going to apply a different set of tools. These will be mostly aimed at reading the reactions of other participants. Instead of company reports, you will be reading and analyzing the charts. Again, these matters will be further analyzed in the *Creating Your Trading System* part.

Finally, your risk control method is going to be governed by this choice. The first question in this regard is going to be: **What are the signs that you are wrong?** This is important to define because different type of events will trigger your action in each case. In the case with a fundamental approach, the sign of being wrong is story change. A company's product losing the market share, the drug being rejected by the FDA, an unfavorable financial situation – this is the kind of event that is going to make you apply risk control by exiting or downsizing your position. In the case of a technical approach, it is a certain price action that is going to make you exit your position. As you observe the chart developing, you define your "uncle point" by the price behavior showing that the market disagrees with you.

The second question in this regard: **How do you manage the risk?** The important factor to realize in this scenario is that the longer your exposure to the market, the bigger your chance to run into some adverse event. Bad news, missed earnings, downgrades by analysts, geopolitical events – occurrences of this kind can make the price drop significantly. It means that in the case with a fundamental approach your major weapon in the risk control department is going to be diversification. The proverbial eggs being put into many baskets will warrant certain safety. In the case with a technical approach, it is a shortening timeframe that will diminish the role of diversification and increase the role of stop loss as an instrument of risk control. For a scalper (the ultimate form of a short term trader), diversification has no real place; a tight stop loss and disciplined application of it, however, is critical to success.

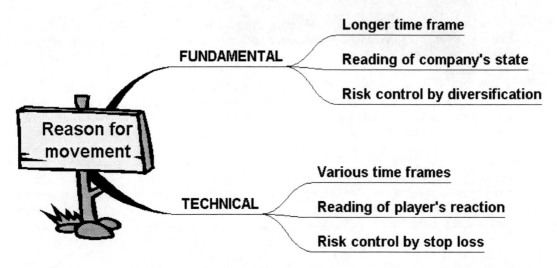

*Mind map of Reasons for Market Movement.*

> When making your choice between a fundamental or technical approach, keep in mind that it is not always "either/or" in these styles of trading. A technical trader might want to initially check the fundamentals before acting on a decision based only on the charts; a fundamental trader often can and should check the charts to time his entry and exit. Such a mix of approaches works for some traders adding a new dimension to their method.

## What is the Market's Reality?

This is one of the cornerstone questions for a trader. If there were a single market reality, objective and measurable by absolute, common standards for each trader, there would not be room for different methods of reading the market. Continuing this line of reasoning, there would not be price change in the market. The very reason for the eternal changing of price for a stock is the disagreement between market participants on the stock's fair value. Having different criteria, opinions and objectives, players interact with each other by executing trades thus impacting the price. Each trade exists by the desire of one side to buy and another side to sell. It means that in order for a trade to occur there should be disagreement on the further direction of a price. In the absence of such disagreement, there are no trades. This leads us to the realization that there is no single reality that would be identical for different traders. Each market participant has their own reality and their trading decisions are based on that reality. Their reality is their map and it can be matching the territory or not. The closer the market movement is to a trader's plan, the closer his map is to the territory. What is the territory then? The market movement itself is. Price movement is the ultimate answer to any question you can ask in the market. This is the final and absolute reality that reveals itself as it develops. You may be right about the company's fundamentals, but if the majority of players disagree with you and force the price down, being right does not help you make money.

As Jesse Livermore, arguably the best trader of all times, stated in Edwin Lefevre's book, *Reminiscences of a Stock Operator*, 'My business is to trade – that is, to stick to the facts before me and not to what I think other people ought to do'.

Such an absolute fact for a trader, in this case, is the price movement not confirming his belief of where the stock would go next. Is it possible that you were right and the market was wrong? The very question is invalid. The market cannot be wrong in the same way that ocean currents carry your raft in an undesirable direction. The market is not right or wrong. It simply does what it does; your job as a trader is to utilize its action, not to fight the market current.

The creation of your 'map', your reality is a process of listening to the market and following its lead. Why is it so important to understand? Because you are going to be one of those traders with a map, and your map can be as right or wrong as the next guy's. Mark Douglas in *The Disciplined Trader* puts it this way, 'The market is never wrong in what it does; it just is. Therefore, you as an individual trader interacting with the market... have to confront an environment where only you can be wrong, and it is never the other way around. As a trader, you have to decide what is more important – being right or making money – because the two are not always compatible or consistent with one another'.

This idea of numerous realities in the market naturally leads us to the next question:

## Is there Certainty in the Markets?

If all that has been stated above has now crystallized into a deep, internal belief, you will not hesitate to answer this question with a resounding NO! Think about it. If the price change is a result of the collective action of many players, then in order to be certain about what happens next, you would have to KNOW all of their intentions. Obviously, this is impossible. It is possible to read those intentions to a certain extent, and the better you are at this skill the closer your read to the market reality. However, there never will be such a thing as KNOWING in the market.

Even if by some magic turn of events you learned everything about the current intentions of all the participants, those intentions will change as price changes. Worse yet, there could be new intentions coming into play that have nothing to do with the market at all. For instance, a big player deciding to re-allocate his funds, dumping stock to free money for a new position in another stock. The consequence is price movement under this market participant's selling pressure, without any other market-related reason.

The important conclusion here is that the market does not work in certainties. It works in probabilities. If your read is right, your map is close to the territory – and probability will work for you. The farther your read from the market reality, the more the odds are stacked against you. Yet, no matter how good your read is, there is always room for a loss. Any read, however good it is, can lead to a loss if unforeseen turn-of-events come along. Any setup, however perfect it, can fail. You can lose on any given trade even if you do everything right. You can lose in any given period, whatever your timeframe, even if you do everything by the rules and your rules are correct. No trader, no matter how competent, can have 100 percent winning trades or 100 percent confidence in the outcome of any particular trade. It is what happens most often that defines your winning or losing overall. This thesis leads to many outcomes as far as a trader's psychology is concerned, and we will get back to this topic in the *Trading Psychology* part. At this point building our trading philosophy we are naturally moving toward defining an answer to the next question:

# What is Loss? Is it Avoidable?

For many traders a loss is a sign of a bad read, bad trade, wrong decision or even a result of someone's manipulation. Sure, everything listed is possible and is often true. However, as your skills grow, your read will become better and your decisions more sophisticated. And yet, as we already saw, losses will be present at any stage of your development as a trader. Thus, it is important to distinguish between the two different kinds of losses.

The first kind is a **loss caused by your wrong decision**. This kind of loss must serve as an indication of something to be learned. If a loss taught you something, then it was not as much a loss as it was tuition. When you repeat the same mistake, over-and-over again, that is a pure loss since you have not learnt from it. In fact, some losses serve as the best lessons learnt by a trader because of the powerful messages they impart. It has been the case with many traders; it certainly has been a case with me as I described in my book *Techniques of Tape Reading*.

The second kind is a **loss caused by market uncertainty**. It means that you lost on a trade where you did everything right. There was the right setup, all the criteria for the trade were met and yet, a trade went sour. This kind of a loss has to be taken as a part of trading probabilities. An experienced trader with a proven approach simply plugs along knowing in the long run that his system will work for him. Even when hitting a cluster of losses, the trader knows that it is just a series of sequential losses and not a pattern. Often there is a need for specific trading corrections when a trader hits such a cluster, and we will discuss those in the following sections of this book. The point to remember here is that when a loss occurs in a setup, there is no need to change your entire approach, learn a different system or switch trading tools.

How do you tell one from another? It is not easy at the beginning, and for a newer trader the first kind of loss is more probable than the second kind. As a trader's experience and knowledge grow, he starts seeing which loss is "deserved" and which is just a tribute to the market uncertainty.

Let us, however, go to the next ensuing matter. If losses are unavoidable, then in order to survive and make money we need to make sure that no loss takes us out of the game. That is why the natural question at this point is:

# How do I Approach Risk?

We already see that risk is an inherent part of trading. It is vital to understand that risk is a necessary part of trading because there would not be any reward if there were no risk. There is a balance between risk and potential reward. The most risky entries often provide the best opportunities because the market works as a discounting machine. Let us go deeper in this thought as it is going to be another crucial cornerstone of your trading.

In many trading books, you will read variations on the following theme. The best time to buy is when a stock is at its darkest time, with bad news, downgrades and the worst outlook possible. It is the right time to sell when a stock has optimistic growth projections, great news, upgrades and the brightest outlook. The market works this way because by the time all the bad news is out, everyone knows things are bad. In practice, it means everyone who is selling has sold already. When there are no more sellers, the stock has hit rock bottom. The stock price has nowhere to go from this moment but up, simply because selling pressure is now absent. We are not talking about extreme cases, such as an announced company bankruptcy. Accumulation starts at this point, first by those that understand this principle. These types of players are usually referred to as Smart Money. As the price is appreciating, action attracts broader attention. More participants pile up. Finally, at some point good news pours in. This is the point at which the stock price rockets and the last batch of participants buy their shares – guess from whom? Of course - from those whom accumulated their stock at that rock bottom, darkest times. Now, when the outlook is the brightest, Smart Money sells to the crowd that came late to the party, and this event marks the top. This cycle repeats itself but now in the opposite direction: the stock price is falling because there are no more buyers and it has nowhere to go but down.

Of course, this is a somewhat simplified scenario I have described, and in reality there are many variations to it. However, it holds true and serves as a fundamental principle of the interaction between Smart Money and the Crowd. It also illustrates the idea of the market being a discounting machine: by the time everyone knows the news it is usually too late to act on it. Finally, it shows us how risk and reward are two faces of the same action. It is in times of the biggest **perceived** risk that you have the highest leverage. We say perceived because in fact it is the safest time. Here is what Justin Mamis says about this in his book *The Nature of Risk*: 'Because the market anticipates, the more you know, the later it is. The later it is, the greater the risk. There is no safety to buying on positive information (or shorting on bad news). Thus all information has a negative bias against the price trend'.

It shows you that there is much to learn and realize about risk in trading. Building your trading philosophy, you need to incorporate your attitude toward risk and your understanding of its mechanics – because risk is what you are going to face and manage on a routine basis in trading.

Now, since we already know that the market is an uncertain environment and that risk is always present, we need to answer the following question:

# What is it that Constitutes the Difference Between Reckless Gambling and Trading?

The simple answer is risk control. This 'difference' is what takes care of that problem we stated earlier: how to make sure that no single loss or string of losses takes us out of the game. Diversification for fundamental traders, stop loss for technical traders and various combinations of those two approaches should be incorporated in each trading transaction. In this way, we ensure a trader's survival in the case of a trade going bad. We are going to go deeper in this matter in the *Creating Your Trading System* part. At the level of our general philosophy, let us state the main principle of risk control:

<u>Stopping out a trade is a function of the reason for a trade not being there anymore.</u>

Earlier we listed the possible reasons for exiting a trade. When the story changes for a fundamental trader or a technical trader observes there is a break of support for a long – those are signs of a reason for a trade ceasing to be worthwhile. The following discussion will show you how this idea applies in practice.

Now, when we are done with the entire line related to risk, there is one more choice to make to round up your general approach:

# What am I Going to Trade in Terms of Market Movement?

The market spends some time in trends and some time in ranges. Those conditions require different approaches, and not many traders feel equally comfortable trading both. Even within each of them, there are different ways to trade. This is part of your trading philosophy that is almost certain to change and adjust as your experience grows. The truth of the matter is that there is no way for a beginner to know which approach suits him best. In the course of practical trading, you are going to get a feel which of those movements is a natural fit for you. Nonetheless, it is very important to understand the difference from the beginning and make deliberate choices. Keep in mind that this is a practical experience, which will show you how comfortable you are with your choice. By approaching it this way, you collect meaningful experience in the sense that you understand which components of your trading approach need to be changed and adjusted. Realize also that as you advance through your learning curve you will reach a stage where you are able to distinguish between different kinds of market movement and apply this or that approach accordingly.

Let us define range and trend, and see what the basic principles of trading in both cases are.

**Range** is a type of movement where the price tops and bottoms at the same levels. Trading in a range will require a classic trading approach, 'buy low, sell high.' It works as long as the stock moves within a range. When the range is broken, moving over the top or below the bottom, the trade will be stopped out.

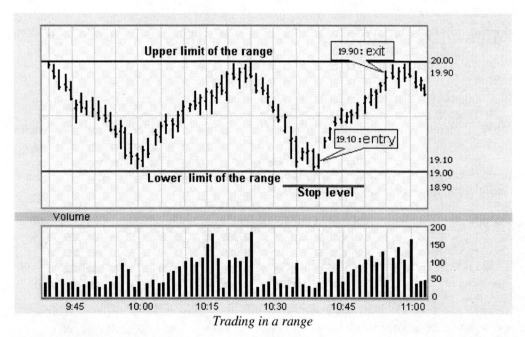

*Trading in a range*

In the example above, a stock moves in a range from $19 to 20. Trading on the long side, a trader will buy it near the support level – the lower limit of the range – and sell near the resistance level – the upper limit of the range. His stop is located below the lower limit in accordance with the idea of getting out of a trade when the reason for it ceases to exist. In this particular case, the reason for this trade is the price difference moving between support and resistance. When the support level is broken, the reason to be in the trade is not there anymore.

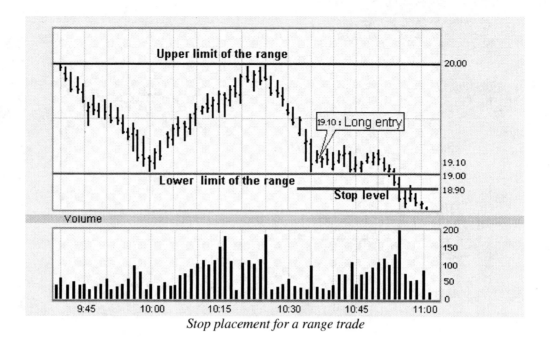

*Stop placement for a range trade*

Obviously, trading on the short side, a trader will short near the resistance level and cover his position near support level. His stop in this case will be just above the upper limit of a range.

**Trend** is a directional type of a movement. There are two self-explanatory kinds of trend: uptrend and downtrend.

**Uptrend** is a type of movement where the price makes higher highs and higher lows. **Downtrend** is a type of movement where the price makes lower highs and lower lows. In the following discussion we will use uptrend examples. Everything said will be equally valid for a downtrend movement with obvious differences in direction.

Trading in a trend presents a trader with more choices compared to a range trade. First, you need to decide if you are going to be a **trend follower** or hunt for **trend reversals**.

A **follower** goes with the trend direction, trying to capitalize on the trend itself. For the follower, the reason for a trade is the price making new highs while support is not broken. In the process of moving higher, the stock forms new support levels. Thus, a break of any of these support levels constitutes the cessation of a reason for the trade. This idea is illustrated by two examples displayed below. Both of them are uptrend examples, the only difference is that in the first example the price is bouncing off a support line right away while in the second example, there are no pronounced pullbacks, so the price is consolidating before making a new high. When trading the uptrend, a trader rather goes with principle 'buy high, sell higher'. When trading the downtrend, it's 'short low, cover lower'. There are variations to the buying high in the sense that you can buy a new high or on a pullback. We are going to discuss them later.

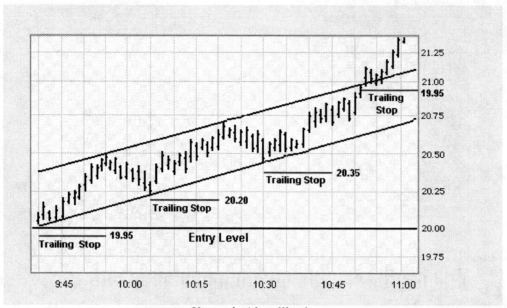

*Uptrend with pullbacks*

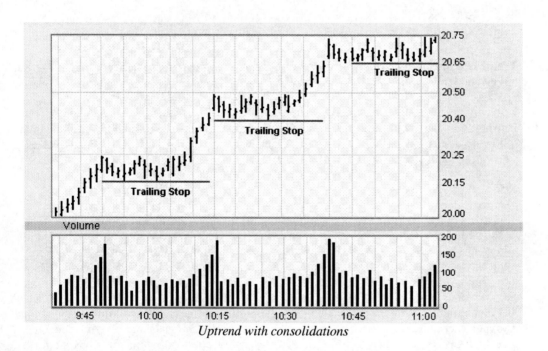

*Uptrend with consolidations*

A **trend reversal** trader, also known as a bottom-fisher, is looking for the point where the selling becomes exhausted and the direction changes.

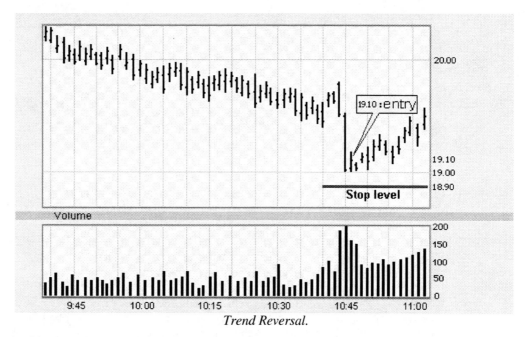

*Trend Reversal.*

In this example, the rationale for this trade is an assumption that the final low has been made and the trend is going to reverse. Thus, any new low after the initial bounce will render the reason for this trade non-existent, so the stop is placed just below the last support level.

Making your choice at this stage, you need to keep in mind that trading for reversals is very risky and requires a good deal of experience. It is not advisable for newer traders to start with this approach, and if you do – remember that the role of stops is even more critical. Bottom fishing is also known as "catching falling knives", and for a very good reason.

As you advance further in your studying, you are going to learn the tools that help you find the points of entry for each type of trade. It is a strong possibility that even at this stage you will change your decision about what you are going to trade as some tools appeal to you more than others. Practical trading will further refine this process. Make your pick now and be open to the changes later on.

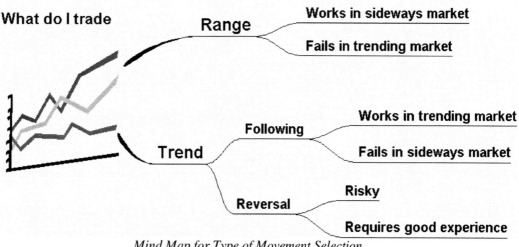

*Mind Map for Type of Movement Selection*

## You Asked

**Question:**

What about different trading vehicles? There are stocks, futures, currencies, commodities and lots more. How do I decide what vehicle is best? What are the advantages and disadvantages to them?

**Answer:**

Let us leave currencies, bonds and commodities out of the framework of this discussion. It is not that they are not tradeable; however, those are quite specific markets. It is quite possible that at some point in your trading career you will get interested in them. I would suggest you start with the classic securities markets where the technology is quite advanced, there is a solid base of knowledge and experience to draw upon and plenty of available material to study. We will focus on stocks and e-mini futures.

E-mini futures reflect the movement of the related market: S&P, Dow or NASDAQ. For all practical purposes, they move and can be traded pretty much like stocks. There are certain advantages to futures. For instance, there is no need to get familiar with the specifics of certain stocks; they trade with constant spread; there is just one vehicle to focus on; their liquidity is fairly deep which makes it easier to increase your trading size as your experience grows. On the other hand, when the market is locked in a tight range or trading in the way that does not cooperate with your trading system you can probably find a stock that provides you with opportunity. Since many brokers allow trading both securities and futures both in single account, I would suggest looking into trading both. If you prefer to focus on one of them, that is fine, too. Considering that stocks involve more variables, most of the further discussion will be about stocks.

**Question:**

How about choosing between the NASDAQ and NYSE? Any preferences?

**Answer:**

The situation is changing lately and it is hard to say how those changes will play out in the near future. These are somewhat different markets. The NASDAQ, is a free competition market where everyone is trading for himself and no one controls the way things go. On the NYSE there is a specialist handling the trades and to a certain degree controlling them. Orders are filled automatically on the NASDAQ which leads to faster executions. The longer your timeframe, the less this difference matters. My personal preference is to trade the NASDAQ. Do not however, assume that this should influence your choice.

The last component of this choice is your **level of aggressiveness**. Let us recall the idea that we discussed earlier, about the balance between the risk and reward. There is similar trade-off in terms of aggressiveness. We will illustrate the concept using an example of a breakout trade which is usually related to the trend following method. First, the illustration of the breakout idea:

In this example, a stock is ranging between support and resistance level. A break of resistance signals an uptrend is starting. Unlike a range trader, a trend follower will wait for this break to enter from a long side. In this particular case, his stop is going to be .25 cents – the break of support rendering the reason for a trade not being there anymore. This is the general idea of the breakout setup.

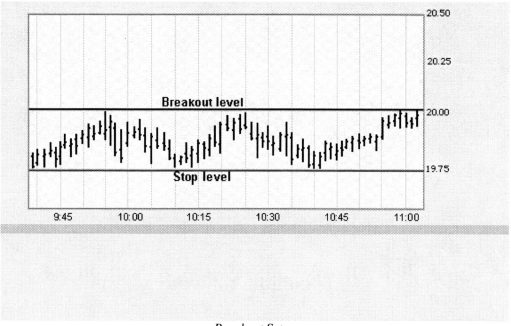

*Breakout Setup*

Now, let us look into different ways to enter the trade from the standpoint of aggressiveness. There are three ways to initiate the trade: **regular**, **aggressive** and **conservative**.

**Regular** entry is the most straightforward. It is simply an entry as the breakout occurs, at the $20 level in this case. This way is more or less "mainstream" in the sense that most traders use it as their primary way to initiate the trade. It means that you are going to compete for shares as you enter this way.

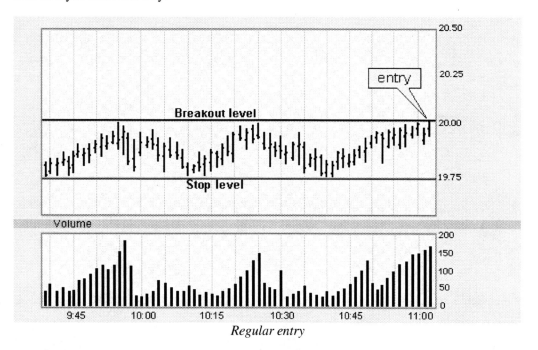

*Regular entry*

**Aggressive** entry means that you are initiating your trade in advance, counting on the breakout in the future.

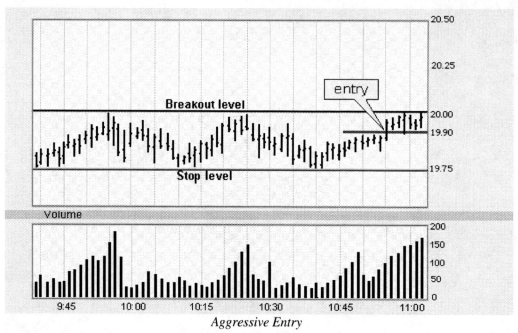

*Aggressive Entry*

In this particular case, the entry is being taken .10 cents below the breakout level. Advantages are obvious: your stop is tighter, your profit potential is bigger and competition for shares is not as fierce. The trade-off is, in accordance with the quote from Justin Mamis that we cited earlier, you have less confidence in the breakout. In other words, your certainty of an eventual breakout is less, while reward in case it occurs is higher and your loss in case of failure is smaller.

**Conservative** entry is taken AFTER the breakout, on a pullback that you expect to occur after the break.

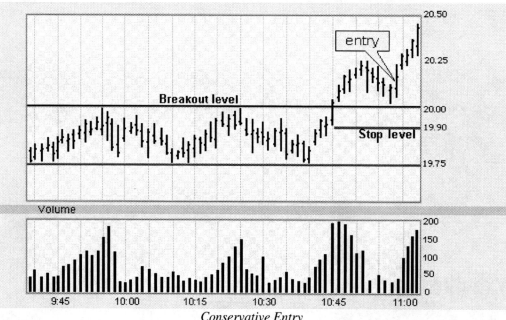

*Conservative Entry*

In this case, you let the breakout go and wait to see if a stock pulls back and holds a new support level formed by the former resistance. The idea of this approach is that if a break is valid, price should not go below that former breakout level significantly. With this approach you place your stop under the new support level as shown on the illustration (this support, if broken, invalidates the reason for a trade). The advantages of this method: you have more confidence in the breakout and the competition for shares is not too big. The trade-offs are, if a stock never looks back you are going to miss the trade altogether and your entry is not as favourable a price as in the two previous cases.

Different ways to enter could be applied to trend reversal as well. For instance, aggressive entry in the case shown for the reversal trade would be an attempt to initiate the trade as soon as selling pauses; regular would be entry on the first upticks; conservative would be letting a stock bounce, wait for pullback and entry if no new low is being made. Let us put all three on a single illustration to see the difference clearly.

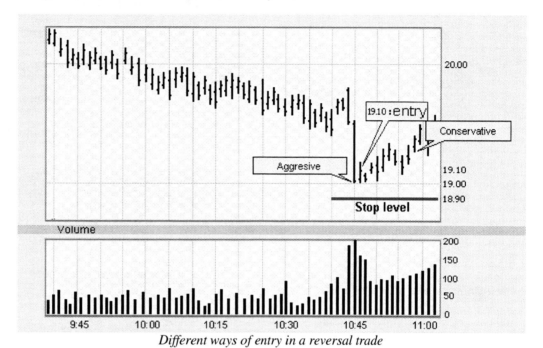

*Different ways of entry in a reversal trade*

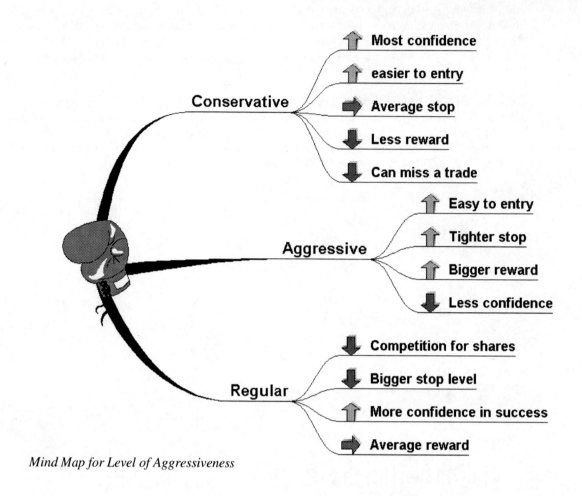

*Mind Map for Level of Aggressiveness*

We went over the major elements of your trading philosophy. Let us sum them up in a mind map and establish the connections that we outlined earlier.

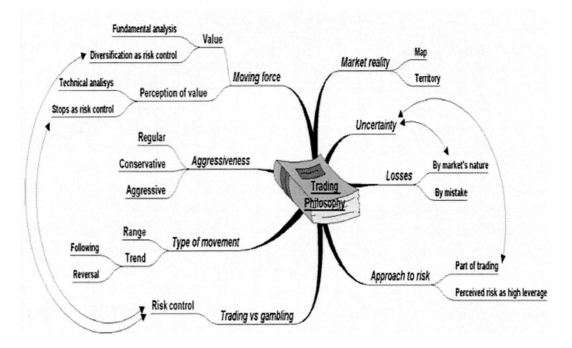

## Resources for Trading Philosophy

http://www.realitytrader.com/Tapereading.asp#dual
http://www.realitytrader.com/Tapereading.asp#philosophy

## Recommended Reading

RR1; RR2; RR4; RR11; RR13; RR19

## Trading Plan

At this stage, we are going to shape up the part of your trading plan describing your adopted trading philosophy.

### Trading Plan Form: My Trading Philosophy

In my approach, the market's action is dictated by

_____

_____

The ultimate market reality for me is the price action. I never consider the market wrong. The market works in probabilities. There is no one hundred percent certainty in the market's action. Losses are unavoidable and an inherent part of trading.

Some losses are just a part of market uncertainty. Others provide a lesson. It is important to distinguish one from another and learn the lesson presented by a loss.

Risk is a necessary part of trading for there would be no reward if there were no risk. I embrace risk and appreciate the fact that it provides me with opportunity.

Risk control is turning trading into a planned activity. When a reason for a trade is not there anymore, a trade must be cancelled entirely.

In my approach, a reason for taking a trade is

_____

Sign(s) of a reason not being there anymore for me is

_____

_____

The type of the movement that I am going to trade is

_____

_____

My level of aggressiveness is

_____

_____

# *Traders Talk – Bo Yoder*

*Trades since 1994, full time since from 1999. Author of Mastering Futures Trading, McGraw Hill, 2004. Speaker at Trading Expos in Las Vegas, New York, Chicago, Anaheim. Leading trader for RealityTrader.com. Swing trader in stocks and futures with trading as main source of income. 29 years old, Maine, USA*

I have always learned best by exploring and experimenting. I learned a great deal about trading from books, peers, mentors, but in the end, I needed to prove these concepts for myself through real-time/real money experimentation. By trading, trading, and then trading some more, I built a database of real world experience that gave me the conviction I needed to trust my edge in the markets. As I taught myself to trade, I went from "A" to "B" via "L". I am sure that if a systematic/curriculum type approach had been available to me it would have saved me a great deal of time and mental anguish. I see how a more structured approach helps jumpstart my consulting clients' learning curves, and feel a bit chagrined that I had to do it the hard way.

I started trading full-time during the bubble years. The edge at this time was so sloppy, that even with errors, mistakes, and trade mismanagement I was still able to make money. So, I take that time for the anomaly it was, and would say that it took two years before I achieved stability and consistency in my trading.

My first trade was 1000 shares long CSCO. I lost $300 in the blink of an eye. Every book I read talked about trading in 1000 share lots. It took a while before I realized I was out of my league, and needed to get small and learn or go broke. When I first started trading in the late '90s, I had less than $10,000 in my account. At this point I was trying to employ a fundamental approach, and thought of myself as an investor, not a trader. I took a position for fundamental reasons in a telecommunications stock. The stock rallied for me in the short term as my entry was well timed. Immediately thereafter, the stock topped out and began to fall slowly but steadily. I went through the common hope-cycle of the greenhorn. Justifying my purchase with the fundamentals, hoping the stock would work its way back to "fair value". The decline continued, and eventually I capitulated after losing about $3,000 on my investment. That loss, while not catastrophic in the grand scheme of things, certainly taught me respect for the market's ability to punish an incorrect opinion. In retrospect, this loss was probably the best thing that could have happened to me. Had I been rewarded for my lack of money management or risk control, I probably would have continued these destructive behaviors until my inevitable come-uppance.

I really feel like I became a trader about two years after I started trading full-time. I experienced the worst losing streak of my career. I lost small amounts of money steadily for a solid month. Not only did I lose every week, but almost every day as well. Two losers, one winner one day. One loser, one winner the next. I never banked a terrible loss; rather it was death by a thousand cuts.

After a month of this misery, I decided I had enough and took a week off. When I returned I looked at my trading loss and discovered there were a few behaviors I should change. I made these changes and began trading again with a fresh mind. I made enough money the week after I returned to completely recover what it took me a month to lose. It was at that point when I really began to believe in myself and my skill set. I feel like that trial by fire "made me" into the trader I wished to become.

I really didn't start formalizing my trading plan until the middle of my third year as a full-time trader. It was during this year that I realized that the consistency in my trading was coming from the consistency in my approach to the markets. Having discovered this, I realized I needed to formalize and quantify my edge. As I began to analyze why I made money, I learned a great deal about myself as a trader and took a giant step forward along my learning curve. I worked out a certain trading philosophy for myself with major points:

- The entry is the only time you have absolute control over your trades.

- Maximize this control and become the best entry technician you can be.

- The market rewards the anticipator; too much confirmation reduces your risk to reward ratio.

- The crowd is always wrong, the richest trade entries will occur just before the crowd makes its incorrect trading decision.

- Your edge is an expression of a mathematical and statistical expectation. Each trade is but a tiny piece of the overall pie. No one trade can make or break you, losses are to be expected, not dreaded.

I call myself a "chart reader". I use candlestick charts of price and time to analyze the supply/demand forces that exist at any given time in the marketplace. I became a chart reader gradually as I began to realize that technical price patterns were becoming more stimulative rather than predictive market events. The price pattern attracted the crowd. Since the crowd is always wrong, if I could interpret their actions and motivations I could fade them successfully for a profitable trade.

I started out as a very fundamentally driven investor. I quickly realized how often the market ignores undervalued stocks and rewards overvalued stocks. As I began to learn more about technical analysis, I was intrigued by the idea of "listening to the market". As a fundamental analyst, I felt I was dictating to the market, and then waiting for it to realize the "rightness" of my opinions. The more I traded, more experience I gained, the more incorrect this approach felt to me. Swing trading became a timeframe with which I felt most comfortable. I find personally that I cannot sustain the focus needed for small timeframe day trading. I'm much more comfortable forming my opinion, setting my stops and letting the broker do the work after that. I am calmer and less emotional when trading the deeper timeframes, my accuracy and risk to reward ratios are much better. As I experimented with different timeframes, the deeper timeframes just "felt" better to me so I began to specialize on daily and weekly swings/position trading.

I trade reversals mostly. I find the market rewards the anticipatory trader the most richly. I would rather accept the lower accuracy that reversal trading delivers in order to obtain a much higher risk to reward ratio. As my experience and confidence grew so did my aggressiveness. Profitable trading takes a bit of arrogance. When you put a trade on, you must feel like the market has made a mistake in offering you your entry price. There is a sense that you are the only one right, and everyone else's market opinion is about to be proven wrong.

I take risk as an inherent part of trading. It's my job; it's why the market offers me a pay check. As a speculator, I am paid to assume the risk that others wish to avoid. It is my job to determine which of these risks are being avoided foolishly. You must be comfortable with risk in order to trade consistently. "Scared money" always loses in the end. You must learn to embrace your risk, not fear it if you wish to succeed in the long-term. I control risk by never endangering more money that I am truly willing to lose. Yet, there is one more aspect of trading related to risk. It's stress. Stress in trading is often caused by feeling out of control. By understanding clearly what you can and cannot be in control of, you can release much attention and frustration trading can cause. I get frustrated and angry when I lose money because of an error or a bit of mismanagement over some aspect of trading that I DO control. If I take a loss due to some unforeseen and uncontrollable force, it doesn't bother me....this is just part of the business.

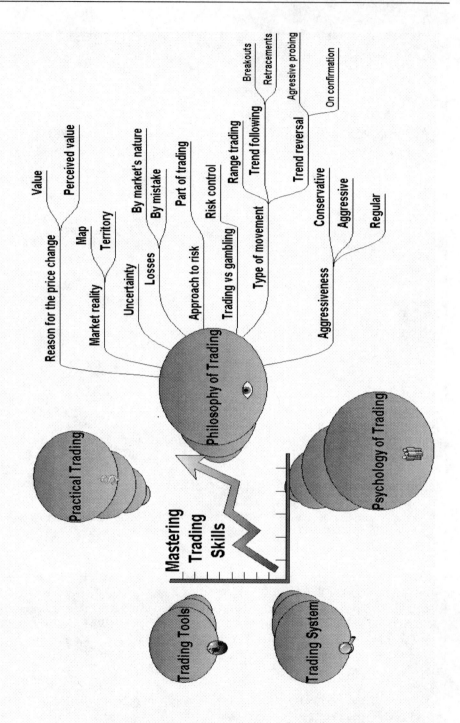

# Part II: Trading Psychology

# Simple vs. Easy

There is a great paradox in trading the markets. Believe it or not, trading can be very simple. Many experienced traders refer to their trading approach as very simple. You do not have to be a rocket scientist in order to build a working trading system. In fact, if you can do as much as connect two dots with a line and can tell a higher number from lower one, you are solidly on your way. There is a great catch to it, however. SIMPLE does not equal EASY. Is trading simple? Yes, it is – if you chose it to be so. Is it easy? Not necessarily. Sometimes it is amazing how something that simple can be that hard. The cause of this paradox is within us. It is simple to understand what needs to be done. It is not always easy to actually do it.

Psychology is another part of a trader's education usually put off until a later time. At the beginning, many do not even suspect how important a role this side plays in their trading achievements. It is only after a certain amount of struggle, and often losses, that traders realize the importance of psychology in trading. There are two sides to the psychology role in trading. First, let us call it **defensive**, which is avoiding an incorrect mindset and putting oneself in the right state of mind necessary for successful trading. The second side, **offensive**, comes into play when a trader is moving to more advanced levels. The offensive side is two-fold. It is directed internally to engage one's intuition as a powerful tool of filtering; and it is directed externally to evaluate another's thinking in order to exploit it.

# Defensive Aspect of Psychology

The difference between a correct and wrong mindset in trading is the difference between success and failure. The problem is, in trading it is not enough to know what to do. It can be very difficult to actually do what you know is right. Almost everyone is successful in paper trading but it is a very different situation when your money is on line. The correct trading requires a somewhat unusual mindset – one that is vastly different from what works for us in all other fields of activity. You need to act with certainty in an uncertain environment; you need to think in probabilities; you need to learn to accept risk; you need to reverse many of the reactions habitual for human beings. You need finally, to learn to do one of the hardest things for an individual with the slightest shred of ambition – suppress your ego.

Let us list major distinctions in the mindset required for trading.

## Obey the Market

In many other areas of activity, we are taught to try to influence the way things go. We convince people around us. We try to impact their decisions. We argue points and defend our position. In other words, we have some power to change the development of events to a certain degree. We are taught this way of thinking from the very beginning of our formal education and even earlier. If you want to be successful - make others understand you, trust you, believe in you and follow your lead. Change things around you. Make things work. Lead. Manage.

This is not the way things work in trading. Here you deal with something that is so much bigger than any particular player, that it is practically impossible to have any significant impact on the market. Any attempt to impose your opinion on the market will lead to your destruction. As we said in the *Trading Philosophy* part, the market is always right. Now we are dealing with the practical implementation of that thesis, and this implication is: Do not try to push what cannot be pushed. If the market is always right, then the key to successful trading is listening to it and obeying it. It is swimming with the current that is going to take you where the current goes. Thinking and acting like this we need to forfeit our ego, admitting that if the market does something opposite to what we expected, we are wrong. As

*Techniques of Tape Reading* says, 'The market is your boss. Obey it and get paid, or rebel and get fired. You do not fight the ocean; you swim in it. If you find yourself in a current that takes you in an undesirable direction, you do not try to change its direction. Look for another current.'

## Control Yourself

If you cannot control the market, then how do you impact the outcome of your actions? The answer is simple: by controlling yourself. If the market does what it does, then it is your responsibility to make your reactions well thought through and not emotionally impulsive. As Stephen R. Covey puts it in *The 7 Habits of Highly Effective People*, 'Between stimulus and response, man has the freedom to choose'. By accepting the thesis that the market is always right, we accept the idea that there is no place for emotional response in trading; we simply need to internalize the thought of necessity to follow the market's lead and execute decisions accordingly.

## Comfort with no Protection

We are accustomed to having a certain safety net in many areas of our life. There is insurance for your health; there is a warranty for your purchase; there is social help for your various needs. We are conditioned to perceive our environment as mostly friendly, a one that limits our options to fail. An environment with no mechanism of protection is perceived by us to be hostile. Yet this is exactly what we face in the markets – it is indifferent to our existence and does not care if we make a mistake. No one is going to stop you from making an error or compensate you for the outcome of poor judgment. This makes us fully responsible for our actions and the consequent outcome. This feeling is uncomfortable at first; however, by accepting the responsibility for our errors we also become entitled to pride in our achievements. This is only natural because on the positive side of the coin no one is going to limit our winning potential or prevent us from making a right decision. Trading is a profession where it is totally up to you whether you win or lose.

<u>Humble toward the market, fully in control of yourself, responsible for your actions and proud of your success – this is your psychological profile as an ideal trader.</u>

## Be a Good Loser

In order to win, a trader has to learn how to correctly lose. We discussed in the *Trading Philosophy* part the different kinds of losses. A good trader has to learn to lose gracefully, with an understanding that loss is a part of trading. He also has to learn to lose easily taking his losses quickly before they grow larger. A stop loss taken correctly is not a loss for him – it is a way to stop the loss from growing. It is his protection, his safety net. Risk control means, among other things, cutting your losses quickly.

## Forget Standard Work Ethics

One of the strong beliefs ingrained in us is the more you work the more you will be rewarded. In trading, this direct connection is not true. We are not talking about learning how to trade here – this is work that has to be done. What many do under the impact of this belief though is they try to trade all of the time. Sitting on their hands doing nothing feels like wasting their time, they almost feel ashamed. This often results in making unnecessary trades and taking incomplete or poor setups. Sitting on the sideline when there are no trades matching your approach is one of the most important skills you can learn. A good trader will take only the best trades and avoid marginal ones, keeping his probabilities for winning as high as possible.

## Learn to Act without Knowing

Our entire education and most of other professions teach us to gather as much information as possible to be able to predict the outcome of our action.

It is necessary for an engineer designing a bridge – he had better know for sure the bridge would hold the load. It does not work this way in trading. There is no way to know what is going to happen as we established in the previous part. You can suggest certain scenarios and prepare your response to each of them.

Do not believe that you cannot win successfully and consistently if you do not know what will happen next. In chess, you never know what your opponent is going to do. In martial arts, you do not know either. Yet obviously, there are chess players and fighters that are consistently better than others. They do not know their opponent's moves in advance. Their winning is based on being good at their game and having prepared reactions – a scenario of 'IF – THEN'. It works exactly this way in trading, too. An ability to act in an uncertain environment is an essential trait of a trader.

## Reverse your Natural Instincts

On this topic, there is a perfect quote in *Reminiscences of a Stock Operator*, by Edwin Lefervre. I will cite it in full as it comprehensively covers what we have just been discussing:

'The speculator's chief enemies are always born from within. It is inseparable from human nature to hope and to fear. In speculation when the market goes against you hope that every day will be the last day – and you lose more than you should had you not listened to hope – to the same ally that is so potent a success-bringer to empire builders and pioneers, big and little. And, when the market goes your way you become fearful that the next day will take away your profit, and you get out – too soon. Fear keeps you from making as much money as you ought to. The successful trader has to fight these two deep-seated instincts. He has to reverse what you might call his natural impulses. Instead of hoping, he must fear; instead of fearing he must hope. He must fear that his loss may develop into much bigger loss, and hope that his profit may become a big profit'.

## How do you do the Change?

All the differences listed above lead us to a conclusion that to trade successfully a trader has to change his psychological makeup. An adjustment of the mindset is necessary in order to learn to listen to the market. We talked about the market's reality and perceived reality earlier. Now we are talking about a process in which your mindset changes allowing you to close the gap between your map and the territory. However, as with all self-change and self-improvement processes, there is a question about how to do it.

It is a two-step process. The first step is to **understand your goal** and visualize the state of mind you have to arrive at. The second step is **actual change**. This is an individual process, in the sense that different people do it in different ways and with various degrees of ease. For some the very understanding of how they should think is enough, they just move into this new state of mind. For others, this process is quite difficult as old habits return after a brief period.

Many traders tend to repeat old mistakes that they seemed to get under control. In some astonishing way, when presented with an opportunity to make an old mistake, well familiar to a trader already, he feels "this time it is different". This is probably one of the most costly thoughts a trader can have. For traders that experience this kind of setback, the realization of the right way to think and act is not enough. There is a need in the practical steps - you can call them tricks - that will make this transition easier and permanent. I have two favorite methods:

**'The Model Trader'** and **'If I Were Smart'**. Let me describe both.

The major change that has to be ingrained is emotional detachment. When you are involved emotionally in a particular trade, it means your thinking has become subjective. The chance of your map distorting significantly is higher. A perception that your opinion is right or wrong becomes vastly different versus the case when you evaluate someone else's opinion. Instead of focusing on the market's action, you risk becoming focused on your being right and on your money. The focus should remain on the subject of your job as a trader, and this subject is the market movement. Money made or lost is an outcome of you doing your job properly or poorly. This is the same as a surgeon focusing on a surgery he performs and not on the monetary reward for that surgery – if he is good surgeon of course. The market, as we said before, has no interest in the state of your trading account – it is not trying to make money for you or take it from you. Thus, focus on the market's action and not on your money. If you act correctly, the money will follow.

It is not an accident that traders do well when paper trading. It is an absence of emotional involvement, which makes paper trading so much more profitable. If you can replicate this state of mind when trading with real money, your chances for success are much greater. My favorite method to achieve this state of detachment is to create a **Model Trader** in your mind.

The following section might seem too esoteric for you as a beginner at this stage. Simply read it, take what you find useful from it and return to it in a month or two after you start practical trading. The method described below is likely to appeal more to you at that point.

## Model Trader

The idea of this method is to envision a person possessing the traits necessary for successful trading. Those traits must be well thought through so this model trader becomes real to you, with reactions that you can see and understand. When you create such a person, simply let him trade your account, acting according to those traits. Remain an observer of his action. Create a role for yourself – you can be his student or his supervisor, or his mentor. The important part is it is not you who is trading. You are detached emotionally since you can remain just an observer. Ask him questions about why he did this or that, and think how he would answer – from a position of model trader. Demand his report about his trading and mark his performance, giving him directions on how to improve it.

There are multiple advantages of this method. You can remain **emotionally detached** as we said before. You become more **flexible** as it is easy to correct those traits that require correction or add new ones as you see the need. You are less likely to focus on money as it is the performance of your model trader that you are observing and evaluating. He, in turn, **focuses on the market action** since he is not trading his own money. Recreating his actions according to the traits you gave him, you become him, and this is exactly what you want to achieve – to become your model trader. Finally, this method creates certain **playfulness**, and this is very important, too. It allows you to decrease your emotional tension, create an **uninhibited state of mind**, and unchain your mind for **objective perception**. Move further with this idea of a playful approach and give him a name. Relaxed George? Robbie Granite-Face? John the Money Grabber? Do not be afraid to be playful – a creative, relaxed mind is very effective. It also opens your mind for intuitive perception – something that is going to come later to you as your skills grow.

Now as we went over major differences of a trading mindset, let us look at a trader's action sequentially in a developing trade and discuss the psychological makeover of each. There are psychological problems a trader often encounters at each stage of a trade. These problems include impulsive trading on marginal reasons; fear of pulling the trigger; premature exit of a profitable trade; an exit for no good reason based on anxiety; failing to keep the stop.

We are going to go over each stage of putting on a trade and managing it and see how our model trader Joe Calm does it. This is going to be your first guideline to creating your own trader within you.

## Model Trader Action

### Stage 1: Looking for a Trade

In the beginning, Joe Calm is scanning the market looking for a trade matching his criteria. He has his trading system, which defines his ideal trading setup. He is not jumping impulsively on anything that moves. He is not acting on tips. He is not entering the trade because someone likes it. A commentator on CNBC or in a newspaper enthusiastic about a stock is not his sole motivation for a trade. Any trading idea that comes from outside is nothing more than a reason to look at the particular stock setup.

Joe does not feel obliged to be in the market all the time. He understands that money inside in his trading account is his tool. The tool has to be ready, sharp, oiled – and used when needed.

For Joe the process of looking for a trade is much like ambush hunting. He is patient while waiting for his prey to come along. It is either the best conditions possible for him or no trade. He is carefully monitoring his state taking care to remain objective and not tempted by a lucrative but marginal setup. If his conditions for a trade are not met in full – he ignores the trade. Long inaction does not bother him. A hot market that does not offer his type of opportunity, his edge, does not make him anxious.

Joe Calm has his trading plan for the day. He goes over market conditions in advance. He has his set of possible scenarios that include possible market actions and his reactions. He knows which sectors are hot and which are not. His attention focuses on the area of the market where he feels opportunity coming.

He knows his risk limitations. He evaluates each trading candidate not only from a reward angle. His first consideration is risk. If he sees that a trade failure will cause him to lose more on the trade than his trading plan assumes – the trade is going to be skipped.

To sum it up, Joe Calm is not imposing his view on the market. He is waiting for a market to come to him. It means that he is going to put on a trade when the market offers him conditions matching his trading system requirements. He is not gambling – he is trading.

### Stage 2: Trade Initiation

When all the conditions for a trade are met, Joe enters the market. He has no fear of engagement. This is his profession; this is what he lives for. He is not eager to be in the market all of the time but when his setup comes along, there is no hesitation. All the work necessary for trade evaluation is complete; a setup is there; risk is assumed and carefully weighed. He sees a signal matching his trading system criteria and this is enough for him to act.

Joe Calm sizes his position accordingly to his risk. His trading plan includes risk as one of the most important elements. No matter how lucrative the reward is, his position size will not exceed what his trading plan defines as his maximum pain tolerance. Joe defines his degree of aggressiveness. Depending on market conditions, he enters aggressively or conservatively.

He knows his tools for order execution and uses them effectively. Different types of orders and their match to different market conditions are well known to him. He picks his way to route an order automatically, without thinking – all the thinking is done during his preparation and learning his tools.

If a setup matching his criteria comes along and for some reason Joe does not get his best shot, he is not chasing the price. He gets his order entry at his price or no trade.

## Stage 3: Riding a Trade

The first thing Joe does when his entry is completed is he enters his stop order. In the case of a quick intraday trade or scalp he might opt for a manual stop which is a stop executed by him not by the computer. However, that is an exception for him because Joe prefers to be on the safe side.

The next thing for Joe Calm to do is to sit tight. He ignores the market's noise. Everything the market does between Joe's stop and target is qualified as noise – meaningless action that requires no reaction on Joe's part. His defined stop level was chosen for a reason, and if this stop is not hit – there is no reason to exit the trade. His exit signal on the profitable side is defined by his trading system – and until such signal is generated, there is no reason to take profits. Joe is not trading looking at his trading account balance – his trade actions are governed by the market actions. He is an ultimate market listener. Joe knows how to be patient. He simply lets the market do its thing. For him the trade's fate from the moment of entering is totally up to the market – he is not trying to engage when there is no reason. All the decisions made before entering the trade are part of the plan – now the plan executes. Joe observes the action with his IF-THEN scenarios in mind. This approach keeps him from premature exiting with unnecessary stops or a little profit not justifying the risk.

If time in a trade is an element of Joe's trading system, he considers it. If a trade is not resolved in a time span provided by his plan, Joe closes the trade. If he is an intraday trader with no plan to hold his position overnight and the trade has still not resolved itself by the market's close, Joe will exit the trade.

## Stage 4: Exiting a Trade

There are two cases for an exit: **stop** and **profit taking**.

### Exit on the stop side

If Joe's stop is hit, it is taken. It is not discussed, questioned or rationalized. A stop is Joe's way to protect his trading account. Stops are taken religiously.

Joe Calm encounters situations where a stock reverses after hitting his stop and returns to a breakeven level or even in the profit zone. Nonetheless, those cases are not making Joe question the reasonability of taking stops. He knows that if he ignores them, his loss at some point is going to wipe out all his profits. He is not frustrated by taking a stop – his trading philosophy includes understanding that loss is a natural part of trading.

If a stock comes into a stop level in a way that would normally signal entry at this level in Joe's trading system, he might wait a little to see if the stock bounces back enough to minimize his loss. If there is no sign of such a bounce, the stop is taken.

Joe never averages down if a trade does not work. He knows there is another trade just around the corner. He does not get involved in his position that much to add funds to a non-working trade.

### Exit on a profit side

When a sell signal is generated by Joe Calm's system, he exits a trade. He does not try to sit in a trade longer than his method of market reading allows. He knows that the profit can evaporate and has to be protected. If his trading approach includes partial exits, he takes them as a way to protect part of the obtained gain, while the remaining part of the position is kept in order to maximize his potential profit.

## Stage 5: After a Trade

When a trade is completed, it is filed in Joe's trading journal. This journal is going to be his tool to analyze his performance, reevaluate his system and make corrections if needed. It also will serve as a window into Joe's inner state to evaluate whether his reactions were correct and his judgment was not clouded by emotions. Joe is confident in his ability to keep his emotions in check; however, he knows very well that an inner enemy can creep up unnoticed. Joe is on guard and always aware of his limitations.

## If I Were Smarter

The second method deals with the following issue which you are likely to encounter as your trading progresses. You learn the right way to act; you do right trades; you know what trades are mistakes – yet you slip now and then and do what you know is the wrong thing to do. It is as if there is an inner enemy within you that makes you do that time and again. It is actually correct: self-change is not something that occurs quickly or easily. In order to return myself on the right track I designed the **If I Were Smarter** method. When I saw myself slipping into a pattern of repeating old mistakes, I made a table with two columns. Trades that matched my trading approach went to the left column. Trades that deviated from my approach, fell into a category "I should know better", and went into the right column. Notice a very important thing: they were not categorized by the label winning or losing. There were winning and losing trades in both columns. They were classified only by the category "matching my approach or not". After the table was completed following a couple of weeks of sloppy trading, I summarized the results to see where my trading balance would be if I were never to deviate from my system. The results were shocking. I was practically robbing myself! This trick does wonders to discipline oneself by this shocking reminder. If you start to categorize trades this way before taking them, the results of that table immediately sober you up.

# *Traders Talk – Alan Farley*

*Trades since late '80s. Author of Master Swing Trader, McGraw Hill, 2000. Speaker at Trading Expos. Columnist for TheStreet.com. Headtrader of www.hardrightedge.com. Swing trader in stocks, trading is main source of Income. 53 years old, Arizona, USA.*

**How did you start trading?**

My last career was in the insurance industry. I was a claims manager for many years. I was one of the first people at my company who was able to put in a modem when modems were very, very expensive. Due to downsizing, there would be stretches of months on end when you would try to find people in management but they'd been laid off. I couldn't get any instructions from my higher-ups, so I'd finish my work and just sit there. I had nothing to do so I taught myself the market and trading as a swing trader.

I think a lot of people, I almost said the less informed, but I think a lot of people have a sense that swing trading is some sort of momentum trading. That's not really true. In a directional market, you play momentum. You buy high. You sell higher. You buy higher. You sell even higher than that.

Swing trading uses the sloppy part of the market a little bit better. It uses support and resistance. It uses market mechanics more than fundamentals, and more than the excitement of a crowd filled with greed or fear.

**How long do you tend to hold stocks?**

My favorite holding period is about two to three days. But, I've held positions for a couple of weeks. I think they set up in different timeframes and you have to be willing to align your holding period to that timeframe if you want to make any money on it.

Sometimes it's the type of setup where, from the chart, it looks like it's going to take a couple weeks to setup. You've got to be able to choose your spots so your stops don't get blown out.

**You taught yourself to do this in the mid '90s?**

It was really back in the late '80s and early '90s. At the beginning you read lots of books. I used to go down to Barnes and Noble, but everything was 60, 70 dollars, and I thought, "The stuff is expensive." So I'd go on a Saturday morning, sit there for three or four hours and just pull things out of the shelves and read them. Eventually I started buying some books.

As the Internet became faster and better, I met some excellent technicians online. I actually joined the staff at Compuserve's Investor's Forum for several years and I wound up reading every post on that site. There were probably three quarters of a million posts that I read in 2 or 3 years while working for them. It was the only place to go. There was no Web environment and it was before Motley Fool. Before AOL. So you talk about learning economics and trading. When you read close to a million posts by professional economists, investors and traders, you really learn a tremendous amount. It was a lot of fun.

**What helped you the most in your learning process?**

It was a man named John Yurko, a very humble technician. John was on the staff of Investor's Forum, too. He introduced me to some really classic, technical analysis principles and even beyond that, he introduced me to a counterintuitive way of thinking. Technical analysis (TA) and trading are two separate skills and I think they are very often confused. A lot of folks think if they learn TA that makes them a trader. So they get in there and they get their clock cleaned.

I believe TA must be used within the context of trading. All the charts in the world won't do you any good unless you have a strategy to deal with price movement at any particular point in time.

**In other words, have a plan before you go in?**

It's even more than a plan. It's a perception. It's a point of view. So much of what the market gives you is counterintuitive, even in respect to the price chart. The price chart will say one thing, but sometimes you have to be willing to do exactly the opposite because you understand that's the hidden reaction message within the chart. It's very difficult to learn, but that is what successful traders do.

They say that profits don't follow the majority in the market. Profits follow the minority and, it follows, the counterintuitive and original thinking process. If you develop the same point of view and the same thinking process as everybody else, well, it's the majority that loses the money. Somebody's got to be taking it. So you want to get on the other side.

**How much do you use the larger macroeconomic picture?**

Almost never. With the large swings in the market, it's important to know what kind of environment we're in. That helps me determine how long I'm willing to hold a stock. You don't want to get in the way of certain economic reports. When there's a lot of fear in the market you don't want to hold overnight, because you don't know what the next day will bring. Macroeconomics affects things from that standpoint in terms of larger swings. But in between those swings, the time is spent mostly with the technicals, not worrying that much about the fundamentals.

**How do you choose what to trade?**

I run my own technical scans, and I probably look at 500 - 600 charts a day. You see something start to develop so you take an interest in it and watch it and there are certain things you expect it to do within the context of your interest. I think that's what creates opportunity in the market, especially on the technical side.

I've found my little niche. I don't trade options, I don't trade futures. There are other people a lot smarter than me when it comes to those things. One of the reasons I'm not crazy about futures is that I know the ratio of professional traders in the futures market. I don't want to compete with them. I'd rather compete with retail traders, retail investors. It's a type of thinking that I understand more. I understand their psychology a little bit better. I understand their point of view a little bit better. I think I can take advantage of that and that is where my edge is in the market.

**When you were first starting off, did you experience losing streaks or other difficulties?**

I still experience losing streaks. I still experience drawdowns. That's just part of trading. It really comes down to, not so much not letting your losses get to you, it comes down to keeping your losses small. I could lose on many, many trades and still make that money back very, very quickly.

It disturbs you when you run 5...6...7 losers in a row. But if you keep those 7 losers managed, you know that when you get a winner and you get a stock moving in your direction that you are going to take a lot more out of the market than you lost with those losers. For me that's really the key. I take more losses now because I'm not willing to sit very long in a losing trade. I'd rather take two or three shots at one particular type of setup to get it right. It may drop and I may get out and I may buy it again and it may drop again and I may get out and then buy it again, before it finally takes off in my direction. So I am running losing streaks, because I am taking losses as I'm trying to find the spot where it's best to own that stock. The percentages aren't really everything. Losses themselves are really part of strategy.

**How far will you let it go down in those cases?**

Not very far. Even on longer trades, I like to keep my losses under a point. I try to find setups where the risk in the market is less than that, and that's not the easiest thing in the world to do. But it can be done. If you're wrong, you should be taking your loss. I can gauge that and I try to find opportunities that have a really good upside and a really definable downside.

A lot of people get stopped out of a stock and then find it hard to buy right back in, even when it's a good setup.

That's a big mistake. That's strictly a psychological issue. If the setup is there, you have to be willing to swallow your pride and do what's necessary.

Very often you are selling out at a bottom. That's human nature. If you sell a stock at the bottom and you see the market giving you signals that it's coming back, that's when you really have to swallow your pride and get in there and buy the thing back. I've done that a few times. Commissions are very low now. It doesn't cost a lot to close out a position and reopen it. You don't lose a lot. I think that is really important, being able to sell a stock at a loss and buy it back in the same vicinity when the same setup is still functioning.

**You describe it as "swallowing your pride". Do you think the main obstacle for people is their pride?**

It's not always pride, because I think pride comes from high self esteem as opposed to low self esteem. At least, that is my interpretation of it. For me, it's my pride. But I think for the losers, it's their loss of confidence. They thought something was going up and it went down. Now they don't believe in themselves. They don't trust themselves. Of course being wrong hurts. But you have to have some belief in your ability to see things, or else you can't be trading.

**How do you keep your confidence?**

If you trade a lot, you see markets come back and you see that you're right. You develop confidence from that. What amazes me is how many times I watch my trading account go down and then come right back. In spite of myself, I'll be making money. In spite of myself. That's the thing that draws confidence to me: you can lose it, but you can sure make it back real fast, too. That's a nice thing.

Once you realize you are able to do that, it's a real confidence-builder. That's when you don't feel it as that much of a loss, when you are down whatever amount of money, because you think, "That is an illusionary number. That number doesn't exist. Even though there is less in your account than you had yesterday, it will be more some day in the future."

Plus, for me, I've built up so much confidence from teaching other people how to trade. I have to show other people what good trading opportunities are. Trading for yourself is one thing. Most traders are closet traders. They are in there making and losing their money in private. And especially they don't want to share their errors with other people. They're embarrassed.

There are not many of us who I call "social traders". Not only are we traders, but we have to do publications, we have to talk to people, we have to educate people, we have to put ourselves on the line and show what we are trading. Not only do we have to deal with our own "humiliation" if we are wrong, the people who are watching us are going to see we are wrong, as well. How does that affect their opinion of us?

**Have there been times when you thought about giving up trading?**

Oh, many times. And I find a week later I still want to do it. That's what it comes down to. It is addictive, like nicotine was for all these years it took me to quit smoking. You quit and feel good. But when temptation comes along the whole "itch-scratch" thing starts again. Well, same thing with trading. If you have a bad day, at the end of the day you feel like garbage. You think, "This is it. I've got to change myself." Then all of a sudden that goes away. Especially because the market is fresh every morning. Every day is a new day and it really wipes the slate clean. That's the thing that draws traders back in.

There are people who shouldn't be trading, but because of the clean slate every morning they are getting sucked back in and putting at risk money they shouldn't be putting at risk. It's that renewal - every day is a new day. The market's never the same two days in a row and it never comes in with the same vibe two days in a row. That's really, really true and that's one of the things that renews traders after their losses.

**How important do you think is psychology in trading?**

I have a saying and it's related to psychology: "Discipline is a lot more important than knowledge when it comes to success in trading." How you manage your decision-making has a lot more to do with success than reading all the books in the world about trading. So much of it is in "time-frame cramp," getting caught up in the moment. You may set a plan for yourself, a very rational plan based on good technical information, where you are going to do A,B,C,and D over the next so many days in order to make money on this stock. Here's where you are going to watch. Here's where you are going to get in. Here's where you are going to get out. And then the market opens and your stomach turns, and the first time things turn against you by two tics you're thinking, "Oh God, I think I'm wrong. Maybe I'll just jump ship now." Or each down tick you think, "I was wrong. That analysis really sucked. I don't know what I'm doing. I'm an idiot."

That's the "timeframe cramp". You are getting caught up in the small wiggles in the market, when you are trying to take a big wiggle out of the market. That's really where psychology comes into play, because it's the difference between signal and noise. Unless you are able to manage yourself, it's so easy to confuse noise for signal in the market. Your ability to digest information collapses when you are not in control of yourself.

**How do you know when you've lost too much control? And what strategies do you use to keep control or get it back?**

I don't lose control a lot. Now, at least, I take my losses very fast. I wouldn't say it's a loss of control.

**What about earlier on? Did you ever struggle with that?**

Yes. Whenever I believed in a company, that's when I used to lose control. When I felt the stock has got to go up, or the stock has got to go down, that's when I lost control.

The market doesn't HAVE to do anything! You can have the most beautiful technicals, the most beautiful setups in the world, and the market is still going to do what it wants to do. If I'm posting a newsletter recommending 4 or 5 stocks, I already know that some of those stocks are going to do exactly the opposite of what I am saying. That's the nature of the market. One of the requirements of success is being able to filter that out. You have to be willing to see why things don't work out and have that be a natural consequence.

Somebody once said when it comes to the market, the difference between winning and losing is very small. It's not based on all the technical information. It's not based on the great stock picking. It's based really on your perception of losing and winning, and how you handle that.

That's a really subtle thing.

**How did you learn not to hope the market would do this or that?**

How does a child learn that a stove burns your hand? You make every mistake more than once. That's really the answer. Maybe at the beginning it doesn't sink in. But eventually, it sinks in, what is causing your pain and what is going to give you your pleasure.

Some people would be filled with despair and give up. But it sounds like you were spurred on to try even harder.

It's not so much the losses, but more the sense of powerlessness that somehow the loss can't be made whole again. For me the real confidence booster is knowing I can make myself whole. That's empowerment.

One of the biggest ways that traders fail is that they are used to working really hard and getting a paycheck every two weeks. So they figure if they come into trading and work real hard, they will get a paycheck. Well, in trading you can work real hard and get absolutely nothing. And it doesn't necessarily mean you are doing the wrong thing.

The market's not going to pay you based on pure effort. The market's going to pay you based on a lot of subtle things, but not necessarily pure effort. Effort is part of it, but also your sense of perception. Your self-control, self-discipline. All this other stuff.

**Have you struggled with that issue?**

Oh yeah. I go back into the 80s and early 90s, starting businesses that had nothing to do with trading and having them fail. There has always been a little of the entrepreneur in me. But all of those failed until I started trading, until I started doing websites, until I started writing. Then it finally clicked. I was the most amazed person around when that happened.

**Even though you failed, you continued to try, which seems like an ingredient in your personality that makes for a successful trader.**

Well, necessity is the mother of invention. I was laid off from my job. That's what put me in trading full time. If I had to do it on my own, and take that risk, I don't know. I'm over 50 years old and I have kids that are going to college in a few years. I've made money in the market over the years. But there is a difference between making money in the market and having to earn your living in the market.

There were two different processes at work here. I had a six-figure job, too. I was one of the highest paid managers in the company, and that's the job I lost. And I was also trading, so I was living pretty well. All of a sudden 100,000 dollars a year is not there anymore. You've got to deal with replacing that. That is an interesting spot to start from, especially when you don't have a choice.

**What was that like?**

It took me the first 6 months to figure out what to do, because first I was thinking, "Do I go back into the insurance industry or don't I?" It was that whole confusing period.

Once I committed to going out on my own, it became easier. I started to know what I needed to do. Literally, for me, I woke up in the middle of the night and understood what I needed to do. I haven't looked back since. I wish other people could experience a realization in that way. It has happened to me three or four times in my life and it has always been right. Related to psychology, it's the idea of inspiration. And when it comes you really appreciate it. It usually comes after a long period of lack of inspiration.

**What do you see as a difference between having to earn your living in the market versus just making money from the market?**

I have to work seven days a week now. I probably work 90 to 100 hours a week. Just a tremendous amount of time.

And how much is that something you have to do versus getting sucked in and wanting to do it.

95% percent is having to do it. That is the price of success. My business, the trading, my book - everything has improved year to year. Every year there has been more to do, more to pay attention to, because people are more dependent on me.

I'm more focused on the market when it is open. I'm writing more. I wrote a 420 page book, and now I'm writing to meet eight deadlines a week for TheStreet.com. Plus I'm watching the market six and a half hours a day and trading it!

One side of my brain is doing one thing and the other side of my brain is doing something else. It's multitasking. It's a challenge. I like staying busy. There's no problem with that. But you've got to stay organized.

I meditate every morning. I've done that for years. Part of it is to keep my head on straight. The physical stuff - over the past few years I've quit smoking, I've lost 45 pounds, I've lowered my cholesterol. Everything to get my health and head in order. It all has an impact.

Especially when you are sitting at a desk, and getting reinforcement with a regular paycheck, I don't think you have the same motivation to take care of yourself as when you are in the situation of, "If I don't do my job I don't get paid." My wife and I are going to go on vacation this year. When I go on vacation, I don't collect a vacation pay check. If I'm away from the market, I don't get paid. If you are earning a paycheck, you don't have that mentality.

**How does meditation help with your trading?**

I'm a type A personality. For me, it suppresses the underlying anxiety that type A's carry around. It quiets down that little voice that may not be working in your favor. Doubt. And also, it addresses a lethargy, an "I don't want to" mentality. It's a focus. I am trying to use more of my brain. Maybe instead of using 14% of my brain I can use 16% of my brain. That means I can possibly work a few hours less per week. For me, it relates to the emotional side of wanting to deal with the anxiety without Prozac, or whatever medication. And it's also to try to function at a little bit higher level.

**Are there times when you find your emotions starting to drive your trading decisions?**

Oh yeah. But I'll feel like my brain's cracking only a couple of times a month. My trading finger starts to move faster than my logic. Or you do revenge trading. Things don't go in your favor and you say, "I'll show them." You don't just hit the keyboard. You hit it hard.

**What triggers your self awareness of that?**

I know right away. It's just a question of whether I'm going to stop it! You're getting some reinforcement from it. When you're angry, how do you choose to not be angry. I stop being angry when I get it out of my system. It is sort of role playing, somewhat. You see yourself on that stage and you know better. You know you're going to have to deal with it. I hate to say it, but I am willing to sacrifice a few dollars to get my personal rage out. It's a positive reinforcement thing. Sometimes the money's worth it!

**What do you do when you see that revenge trading is taking over, or you're hitting the "Buy" key too much? How do you stop?**

You have to stop trading for that day. I may do some writing or some other stuff. Deadlines kick in. It doesn't go on for days, for me. It's usually a one day phenomenon. As soon as I turn around, it's gone. That's a funny thing. It surprises me how quickly it disappears. I take my mind off it for a while and suddenly it's gone. I think that's important.

**Have you noticed others having an ongoing problem with emotions driving their trading?**

Well, I talk to most of the people I teach and it's a huge problem. I expect most of them to wash out because of it. An inability to get control of themselves, to deal with that kind of thing. It's just human nature. Especially when you are teaching, you understand how many people - it's not that they're not cut out for it - you're not judging and saying, "This person's going to succeed and this person's going to fail." By the questions you get and the concerns you get, you know somebody is going to have a hard time. You get the sense they are not getting it. I think that's a big part of it.

**Can you give an example of someone "not getting it"?**

A lot of people want the market to be perfect, to give them a nice linear experience. If I do A, I get B. If I do B, I get C. That kind of mentality is just very destructive to success, because that is not how the market works. The market is a gem of nonlinear thinking. The ones who are the most logical suffer the most. I hate to say it, but a classic example is engineers. Engineers believe they make great traders, but their whole thought process is so black and white, it is very, very difficult for them to succeed. You can't trade the way you build bridges. They try to apply to trading the same skills they apply to their engineering, and they just fall on their face.

**What are some of the mistakes they'll make, based on linear thinking?**

They'll try to put everything into a formula that is repeatable and observable. Over and over again. They can't deal with fuzzy logic. They can't deal with their intuitive side. And it's very important, if you're trading, to develop your intuition. You have to! Your intuition is extremely important to trading because it helps to place all the logical stuff into perspective. It is a missing piece. You do your homework. You think you see something and you use your intuition to tell you whether or not you really see it.

**How do you feel about the intuitive part of trading?**

I like the gray of the market. I like the voodoo of the market. There is market superstition. There are people who put pseudo sciences into trading systems. I love all that, because there is an aspect of it that is very powerful. Some of it makes no sense, but part of the market has a religious aspect to it - it is bigger than human. It moves like a very complex machine, and anybody trying to reduce it is in for trouble.

We need to use both sides of the brain. I don't make it a mystery. You either get it or not. I think a lot of people really can't deal with that part. In their own sense of who they are, they can't deal with that kind of thing. For me, that's their issue.

**What about overconfidence?**

You know who gets overconfident? The 40-ish white male exercising his testosterone. He thinks: "I'm good at sports. I'm good at my job. I'm good with the ladies. So I'll be good with trading." That's a classic. They're going to force it to their will, force it to work, because they've forced everything. How do you get the ladies? You talk them into it. How are you going to be a successful trader? Talk the market into it? There's a lot of that going around, that bravado thing. It's a great way to get humbled by the market. Markets don't respond to talk.

To them, I say, "It's not about testosterone." Some of the best traders in the world are females, for a very important reason: they have the flexibility to take what the market gives them without trying to force their will on the market. That is urgent for people to understand.

**What about becoming overconfident temporarily based on large profits?**

Yeah. Well, the market will take that away from you fast enough.

Most of my winning streaks end with a series of losses, because I lose my timing. It's a balancing act. Losses from overconfidence wake you up to the fact that you were out of balance.

**Where do you find the emotional/psychological strength to make difficult trades?**

I like making the trades because they are uncomfortable. Those are usually the best ones. That's counterintuitive, but true. The trades that scare me the most are usually the ones I want the most, because those are usually the ones that work out the best.

People want to avoid pain, avoid discomfort. But you have to dive into that pain. That's another thing about the market and why it makes you crazy. That pain is very often a message that something should be traded, because the pain is not only the pain of loss but the pain of being right, too. A lot of people don't want to be right on some level. That is what part of their pain is about, that 'flip side' to their intuition. A lot of times, intuition hurts.

**Do you carry your gains and losses with you, emotionally, after the market closes?**

I carry them with me until I go to bed, no doubt. I don't carry them with me much longer, because I really like what I do. So I'm able to give it up, to some extent. I like role playing it out, too. I like being upset when I have to be.

Longer term, things don't bother me as much as they did years ago. I don't think I carry things around for very long. Maybe my wife would think differently. That would be my perception of it.

**What do you like most and least about trading?**

I love the market because it is so fascinating. It covers so much of the gamut of human existence. That's what I love about it the most. The time management problem bothers me the most. You have to use time properly or you can't make money, and a lot of time the market is telling you to do nothing. It really is disturbing when the market is telling you that, because you don't want to wait for your money. When you want to get paid, you want to get paid. I hate to have to go according to the market clock, rather than my own. If it was up to me, I'd rather be trading from 7:30 in the morning until 2:00 in the afternoon. I'd have Denver hours for the New York markets.

**What gives you your edge as a trader?**

I'm counterintuitive, going my own path. That's something you learn in the market the hard way. You learn that doing what everybody else does, does not work.

**Have you seen shrinkage of the trading community as a whole?**

Not any more than in the past. Go back to a 1980s example, when everybody was into "psychic channeling". The end of channeling came when Time magazine did a cover story on it. I remember telling my wife: "That's the end of channeling." And sure enough that was it.

Trading was on the front pages in 1999 and 2000. And when it really made the front pages big time, you knew the public fascination with it was pretty much past. It's really gone off the front pages now. The people who thought it was easy money are gone. Now you have the basic trading community back. It has always been there and it will always be there. Everybody else is gone.

**What emotional, psychological advice would you give to new traders?**

Start small. Stay small until you know what the hell you're doing. But that's hard for new traders to do, because they come into trading to try to make big money. They shouldn't be doing that. They should be trying to trade well. It's a big difference.

# Offensive Aspect of Psychology

The first part of this aspect is engaging one's **intuition**. We put it in the offensive part because this is the way to enhance your trading performance when you are already a stable, confident trader. This is an advanced concept that becomes available to you only after your mindset is correctly conditioned and, most importantly, when your trading skills mature. Trading intuition is researched quite extensively in several great books referred to at the end of this part.

Intuition in trading is not some mystical power coming to you from outside. It is your experience that is the source of intuitive impulse. You learn to work with information faster as you internalize it. It is processed on a subconscious level, much as you process road information without thinking when you are an experienced driver. However, it is not so easy when you just start driving. Every turn of the wheel, every gear switch braking or accelerating, interaction with other vehicles, traffic lights and road signs – all this has to be processed consciously by a beginner. The more experience he gains, the more he is able to talk, to listen to music and to think of unrelated topics to road conditions while driving. Most of us know the feeling when we start our car and then find out we are at our destination with practically no recollection of how we got there. Meanwhile, we stopped at intersections, checked the traffic, yielded the way to crossing pedestrians and did a thousand other things to get through to our target. All these things became familiar and recognizable to us over time to the degree when we are able to process them and react on them without conscious thinking.

In trading, it is not much different. Over time, situations become so familiar to you that when you see them you just react. The speed of this recognition and reaction can be amazing for an observer. Experienced traders react to a familiar setup in a way that seems almost mystical even to them. It seems as if their fingers push buy and sell buttons on their own. I met traders that could not even tell what they saw in a trade they just did. They would say things like: "I just saw a trade, I entered, it worked", or "I can't even tell you what it was that made me do it, I just did it". If you have ever observed good chess players during a blitz game, this is very similar. Nothing mystical happens. It is simply another way to process information, one that becomes available with experience.

One warning must be made here. Intuition does not come by one's will. You cannot push for it. You will not be able to tell true intuitive impulse from wishful thinking if you are trying hard to wake your intuition up so it "tells you what to do". It will come naturally, by itself, and when it is there you will recognize it by the way you trade. It becomes an easy, joyful, flowing experience, not tense, not stressful. Making money AND having fun – this is what intuition brings you when it comes.

The second aspect of offensive psychology is **understanding other traders' thinking**. The concept is simple: knowing the standard reactions and understanding the emotional aspect of trading, you are able to understand and exploit those emotions. After all, any chart is a reflection of a trader conglomerate's thinking and emotions. Being emotionally detached you can observe your own emotions muted by self-control and use them to evaluate emotions of other market participants. When a stock drops big with very high speed, you can almost feel the panic and hear a frantic "Get me out at any cost!" When it goes up and up, breaking one resistance level after another, you can feel the happiness of long side players and the frustration of shorters. Try to listen to your emotions even though at this stage of your development they are going to be pretty much muted – it still will help you identify the feelings experienced by the broad public.

Again, as with intuition, many familiar situations will appear when you gain experience. You will see the resistance getting broken after it is tested several times, and the price spiking sharply – this behavior is related to those traders who shorted before taking their stops, and to those who waited for that break to happily enter their positions. You will see a big bounce after the support held – this is hopeful bottom fishers making their bets when they see support holding, and those who sold before re-establishing their positions; those who shorted in hope for a break of support, take their stops. All these scenarios and many more will become readable for you over time.

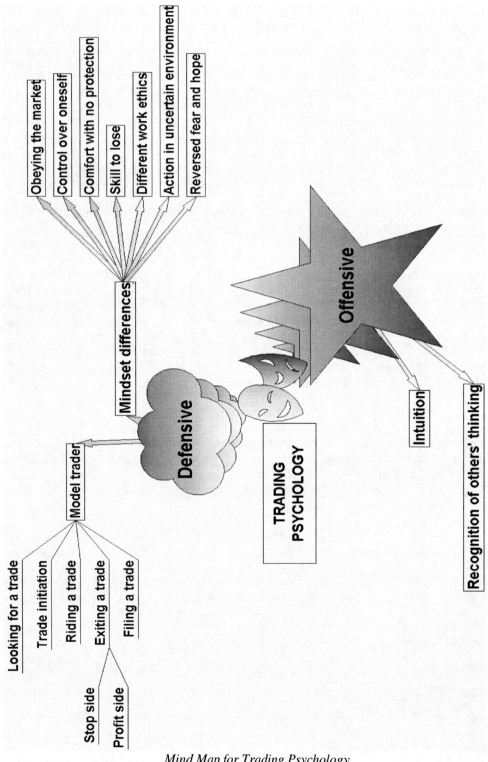

*Mind Map for Trading Psychology*

## Resources for Trading Psychology

http://www.realitytrader.com/Tapereading.asp#mentalstate

## Recommended Reading

RR1; RR4; RR8; RR9; RR10; RR11; RR12

# Trading Plan

In this part of the plan, we are going to outline your approach to the psychology of trading.

## Trading Plan Form: My Trading Psychology

The market is my guide. I am not going to impose my opinions on it. I am going to listen to it and obey it.

Self-control is my major weapon in trading. The market provides the guidance; I control myself to follow it.

I am comfortable with taking responsibility for my actions. This is what gives me strength and makes me self-reliant.

I take losses with no hesitation and no hard feelings. They become a lesson to learn for me.

I do not feel obliged to trade all the time.

I am comfortable with the market's uncertainty. I act on IF-Then scenarios, not expecting to know the outcome in advance.

I am uncomfortable with a losing position and cut my losses with no hesitation when my stop is hit. I am comfortable with a winning position and ride it without anxiety until my profit-taking signal is generated.

My correct mindset is:

- Emotional detachment

- Focus on market action and not money

_____

_____

_____

My method to achieve the correct mindset is

_____

_____

_____

_____

When I am looking for a trade, I

_____

_____

_____

When my entry signal is generated, I

_____

_____

When I am in a trade, I

_____

_____

When a trade is going against me, I

_____

_____

When a trade is going in my favor, I

_____

_____

I am going to use my emotional detachment in order to let my intuition work. I am going to use my understanding of the emotional side of trading to read the action of other players and define my action.

# Traders Talk – Chuck Collins

*Trades since 2001, full time since 2002. Mix of intraday trading, scalping and about 10% of swing trades in stocks and futures. Trading is a primary source of income. 47 years old, Massachusetts, USA*

I became interested in trading after getting laid off from a couple of jobs in tech. In August 2001, I thought the market was probably about washed out (ha!), and it would be a good time to exploring trading as a potential occupation. I started by reading a couple of books on day trading and subscribing to a service commenting on daily market movements. I had made a couple of trades on my own, but it was apparent early on that some sort of real-time training and guidance was required.

Even so, it still took me about 2 years to become consistently profitable. The $25,000 day trading minimum account size had just gone into effect, and since I had started with a fairly small account size only a couple of thousand dollars over the minimum, the biggest obstacle I had to overcome was fear of loss, which resulted in me not entering good trades, and stopping out of trades too early, taking losses on trades which would have been profitable had I not closed them early. Eventually, I borrowed money at very favorable interest rates to boost my account size and ease that particular pressure.

I also scaled back my trade lot size from 1,000 shares to 500 shares. Currently, about 60% of my trades are 500 share lots, 20% are 1,000 shares, and 20% are less than 500 shares. The vast majority of my stop limits are .20 to .25 cents.

In the first year or so, I did have one disaster trade, where I shorted 1,000 shares of a stock at $8.00 after hours when its earnings report came out. I correctly judged that the earnings report was poor, but I did not have any idea of its float or short interest. The stock squeezed, and I covered it at $10, for a $2,000 loss. The stock eventually traded up to $10.50 minutes later, but closed the next day at $7, after trading as low at $6.50. I don't think I traded after hours again for about a year after that one. That also taught me that the 30 seconds or so it takes to look up the details of a stock you aren't familiar with are well worth it before you plunge.

I don't have an overall written trading plan, such as a business plan. I do prepare a daily "cheat sheet" with a list of stocks to watch, index performance and expectations, etc. I write this after the market closes, and then update it before the market opens the next day. I keep this attached to one of my monitors. I also have a list of trading "mantras" attached to one monitor to help keep discipline and avoid stupid mistakes. It's not foolproof, but it helps.

I don't think I have been trading long enough to have developed what could be considered a defined trading philosophy. Instead, I would say that I am still in the process of ingraining habits and discipline to the point where trading becomes as mechanical as possible. In this respect, the most important points are:

- Always define the risk before you enter the trade.

- Be patient; wait for market to fulfil your requirements for taking a trade.

- If the setup is there, take it without hesitation.

- Don't chase; there's always another trade coming.

- Stop or target.

To the extent I am risk-averse, and also given the market environment since I have been trading (just prior to September 11), I prefer day trading simply for the notion that the shorter the timeframe, the lower the risk.

For day trading NASDAQ stocks, I prefer trend following and basing setups, because the risk parameters normally can be clearly defined. I tend not to take capitulation-type in individual stocks because I am still not very adept at reading their reversal points.

On the other hand, I will often trade index futures and ETFs (Exchange Traded Funds) for reversals at support or resistance because I find they are much more reliable and the risk at the turning points is often very small. I have become more aggressive on taking these trades over time, simply because the risk/reward profile is so great and their track record is so good. I also find it much easier to read the tape on these at the reversal points than I do with individual stocks, probably because the battle takes place in a very narrow price range, as opposed to stocks which can be very spready at the turns.

I think the only time I really pay attention to "fundamentals" is on news plays. When a piece of news comes out on a stock during the day, it's absolutely critical to me to know the "history" of that news, and whether it is already priced in to the stock. How many times have you seen a drug stock get an FDA approval intraday and proceed to sell off after a few unfortunate traders jump to buy?

I suppose the only other fundamentals I pay attention to are the float and short interest, for the cheapie stocks that run from time to time. Otherwise, fundamentals are for investors as far as I can tell. I trade mostly on technical indicators and charts.

I have a certain amount of capital I am willing to lose on a trade. When I consider a trade, I find where the entry and the stop should be, and then adjust my position size accordingly. I try not to set my stop at an obvious level that could be easily rinsed, but if it is hit, I get out and try not to look back. I see many traders get rinsed and get mad and then take a bad trade, and I've done it myself. Normally if a trade stops out, I take the stock off my screen immediately. I'll look back at the chart later to see if there was any particular lesson to be learned from the price action, but I doubt there's any trader who hasn't been rinsed by a few cents only to have the trade reverse and go the right way.

The first year or so of trading was pretty stressful, due to having what I now consider being an undercapitalized account, as well as basically making the transition from a regular job to trading full-time cold turkey. Getting to the realization that a few losing trades in a row was not going to break me was a big step. Getting the elements of trading discipline in place, piece by piece is also a big deal. I don't do any yoga or breathing exercises or anything like that, but I also don't just sit and stare at the screens all day, either. There are days here and there when the market is just telling you it is not likely to offer much, and there are other days when you just are not in sync with the flow, in which case it can be advisable to just find something else to do. This is not to say I don't treat trading as my job, I spend as much time on trading as I ever have on any regular job I've ever had. But it's more enjoyable and more flexible than any other job I've had.

When starting out, I'd say it's critical to have real-time guidance, such as a chat room (and one that treats trading as a profession, not just a bunch of gunslinger types), if you want to learn to day trade. You can read all the books you want, and I'd suggest all the usual suspects, but I found every book I ever read was much more useful to me AFTER I'd been trading for a year or so. Just like you can tell a kid over and over again not to touch the hot stove, he isn't really going to learn until he gets burned. Then he says, "Oh, NOW I know what you were talking about." I think the thing that surprised me the most is that trading is just as difficult to get the hang of as everyone says. It has been more difficult than anything else I've ever done.

I think the realization that has been most important to me so far is that I enjoy trading so much that I am willing to put in time far above what I have spent on any other job, so I can continue to improve and continue doing it.

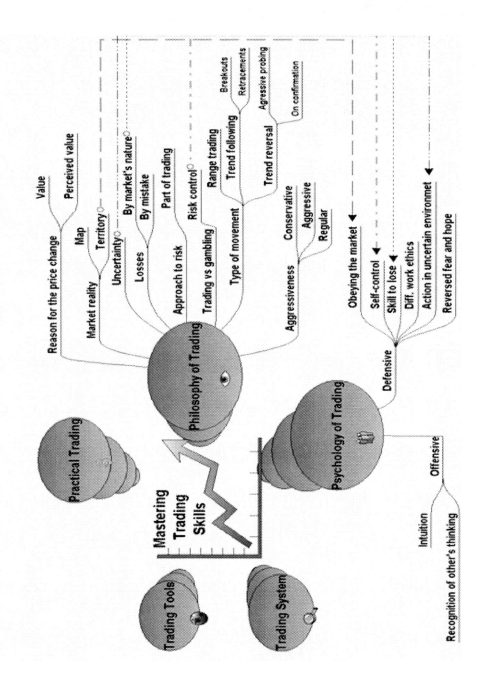

# Part III: Creating your Trading System

# Necessary Comments

Before you start building your trading system, we need to establish several important points.

First, when we are talking about a trading system, we do not mean an automated system of any kind. Programming your computer to trade is an entirely different topic and is beyond the scope of this book. What we are discussing here is a trading system that you create for yourself according to your preferences and circumstances. It will be to a certain degree a discretionary system, in a sense that you will make the ultimate filtering when deciding which signals you are going to take and which to ignore. Your system will change and evolve, becoming more complicated or more simple with time and experience.

Second, as you already know, your ability to stick to your system and execute it in a disciplined fashion is a crucial element of your trading. A sloppy trader will ruin the performance of the best system, and a highly disciplined trader will probably make money with mediocre one.

Third, do not focus too much on creating a *perfect* system at this point. An important realization at this stage is that there can be, and is, a universe of systems. You do not have to find the best. There simply is no "best". It does not have to be truly unique; it does not have to be highly sophisticated; it does not even have to be fully designed by you from scratch. What it really needs to be is a logical fit to your philosophy and general approach. Elements of your system should be in agreement with each other. As a basis for your initial attempt, you can simply use one of many published systems. However, before doing that, you do need to go over the entire process described in this part. Understanding the system's elements and their interaction will make it possible for you to analyze any other system, to see if it fits you, and to apply your own tweaks to it. Without this understanding, you will be destined to lose money with bad systems and even with good ones – simply because you will not understand how and why the system works.

Now that you have defined how you approach the market in general, it is time to shape up the method of selecting your trading candidates. There are three major parts in this process.

The first is **the timeframe** in which you are going to trade. The second is your **risk evaluation method**. The third is **the method** you are going to apply to read the markets. After going over all of these elements, we are going to put them together. This will take us to creation of the heart of your trading – your trading system.

Let us create a mind map for this part. At the end of this part, we will recreate it with new elements that we learn about in the course of study.

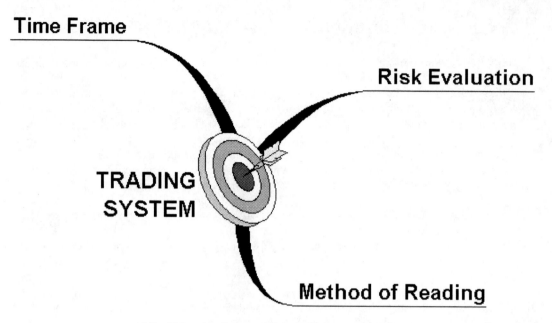

*Mind Map for Creating Your Trading System*

# Timeframe

The major consideration in this aspect is whether you are going to be an intraday trader, or your holding period is going to be multi-day. This is a very important decision as it is going to affect many aspects of your strategy: your basis for stock selection, money and risk management and position sizing. This choice also has to suit your personality. You made a choice earlier deciding what you base your approach on: fundamental data or technical analysis. Now that choice is going to impact your decision on timeframe, too. Adding new factors to that choice at this point, you have one more chance to review that decision and make sure you are comfortable with it.

In basic terms, you have a choice between **long term trading**, **swing trading** and **intraday trading**.

Let us define them for the purpose of this book.

*Long term trading*: can be done in months or weeks, sometimes even in years. This type of trading is as close to long term investment as it gets. In this situation, you will have to diversify your positions, choose small share sizes and research both the particular company and industry fundamentals. Company reports, financial statements, state of the industry, company position in its relative market, general state of economy, trend in different sectors will be governing your picks. The timing of your entry and exit are based on charts displayed according to your timeframe, and this is the main criterion that distinguishes your share purchases as a form of trading and not an investment.

*Swing trading*: generally done in weeks or days. Trading this style, you are going to rely heavily on technical analysis. Company fundamentals matter less although it is still important to make sure you are dealing with a financially sound company that is not going to disappear overnight. Sector trends matter in this approach as well, as does general market direction. Although it still could be somewhat a mix of fundamentals and technical analysis, the latter is having a much bigger impact on your trading decisions in comparison to long term trading. You are still going to hold your positions overnight, so you will be subject to possible negative developments occurring in a manner that will not allow you to keep your stop. It will influence your risk management, which is going to be discussed in the next section.

*Intraday trading*: an approach where your positions are generally opened and closed within a day. In most cases, you are in cash overnight, not worrying about possible adverse news events. Intraday trading also includes *scalping* – a trading style where you are taking your profits on a single stage of movement, not sitting through pullbacks. Scalping is the most "clean" form of short term trading, with very tight risk control (Recommended Reading #5). Both day trading and especially scalping have little to do with company fundamentals and rely on technical analysis, tape reading and momentum. Risk control is done in a very different way than with long term and swing trading.

You might see somewhat different definitions of these terms somewhere else but in the framework of this book, the definitions above are quite sufficient.

There is no better or worse choice here; they are simply quite different approaches and there are many factors that will impact your decision. One thing has to be said in advance though: your choice should be made by you and not by the trade gone badly. By this I mean that a trade that started as an intraday trade and showed a loss toward the end of the day should not be taken overnight or until it recovers, just because you do not want to take a loss. This is the worst possible solution that paralyzes you, ties down your trading capital and potentially can turn into a total disaster.

Let us see what factors impact your choice.

## External Circumstances and Influences

Do you intend to become a full time trader or add trading to your day-to-day routine? Is trading supposed to be your main or supplementary source of income? What kind of capital are you going to devote to trading?

If you are working full time and busy throughout the day, your choices are going to be between long term and a limited form of swing trading. Being able to watch your stocks on an intraday basis, you can choose between swing and intraday trading. You can also use longer timeframes as a "trial period" to see whether this is a kind of business you want to be in instead of jumping in with both feet right away. Or, you can use longer timeframes during your initial learning period to ease into full time trading. Consider also that such an approach involves fewer expenses, so it is generally a good idea to start this way, not spending much while you are in a testing period.

Having trading as a main source of your income you are going to have to withdraw money for a living more frequently than in the case where trading is a supplemental source. This factor makes shorter timeframes more attractive.

The impact of capital available for trading is more complicated. With just several thousand dollars, you can go for long term trades aiming for bigger gains over time with a well diversified portfolio, and you can go for fast scalping, turning over your capital several times a day. There are restrictions for active stock trading with small accounts, but with futures it is possible to accomplish this. Bigger accounts can be used in longer or shorter timeframes. In any case, I strongly recommend you start small and add money to your account after you prove to yourself you can trade profitably.

## Inner Factors

Your *type of personality* and **risk tolerance** are going to be considerations in this choice as well.

If you are the steady, patient, analytical type, you are not likely to be comfortable with scalping. Long term and swing trading is your most probable choice. Being a fast thinker with a strong intuitive side, you will get bored with longer timeframes and are more likely to be comfortable with intraday trading and scalping. It does not mean that only intuitive types can day trade; it rather indicates that individuals with an intuitive personality type will be less inclined to handle longer term trades that require more analytical work.

Risk tolerance is a multifold factor. Short term trading is perceived as a higher risk endeavor, although in reality this is not necessarily the case. There is common confusion between trading overall, as being risky, and a particular timeframe as being more or less risky. Since you have already decided what you want to try your hand at, that risk consideration is already factored in. In choosing your timeframe, consider that in a shorter timeframe, you have more control over events. If you are an intraday trader, you are not subject to overnight gaps caused by the news. If you are a scalper, your market exposure is so limited in time that your control is almost absolute. As a long term trader who is considering all of the risks of adverse events, you are going to control your risk by position sizing and diversification. As a general rule, a shorter timeframe gives you a greater degree of control. Shorter timeframes, on the other hand, lead to more frequent entries and exits which might or might not be your objective. So eventually, it comes to the question of how you want to control your risk – by time exposure (day trading and scalping) or by position size and diversification (long term and swing trading).

The following mind map puts together the factors influencing your choice of timeframe and impacts by it. The explanations for this diagram are simple: **L** stands for Long term, **S** for Swing Trading and **D** for Day Trading. Mark your choices and see what timeframes the map suggests to you. Then see what factors your choice impacts and decide how comfortable you are with them. Making your choice, keep in mind that it is not necessarily an ultimate choice that you are going to be tied to. Like everything, this aspect is flexible.

Also, keep in mind the fact that in order to manage your trade in a smaller timeframe, you often need to see the bigger picture, too. Even trading on an intraday basis, a trader usually needs to see where the stock is positioned on a daily chart over the course of weeks and months.

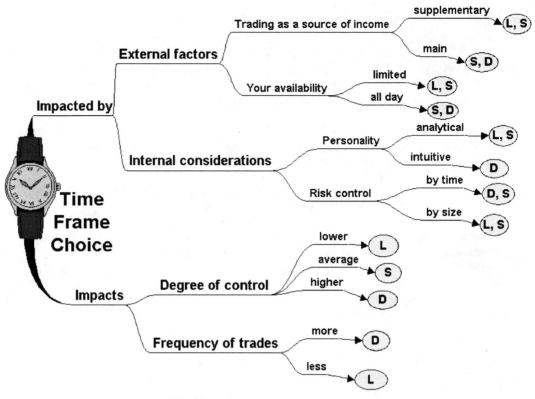

*Mind Map for timeframe selection*

# Risk Evaluation and Control

Risk evaluation is one of the crucial elements of your preparation, and probably the most critical. This is your safety net, the way to make sure you survive your learning curve. Its importance is not going to diminish at the later stages, too. The absence of proper risk control is solely responsible for the most failures.

Let us set the ground rule from the onset: RISK EVALUATION COMES FIRST; PROFIT POTENTIAL SECOND. In practice, it means that if any particular trade shows the risk exceeding what you have planned, a trade should be skipped or its parameters should be adjusted, no matter how lucrative the profit potential appears to be. An "all or nothing" approach results in "nothing" much more frequently than it does in "all". By adjusting, we mean risk control that puts a trade back in your affordability range, even if this leads to decreasing the profit potential. Decreasing the number of shares could serve as such an adjustment. There is a natural relation between risk and potential; decreasing one and you decrease another. The trick is to find high leverage areas where tight risk control still leaves you with enough profit potential for a trade to be worthwhile.

Elements of your risk control are: **money management**; **trade evaluation**; **stock evaluation**; **risk management**. The first three are defined before the trade is initiated and in fact are part of your pre-trading decision. The fourth element kicks in when you are in a trade and serves as your guideline to managing a trade itself. All four form the most important part of your trading plan. Any other aspects of the plan can easily be adjusted as you develop as a trader, and if you do not get them right from the start, it is not a big, and even expected, problem. It is much more critical with risk control. It had better be done as close to "right" as possible from the very beginning, and if there is a need to correct it, it better be corrected as early as possible. Mistakes or deviations from the optimum in all other aspects will be just something to correct; mistakes in this aspect, if not spotted and corrected fast, will result in real troubles.

## Money Management

*Let me say in advance that we are not going in deep waters of the complex math of money management. If you are a mathematically inclined person, you will find in-depth analysis of such approaches in the books devoted specifically to this aspect. If you, however, are like most people and prefer a common sense approach, basics will be quite enough for the first years of your trading, and probably for your entire trading career.*

Your capital should be managed differently in different timeframes. As said above, longer timeframes require diversification and a smaller size of position; shorter timeframes allow for a bigger position size. Let us break this element down into two:

1. Size of loss you plan to take in the case of a trade goes badly.
2. Size of capital committed to a particular trade.

The first component is a crucial element of your trading. Generally speaking, it is recommended to keep the size of your loss for any particular trade within 2% of your trading capital. This is a sound recommendation for a seasoned trader, and for the beginner this number should be limited to 1%. In order to survive your learning curve, where you are likely to take more losses than at later stages, it is wise to apply strict risk control to make more room for those initial losses. In the *Practical Trading* part, we are going to go further into this matter and tighten up this parameter even more for your first steps.

The second component is more crucial for longer timeframes. In day trading and scalping, you can devote a significant portion of your trading account to a single trade because you will be closing your position soon enough, freeing your money for another trade. In longer timeframes, you will need to spread your capital between several positions. Since you are reading the movement in a wider timeframe, your stops are going to be much bigger. There is no strict guideline to what portion to devote to each trade. As a rule of thumb, you can consider spreading your capital in such a way that it would cover about ten - fifteen simultaneous trades for long term and about five - ten for swing trading. If stop placement and capital spreading gives you different numbers, go with the one that limits your risk in a tighter way.

> **Margin consideration**. Margin is a powerful and very dangerous weapon. It increases your buying power greatly, but at the same time, it carries potential risk to lose more than you have and find yourself in debt. It is recommended that you carefully read your particular broker's margin requirements. Margin can be used with less risk in intraday trading. However, with longer terms it is generally better to stay within your capital. In all cases, a beginner should avoid using margin in longer term trades and be wary of it when trading on an intraday basis.

## Trade Evaluation

This part of the process is closely tied with the previous one. Having defined your money management policy, you now need to evaluate how the stock fits into your criteria.

The method of evaluation of the risk for any particular trade depends on your timeframe. For a long term trader, fundamental data will play an important role in this process. Intent to hold a stock in your portfolio for months should be supported by company financial data and perspectives. Your research will have to answer the question, how probable is it that a company will run out of money, not be able to secure financing or run into other kind of troubles.

For a shorter timeframe trader, technical analysis will answer the question of how big the risk is on this particular trade. As we defined above, we are going to keep our loss on any particular trade within 1%. But wait; didn't we say in the *Trading Philosophy* part that a level of a stop placement was a function of the reason for a trade not being there anymore, and not a function of your capital? We did, and there is no contradiction here. This is where position sizing kicks in: you place a stop where support level on your chart, for instance, says to do so, and to fit into your risk requirements you size your position accordingly.

Let us illustrate this with an example. For simplicity's sake, we are not taking into account such concerns as commissions and slippage at this moment. If your trading capital is $25,000, as a beginner you will want to risk not more than $250 dollars on any single trade. If your setup shows you a stop level at .25 cents below your entry, you can trade 1,000 shares. If this stop level is .50 cents below your entry, you will have to adjust the shares size to 500 to keep your risk tolerance within the parameter set.

Acting in this way, a trader compares a trade risk evaluation to money management decisions made earlier and incorporates proper position sizing in his plan for this particular trade.

## Stock Evaluation

This stage of risk assessment measures danger hidden in the behavior of a particular stock. The target of this stage is to evaluate possible slippage. Slippage occurs when there are not enough shares at a targeted level, thus you are likely to get a worse fill than intended. Stocks prone to slippage are called thin or thinly traded. There are four factors to look at in this regard:

1. Float
2. Trading volume
3. Chart bars or candlesticks
4. Level II

**Float** is the amount of shares available for trading for a particular stock. It is easy to find from any financial site. The general rule is that the smaller the float, the bigger the stock's volatility. A stock with a small float, up to ten million, is going to trade in spurts when it attracts attention. It can move very fast making it difficult to keep a stop. Slippage is very likely to occur on such a stock. Huge floats, such as hundreds of millions of shares, warrant slow, steady movement that is easy to handle. Slippage is unlikely on such stocks.

**Trading volume** is a good indicator of a stock's degree of being dangerous. Volume under 100,000 shares for the day is very low. Average volume for a stock matters, although when a stock gets the public's attention, it could increase its volume greatly. Generally speaking, stocks with several millions of daily volume tend to move in a much smoother way.

**Chart bars or candlesticks.** Look at the chart to evaluate whether it looks smooth or the bars are wild, with huge differences between active and sleepy days. Stocks with disorderly, disconnected bars or candles are more dangerous.

Let us compare two charts. The first is for Sepracor Inc (SEPR)

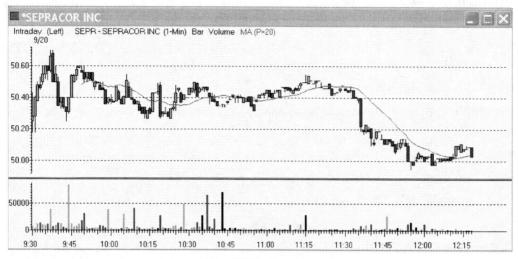

*SEPR chart*

With a .60 cent intraday range, the stock has a candle .20 cents long. The candles are chaotic and change direction suddenly. Now, compare this chart to the chart of Intel Corporation (INTC):

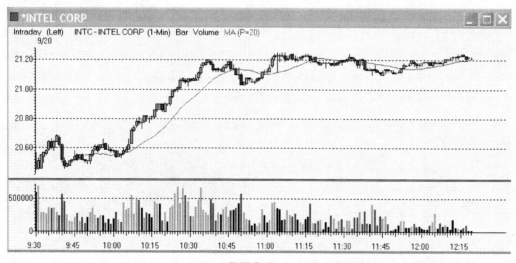

*INTC chart*

You can see a much more orderly move within approximately the same intraday range. The stock is obviously much safer comparing to SEPR. Volume is also higher and distributed more evenly.

**Level II.** This is a great tool to evaluate the probability and size of possible slippage. The major signs to look at are spread, amount of market participants at each price level, order sizes shown by participants and gap between price levels. The following three screenshots show clearly the difference between a safe stock and a stock with a high probability of slippage. The first screenshot is for Dell Inc (DELL).

| DELL | ▲ Last: 35.93 | Change: 0.39 | Volume: 5,036,896 |
|---|---|---|---|
| High: 36.0055 | Low: 35.46 | Open: 35.54 | Last Trade: 11:51:30 |
| Bid: 35.93 | Ask: 35.94 | Close: 35.54 | Last Vol.: 350 |
| Size: 7,700 | Size: 4,600 | Spread: 0.01 | Mkt: NNM |

| MPID | Price | Size | MPID | Price | Size | |
|---|---|---|---|---|---|---|
| BRUT | 35.93 | 6500 | CINN | 35.94 | 2400 | |
| CINN | 35.93 | 3600 | NITE | 35.94 | 2200 | |
| ARCX | 35.93 | 3500 | BRUT | 35.94 | 1000 | |
| SIZE | 35.93 | 1200 | TDCM | 35.94 | 800 | |
| NOCI | 35.92 | 500 | SIZE | 35.94 | 500 | |
| ASE | 35.91 | 5000 | ARCX | 35.94 | 200 | |
| COWN | 35.91 | 100 | HRNB | 35.94 | 100 | |
| GVRC | 35.90 | 5000 | NOCI | 35.95 | 500 | |
| SBSH | 35.88 | 3900 | MADF | 35.95 | 100 | |
| FBCO | 35.88 | 1000 | ASE | 35.96 | 5000 | |
| BTRD | 35.87 | 500 | FBCO | 35.96 | 1000 | |
| TMBR | 35.86 | 5000 | WCHV | 35.96 | 100 | ▼ |

*DELL Level II*

The spread is .01 cent; there are plenty of players at each level; they show nice sizes of orders; the gap between the price levels is .01 cent. Obviously it is easy to move 1,000 shares and more, with minimal or with no slippage. The DELL float is 2,253 million shares.

The next screenshot is for Corinthian Colleges, Inc (COCO). The spread is .02 cents, there are less participants and they show not as great sizes; some gaps between price levels are wider. The probability of slippage is higher. Notice that the volume is also lower. If we look at its float, it is 83 million – not bad, but it is lower than DELL's, and it shows. With this stock you can count on slippage probably around .02-.05 cents if things go badly.

| COCO | ▲ Last: 13.51 | Change: -0.54 | Volume: 1,867,110 |
|---|---|---|---|
| High: 13.98 | Low: 13.31 | Open: 13.97 | Last Trade: 11:56:04 |
| Bid: 13.51 | Ask: 13.53 | Close: 14.05 | Last Vol.: 900 |
| Size: 400 | Size: 600 | Spread: 0.02 | Mkt: NNM |

| MPID | Price | Size | MPID | Price | Size | |
|---|---|---|---|---|---|---|
| SCHB | 13.51 | 400 | CINN | 13.53 | 600 | |
| CINN | 13.51 | 200 | BRUT | 13.53 | 400 | |
| ARCX | 13.50 | 1000 | ARCX | 13.53 | 200 | |
| BRUT | 13.50 | 700 | UBSW | 13.55 | 100 | |
| COWN | 13.50 | 100 | NITE | 13.56 | 100 | |
| SIZE | 13.49 | 2900 | SIZE | 13.61 | 200 | |
| NFSC | 13.49 | 100 | COWN | 13.65 | 100 | |
| BEST | 13.45 | 100 | SCHB | 13.70 | 1000 | |
| NITE | 13.40 | 7600 | WCHV | 13.82 | 100 | |
| GVRC | 13.40 | 900 | PIPR | 13.95 | 100 | |
| CANT | 13.38 | 100 | BEST | 13.96 | 100 | |
| BOFA | 13.36 | 100 | PRUS | 14.00 | 100 | ▼ |

*COCO Level II*

Finally, the third screenshot is for InfoSpace, Inc (INSP)

| MPID | Price | Size | MPID | Price | Size | |
|------|-------|------|------|-------|------|---|
| SIZE | 46.24 | 400 | ARCX | 46.31 | 500 | ▲ |
| ARCX | 46.24 | 100 | SIZE | 46.31 | 100 | |
| CINN | 46.22 | 500 | BRUT | 46.33 | 300 | |
| BRUT | 46.15 | 900 | CINN | 46.34 | 500 | |
| GSCO | 46.14 | 100 | PERT | 46.40 | 100 | |
| SCHB | 46.10 | 300 | GVRC | 46.50 | 400 | |
| SBSH | 46.10 | 100 | NITE | 46.50 | 300 | |
| GVRC | 46.05 | 1000 | PRUS | 46.50 | 100 | |
| NITE | 46.00 | 1000 | GSCO | 46.51 | 100 | |
| DBAB | 45.78 | 100 | MADF | 46.54 | 300 | |
| PRUS | 45.75 | 100 | SBSH | 46.60 | 100 | |
| PERT | 45.73 | 1700 | BOFA | 46.70 | 100 | ▼ |

Top info box:
INSP  ▼ Last: 46.27  Change: 1.88  Volume: 1,327,027
High: 46.90  Low: 44.29  Open: 44.74  Last Trade: 12:06:10
Bid: 46.24  Ask: 46.31  Close: 44.39  Last Vol.: 100
Size: 400  Size: 500  Spread: 0.07  Mkt: NNM

*INSP Level II*

It is easy to see that this stock is even more dangerous, with the spread being .07 cents at the moment, with little participation and gaps between levels reaching .10 cents. It is not an accident that trading volume is lower and the float is 31.7 million shares. INSP can cause slippage around .10 cents.

On the most jumpy stocks you can even find spreads reaching 0.20 -.30 cents and wider. Those are usually very thin stocks with tiny floats and little volume.

As you can see, these four factors are inter-connected and usually go hand in hand. Together they allow you to evaluate the danger of a stock fairly well.

Let us try now and put these three elements of preparation together. You have defined that your maximum loss for any single trade is going to be $250. You evaluated the trade and defined that with a stop being .25 cents you can trade 1,000 shares. Then you evaluated the possible slippage and decided that it is likely to be about .10 cents, for instance. It gives you a total stop of .35 cents, and you need to adjust your shares size from 1,000 to 700. Now your preparation risk-wise is complete.

---

### You Asked

*Question:*
Where do I find a particular stock's float?

*Answer:*
Many charting tools provide this information. You can also find it on any financial site, like Yahoo!, and some of them are listed in *Resources.*

---

Finally, our last element is risk control itself. Knowing about our trade and a stock, everything analyzed above and having your money management strategy in place, you need to manage your risk while in a trade. This element is a part of our last part, Practical Trading. We are mentioning it here since it is going to be based on everything that we just discussed, so there is a logical continuation of the thought. In that last part we are going to break this element down by components and show how such management should be done.

# Method of Reading

This is the element of your trading plan that defines how you are going to read the market movement. There is an endless variety of methods, and you will adjust and hone your approach throughout your entire trading career. Even within a single method, you can find infinite variations. Starting with learning of existing methods, a trader finds a combination that he is comfortable with, and then tweaks it until he gets the results he wants. This process slows down after a while but never really ends. Let us break the existing methods into three large groups and review them. There is **fundamental analysis**, **tape reading** and **technical analysis**. The difference between them can be defined in simple terms: trading by fundamental analysis stems from company and product quality while tape reading and technical analysis play the players.

*Fundamental data* is information on the company and its relation to the general market in terms of company performance and perspectives. This is an inalienable part of long term trading. Although some elements of it could be applied in shorter timeframes, their significance is less for swing traders and especially intraday traders, and becomes practically non-existent for scalpers.

*Tape reading*, unlike what the name implies, it is not just observing the ticker. Ticker, or tape, was the medium that gave a name to this method, but in modern times, there are more convenient tools to effectively apply this method. This is a raw form of technical analysis dealing with the very roots of any movement – price and volume. In this or that form tape reading is presented in any approach, and no matter which trading approach you choose, basics of tape reading should be learned. Tape reading deals with the element of the offensive aspect of trading psychology that we discussed earlier – reading the emotions of other market participants.

*Technical analysis* – the method of reading based on a chart configurations, indicators and studies that track certain patterns and establish the most probable direction of further movement.

---

## Trading Plan

### Trading Plan Form: My Trading System

My planned timeframe is

_____

I limit my losses to _____

I control my risk by limiting my position size so that with my planned stop size, my loss would not exceed _____

At any given time I am trading _____ positions.

Portion of my capital devoted to any single trade is _____

---

My daily (weekly, monthly) loss is limited to  _____

In relation to margin, I am  _____

I set the following criteria to limit the risk of each particular trade:

Volume: _____

Spread: _____

Float: _____

Max length of bar or candle: _____

Order sizes on Level II: _____

I am not taking a trade if possible slippage is evaluated as more than

_____

I apply  _____ method of reading the market.

## Basics of Fundamental Analysis

An introduction to fundamental analysis presented by Andrew Greta on Thestreet.com provides a perfect description to the basis of this approach.

'The intrinsic value approach to the markets is based on a couple of big assumptions. The first is that the intrinsic value of an asset can differ from its market price. Purists of the "efficient market hypothesis" find this concept ridiculous. They feel that market price is the *only* reflection of true value for an asset and reflects all information available about its future prospects at any point in time.

Detractors say the efficiency theory might hold in an ideal laboratory setting. But, go out in the real world and things get a little sticky. Information flows get delayed, altered or incompletely disseminated. More importantly, human beings act on their personal, often illogical, perceptions about the world around them. How else can you explain events like Holland's classic 17th century tulip fiasco where citizens, delirious with speculative fever, bid prices for single bulbs up to an equivalent of $40,000 today? Or, more recently, the **Netscape** where traders paid $70 per share or more for a company that has barely showed positive income to this day?

Assuming you accept the notion of intrinsic value, the second big assumption of fundamental analysis is that, even though things get out of whack from time to time, the market price of an asset will gravitate toward its true value eventually. Again, probably a safe bet considering the long upward march of quality stocks in general despite regular setbacks and periods of irrational exuberance. The key strategy for the fundamentalist is to buy when prices are at or below this intrinsic value and sell when they get overpriced.'

The first step is analyzing the company's **balance sheet**.

**A balance sheet** of a company is a listing of all of the company's assets and liabilities and represents a summary of the financial structure of the company. It is a document that shows how financially sound the company is. The balance sheet is divided into three sections and the two sides of the balance sheet must equal each other:

| | |
|---|---|
| **Assets**: What the company owns. | **Liabilities**: What the company owes. |
| | **Shareholder's Equity**: The "net worth" of the company. |

===============================================================

| **Assets** | **=** | **Liabilities + Shareholder's Equity** |
|---|---|---|

A balance sheet lists assets in descending order of liquidity, from cash to real estate owned by the company. The same order is maintained for liabilities (accounts payable first followed by longer term debts). "Current" asset is anything collectible in the short term (usually under one year); anything owed by the company in the same timeframe is a current liability. The most important accounting terms to focus on are:

- Book Value per share
- Price to Book value
- Cash per share
- Current ratio
- Debt to Equity Ratio

- Total Cash
- Total Debt

**Book value** is the assets in a balance sheet, calculated as the original cost minus depreciation over time. Book value gives an idea of a basic company worth in case of liquidation. If you divide book value by number of shares outstanding, you find **Book Value per share**. If a market price for company shares is significantly higher, a stock is probably overpriced (although this is a somewhat oversimplified way to look at this factor).

Divide a stock price by book value per share, and you receive **Price to Book value**. Compare it to the average for a given industry. A result that is significantly higher than the industry average suggests that the stock is overvalued. A significantly lower result suggests an opportunity of buying a currently undervalued stock.

**Current ratio** is the ratio of the current assets to the current liabilities. It serves as a measurement of a company's ability to pay bills and finance the operations and growth. A ratio of 2 is regarded generally as sufficient, although some industries require a higher number for a smooth operation. Also, high-growth companies need a bigger ratio to sustain the expansion while established companies can operate with less.

**Debt to Equity ratio** is found by dividing the amount of long-term debt by shareholder's equity (excess of total assets over total liabilities). Compare it to industry average. A ratio that is significantly higher than average is a matter of concern. An attractive buying opportunity will be found among companies with a ratio that is lower than average. Generally speaking, a ratio higher than 1 is a reason to be careful.

After going over resources and books listed below and learning the basic terminology the reader should be able to quickly evaluate a simple balance sheet and determine the financial strength of a company. To evaluate a large complex company will obviously take more time and effort. You will have to decide how sophisticated this analysis process will become. You may decide to stick with stocks whose balance sheets are easily analyzed and avoid companies with very complex capital structures. There is certainly no shortage of companies in either category.

The second step of fundamental analysis is analyzing the **income statement**.

The **income statement** is a document showing how much money the company is making. It plays a significant role in forecasting future profits. It is a summary of revenues and expenses that are presented in a particular order. Revenues are listed first followed by the expenses (costs of doing business). When the expenses are subtracted from the revenues, there will either be a profit or a loss. The income statement is usually presented every quarter (three months) and at the end of the year (12 months).

Keep in mind one important distinction that somewhat complicates analysis of an income statement. The income recorded in it is not necessarily firm cash obtained by the company. When a company sells its products or services, it can put a record of income in the statement even though actual payment is not received yet. Similarly, expenses can be recorded when the purchased assets are actually used and not necessarily when a company paid for them.

The most important accounting terms to focus on are:

- Price to Earnings Ratio
- Price to Sales Ratio
- Interest Coverage ratio
- Revenue Growth

- Earnings Growth
- Profit Margin

**Price to Earnings (P/E)** ratio is calculated by dividing a stock's price by **Earnings per Share**, which, in turn, is net income divided by number of shares issued. P/E is a relative measurement for a company versus industry average. A perception that a company with a low P/E is a bargain versus a company with a high P/E is somewhat oversimplified, although it can serve as a good starting point.

**Price to sales** ratio is found by dividing a company stock's price by gross revenue. It reflects a company's market valuation on a relative basis, the same way as P/E.

**Interest Coverage** ratio shows whether a company is able to make its interest payments. It is calculated by dividing earnings before taxes and interest payments by interest expense. The number obtained shows how many payments a company can make with current income. Generally, this ratio is considered sufficient if it exceeds 3-4.

**Profit Margin** is the net income divided by sales (gross revenue). It reflects the profit made by a company from sales. Compared to industry average, this number shows a company's relative effectiveness.

Analyze the dynamics of all of the numbers above, over a period of time, to see how a company is developing.

**Revenue Growth** and **Earnings Growth** reflect a company's dynamics over a period of time.

These two parts are just basics of fundamental analysis. As you can see, there is no exact science to it. Discussed numbers and ratios could be interpreted in different ways. There are also factors to consider that could be additional elements of your research or even trigger for research itself – the product, the technology, the invention, the innovation and many others. You may want to know more about the management, and track inside buying and selling.

## Resources for Fundamental Analysis

http://news.yahoo.com/news?tmpl=index2&cid=749
Simply type the stock symbol in the box and click the "Get Quotes" button. A window will come up that has many options listed on the left side of the page. Click on "Balance Sheet" and the latest Balance Sheet will appear.

http://www.nasdaq.com/asp/quotes_sec.asp?symbol=INTC&selected=INTC&page=filings
Type the stock symbol into the box next to "ADD" and click on "ADD" and the most current SEC filings will appear. Quarterly Balance Sheet data will be found in Form 10-Q's and yearly Balance Sheet data will be found in Form 10-K's.

## Recommended Reading for Fundamental Analysis

RR14; RR15

## Trading Plan

### Trading Plan Form: Trading System for Fundamental Trader

I am interested in stocks that match the following criteria:

Sectors: _____

Stock Price: _____

Products: _____

My criteria for entry:

_____
_____
_____
_____

My criteria for exit:

_____
_____
_____
_____

My criteria for applying a stop loss:

_____
_____

## Basics of Tape Reading

The principles of Tape Reading date back nearly 400 years. Whenever there is a disagreement on the perceived or intrinsic value of a product or instrument, there is cause for speculation about where that price will move. Principles of Tape Reading take you right to the heart of this speculative arena. They match price movement to crowd behavior in the form of rate of volume.

Tape readers see price movement in relation to the rate of volume and can determine what kind of footprints in a stock action are being made. It allows an observer to understand the actions of the minority and finally when the majority climbs in. These principles are applied both in an individual security's behavior as well as the broader market trend's behavior.

Tape reading principles suggest that the majority is usually wrong. Evidence of accumulation and distribution in the market at levels where the minority (smart money) is participating to a greater degree are often masked to the public until the time is right; then the minority unloads positions as the majority catches on. This can be seen in numerous examples in any given time interval. The market is a discounting mechanism by which the majority usually enters and exits the markets at the wrong time. The major idea is that the public is the last to participate, so when the public comes to buy there is no one else to buy from them. Thus, majority participation creates the final stage of the movement and is followed by a reversal. It is the same way when the majority sells, there is no one left but buyers.

We see examples of this during times of capitulation, where the majority creates selling pressure that is so strong as to exhaust selling. They participate in this aggregate selling phase as a crowd. Meanwhile, the minority (smart money) finds this point where selling becomes exhausted - and smart money reverses and goes long. The same is seen on the long side where the majority feels as if they missed out on a major market or stock move and cannot stand to see it raising more without them. This brings in majority buying and euphoria, where buying becomes exhausted. The minority then begins to distribute shares to the crowd of buyers from positions they have accumulated at lower levels.

This cycle of accumulation and distribution favors the minority that can read the tape of the market and participate at levels that feed off the usual ignorance of the majority. Tape reading principles allow you to watch how the minority is participating and how to profit from the majority that creates the herd movement, thus signaling a short-term stop to the current trend.

The major difference that allows us to distinguish the action of smart money from that of the public is the **character of price movement and volume changes**. As a rule, _smart money action can be seen as a slow gradual price movement with steady or slowly increasing volume._ _The Public's action is characterized by hysterical parabolic price spikes, almost vertical movements with sharp volume increases._

## Principles of Tape Reading

### 1. Trend Beginning (Active accumulation or distribution)
**Slow steady movement upward with consistent volume** indicates the so-called "good buying" and **means starting upward momentum**.

This is the stage where the minority, a.k.a. Smart Money, starts quiet accumulation. Buying is carefully done in order not to cause a sharp price rise and to avoid attracting broad attention.

> In the case of distribution, the scenario will be the same except movement is in the opposite direction (downward).

### 2. Trend Confirmation (Active accumulation or distribution)
**Slow price advance with steady increasing volume** indicates **continuing upward momentum**.

This is the next stage of the movement, where a price rise attracts first attention from broader public. Joining the move it creates a volume increase while the price advance is somewhat accelerating, although it still remains relatively slow.

> In the case of distribution, the scenario will be the same except movement is in the opposite direction (downward).

### 3. Euphoria/Capitulation
An **acceleration** in the price **advance**, almost vertical movement accompanied by a **volume surge**, is usually not sustained and indicates the **end** of this stage of the move (**euphoria stage**).

At this stage, price movement or news released to the public attracts broad attention and participation. The crowd rushes in, taking the stock out of the hands of Smart Money, which accumulated it in the first two stages of the movement.

The first three principles described major phases of a price movement. Following principles help understand certain interim price patterns that occur within those phases.

An acceleration in the price **drop**, almost vertical movement accompanied by a volume surge, is usually not sustained and indicates the end of this stage of the move (**capitulation stage**). This is the final stage of the same scenario in the opposite direction (downward).

### 4. Shallow Retracement Trend Continuation

**Volume increase on the price advance** combined with **shallow volume on the pullback** indicating **a continuing uptrend**.

This scenario shows that the buyers are more aggressive and willing to commit than the sellers. A price advance encourages them, attracting broader participation. A pullback, on the other hand, does not attract too many sellers and finds strong support.

### 5. Decreasing Volume Reversal

**A slowing pace of buying with decreasing volume** indicates that the top of this stage of movement is near.

This is usually referred to as "buying is drying up". The price rise fails to attract attention and, not being fed by new participation, the movement reverses.

### 6. Passive Accumulation/Distribution

**Big buying volume without price changing** indicates **distribution** and means resistance level.

**Big selling volume without price changing** indicates **accumulation** and means support level.

Distribution and accumulation by themselves do not indicate what action you should take. They just mark certain levels of support and resistance that can be used to form setups – structures that we build to define our entries and exits.

Let us look deeper into what tape reading really is. This is the method to analyze the action from the standpoint of distinguishing the action of Smart Money from that of the Public. It can be used as a standalone method of reading or as a foundation or supplementary method for any other method, be it fundamental or technical analysis. It is often asked how tape reading relates to technical analysis. They should not be interpreted as mutually exclusive. Tape reading is the root, technical studies and indicators are derivatives. They play a role of interpreters. The market talks to us in its original language – price, volume and pace. You can read this language itself or you can use the help of interpreters to this or that degree. No matter which method you eventually elect as your primary weapon, tape reading is a great measurement against which you should check your conclusions.

### Resources for Tape Reading

http://www.realitytrader.com/Tapereading.asp#tapereading

### Recommended Reading for Tape Reading

RR1; RR3; RR4; RR18; RR19

## Basics of Technical Analysis

*Before we get into technical analysis (TA), I would like to address an issue that surfaces regularly. This issue traditionally starts with statement "TA doesn't work". One who claims that then cites numerous examples of 'indicator showing this direction, yet the price goes opposite" or "chart pattern predicts certain action, yet opposite happens". This is a common misunderstanding stemming from a mistaken concept that TA has a purpose of prediction; thus, any case when prediction does not work is counted as TA's failure. Let us be clear: there is no tool that PREDICTS which way a price is going to move. This is not the purpose of TA. Its purpose is to analyze the action and give you the results of analysis in a form that helps you make a decision. It is your decision that is going to work or not. Just as a thermometer will show you the temperature outside, it cannot tell you if you will get colder and a technical indicator cannot tell you what will happen next. In the case with the thermometer, it is your action that defines whether you get cold going outside; you can wear a sweater or a swimming suit, and if your choice is wrong you are going to be uncomfortable. An indicator, just like a thermometer, indicates something – it is designed to do just that. It is how you utilize its indication in your trading system that will define the outcome of your action. Therefore, the very question "Does TA work?" makes no sense. It does in the sense that it gives you certain information to act upon. And, no, it does not work in the sense that it is not foretelling the future for you.*

*The premise of technical analysis is the following. Market change is a result of combined actions of a traders' conglomerate; if human behavior submits to certain patterns, then so should the market. Thus, a chart is a graphical representation of such behavior and those patterns could be found on it, too. Naturally, while patterns work statistically, each separate case cannot be predicted.*

Technical analysis is the study of price movement based on charts and done in an effort to determine probable future price. The roots of technical analysis stem from the **Dow Theory**, developed around 1900 by Charles Dow. These roots include such principles as the trending nature of prices, prices discounting all known information, confirmation and divergence, volume mirroring changes in price, and support/resistance. As you can see, there is a clear relation between tape reading and technical analysis. Let us review the main principles of the **Dow Theory**, as such a review provides a perfect transition from **tape reading** to **technical analysis.**

### 1. The Averages Discount Everything.

An individual stock's price reflects everything known about the security. As new information arrives, market participants quickly disseminate the information and the price adjusts accordingly. Likewise, the market averages discount and reflect everything known by all stock market participants.

### 2. The Market Is Comprised of Three Trends.

At any given time in the stock market, three forces are in effect: the Primary trend, Secondary trends, and Minor trends.

The Primary trend can either be a bullish (rising) market or a bearish (falling) market. The Primary trend usually lasts more than one year and may last for several years. If the market is making successive higher-highs and higher-lows the primary trend is up. If the market is making successive lower-highs and lower-lows, the primary trend is down.

Secondary trends are intermediate, corrective reactions to the Primary trend. These reactions typically last from one to three months and retrace from one-third to two-thirds of the previous Secondary trend.

Minor trends are short-term movements lasting from one day to three weeks. Secondary trends are typically comprised of a number of Minor trends. The Dow Theory holds that, since stock prices over the short-term are subject to some degree of manipulation (Primary and Secondary trends are not), Minor trends are unimportant and can be misleading.

### 3. Primary Trends Have Three Phases.

The Dow Theory says that the First phase is made up of aggressive buying by informed investors in anticipation of economic recovery and long-term growth. The general feeling among most investors during this phase is one of "gloom and doom" and "disgust." The informed investors, realizing that a turnaround is inevitable, aggressively buy from these distressed sellers.

The Second phase is characterized by increasing corporate earnings and improved economic conditions. Investors will begin to accumulate stock as conditions improve.

The Third phase is characterized by record corporate earnings and peak economic conditions. The general public (having had enough time to forget about their last "scathing") now feels comfortable participating in the stock market--fully convinced that the stock market is headed for the moon. They now buy even more stock, creating a buying frenzy. It is during this phase that those few investors who did the aggressive buying during the First phase begin to liquidate their holdings in anticipation of a downturn.

### 4. The Averages Must Confirm Each Other.

The Industrials and Transports must confirm each other in order for a valid change of trend to occur. Both averages must extend beyond their previous secondary peak (or trough) in order for a change of trend to be confirmed.

### 5. The Volume Confirms the Trend.

The Dow Theory focuses primarily on price action. Volume is only used to confirm uncertain situations.

Volume should expand in the direction of the primary trend. If the primary trend is down, volume should increase during market declines. If the primary trend is up, volume should increase during market advances.

### 6. A Trend Remains Intact Until It Gives a Definite Reversal Signal.

An up-trend is defined by a series of higher-highs and higher-lows. In order for an up-trend to reverse, prices must have at least one lower high and one lower low (the reverse is true of a downtrend).

When a reversal in the primary trend is signalled by both the Industrials and Transports, the odds of the new trend continuing are at their greatest. However, the longer a trend continues, the odds of the trend remaining intact become progressively smaller.

The world of technical analysis is huge. There is no way to describe it within the framework of this book or any other single book for that matter. We are going to go over major classifications and present the basics. If this is a direction you are going to move in, there won't be a shortage of books and resources.

Let us start with basic definitions. Those are:

> **Open** - This is the price of the first trade for the period (e.g., the first trade of the day). When analyzing daily data, the Open is important as an indication of consensus price after all the events of previous time period were absorbed and analyzed.

**High** - This is the highest price that the security traded during the period. It is the point at which there were more sellers than buyers (i.e., there are always sellers willing to sell at higher prices, but the High represents the highest price buyers were willing to pay).

**Low** - This is the lowest price that the security traded during the period. It is the point at which there were more buyers than sellers (i.e., there are always buyers willing to buy at lower prices, but the Low represents the lowest price sellers were willing to accept).

**Close** - This is the last price that the security traded during the period. The relationship between the Open (the first price) and the Close (the last price) are considered significant by most technicians. This relationship is emphasized in candlestick charts.

Those price points are represented graphically in the bars or candles. For a bar, a reading is as shown on the following image:

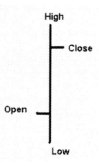

For a candle, a reading is as on the following image:

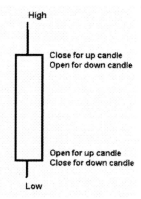

The color of the candle shows whether this is an up or down candle. A white or green (empty body) candle indicates an upward direction (close is higher than open), black or red (filled-in body) – downward (close is lower than open).

## Support and Resistance

1. Support levels occur when the consensus is that the price will not move lower. It is the point where buyers outnumber sellers.
2. Resistance levels occur when the consensus is that the price will not move higher. It is the point where sellers outnumber buyers.

3. The break of a support or resistance level indicates a change in investor expectations.
4. Volume is useful in determining how strong the change of expectation really is.
5. When a resistance level is successfully broken, it becomes a new support level. Similarly, when a support level is broken it becomes a new resistance level.

## Technical Analysis Tools

We will list some of the most popular studies and indicators. By no means should you expect to learn everything about those tools from this overview. This is just to give you a first idea of what is available. Those tools that you get interested in require deeper research.

### Moving Averages

A moving average is the average price of a security at a given time. When calculating a moving average, you specify the time span to calculate the average price (e.g., 200 days or 50 minutes, etc). Moving average lines are drawn on your charts by your charting software automatically, accordingly to the settings that you define. If for instance, you set a daily chart to track the moving average with a 50 day period, you will analyze it as follows.

If the security's price is above its moving average, it means that investor's current expectations are higher than their average expectations over the last 50 days, and that investors are becoming increasingly bullish on the security. Conversely, if today's price is below its moving average, it shows that current expectations are below average expectations over the last 50 days.

Moving averages set certain expectations for support and resistance levels. A break of the moving average is considered an indicative point for the future price change.

### Envelopes (Trading Bands)

Envelopes define the upper and lower boundaries of a security's normal trading range. A sell signal is generated when the security reaches the upper band whereas a buy signal is generated at the lower band. The optimum percentage shift depends on the volatility of the security--the more volatile, the larger the percentage.

The logic behind envelopes is that overzealous buyers and sellers push the price to the extremes (i.e., the upper and lower bands), at which point the prices often stabilize by moving to more realistic levels.

### Bollinger Bands

The basic interpretation of Bollinger Bands is that prices tend to stay within the upper- and lower-band. The distinctive characteristic of Bollinger Bands is that the spacing between the bands varies based on the volatility of the prices. During periods of extreme price changes (i.e., high volatility), the bands widen to become more forgiving. During periods of stagnant pricing (i.e., low volatility), the bands narrow to contain prices.

Characteristics of Bollinger Bands.

- Sharp price changes tend to occur after the bands tighten, as volatility lessens.
- When prices move outside the bands, a continuation of the current trend is implied.
- Bottoms and tops made outside the bands followed by bottoms and tops made inside the bands call for reversals in the trend.
- A move that originates at one band tends to go all the way to the other band. This observation is useful when projecting price targets.

## On Balance Volume

On Balance Volume ("OBV") is a momentum indicator that relates volume to price change. It shows if volume is flowing into or out of a security. When the security closes higher than the previous close, all of the time period's volume is considered up-volume. When the security closes lower than the previous close, all of the time period's volume is considered down-volume.

The basic assumption is that OBV changes precede price changes. The theory is that smart money can be seen flowing into the security by a rising OBV. When the public then moves into the security, both the security and the OBV will advance faster. You can see here a clear similarity to tape reading ideas.

## Average Directional Index (ADX)

ADX is designed to evaluate the strength of the current trend. Low readings, below 20, indicate a weak trend and high readings, above 40, indicate a strong trend. The indicator does not grade the trend as bullish or bearish. ADX can be used to identify potential changes in a market from trending to non-trending. When ADX begins to strengthen from below 20 and/or moves above 20, it is a sign that the trading range is ending and a trend could be developing. When ADX begins to weaken from above 40 and/or moves below 40, it is a sign that the current trend is losing strength and a trading range could develop.

## MACD

The MACD ("Moving Average Convergence/Divergence") is a trend following momentum indicator that shows the relationship between two moving averages of prices. The MACD is most effective in wide-swinging trading markets. There are three popular ways to use the MACD: crossovers, overbought/oversold conditions, and divergences.

### Crossovers

The basic MACD trading rule is to sell when the MACD falls below its signal line. Similarly, a buy signal occurs when the MACD rises above its signal line. It is also popular to buy/sell when the MACD goes above/below zero.

### Overbought/Oversold Conditions

The MACD can also be used as an overbought/oversold indicator. When the shorter moving average pulls away dramatically from the longer moving average (i.e., the MACD rises), it is likely that the security price is overextending and will soon stall at more realistic levels. MACD overbought and oversold conditions vary from security to security.

## Divergences

An indication that an end to the current trend may be near occurs when the MACD diverges from the security. A bearish divergence occurs when the MACD is making new lows while prices fail to reach new lows. A bullish divergence occurs when the MACD is making new highs while prices fail to reach new highs. Both of these divergences are most significant when they occur at relatively overbought/oversold levels.

## Fibonacci Numbers

Fibonacci numbers are a sequence of numbers in which each successive number is the sum of the two previous numbers:

1, 1, 2, 3, 5, 8, 13, 21, 34, 55, 89, 144, 610, etc.

There are four Fibonacci studies: arcs, fans, retracements, and time zones. The interpretation of these studies involves anticipating changes in trends as prices near the lines created by the

Fibonacci studies. One of the most popular is retracements. Fibonacci Retracements are displayed by first drawing a trend line between two extreme points, for example, a trough and opposing peak. A series of nine horizontal lines are drawn intersecting the trend line at the Fibonacci levels of 0.0%, 23.6%, 38.2%, 50%, 61.8%, 100%, 161.8%, 261.8%, and 423.6%. After a significant price move (either up or down), prices will often retrace a significant portion (if not all) of the original move. As prices retrace, support and resistance levels often occur at or near the Fibonacci Retracement levels.

## Stochastic Oscillator

The Stochastic Oscillator compares where a security's price closed relative to its price range over a given time period. The Stochastic Oscillator is displayed as two lines. The main line is called "%K." The second line, called "%D," is a moving average of %K. The %K line is usually displayed as a solid line and the %D line is usually displayed as a dotted line.

There are several ways to interpret a Stochastic Oscillator. Three popular methods include:

1. Buy when the Oscillator (either %K or %D) falls below a specific level (e.g., 20) and then rises above that level. Sell when the Oscillator rises above a specific level (e.g., 80) and then falls below that level.
2. Buy when the %K line rises above the %D line and sell when the %K line falls below the %D line.
3. Look for divergences. For example, where prices are making a series of new highs and the Stochastic Oscillator is failing to surpass its previous highs.

## Relative Strength Index

The RSI is a price-following oscillator that ranges between 0 and 100. A popular method of analyzing the RSI is to look for a divergence in which the security is making a new high, but the RSI is failing to surpass its previous high. This divergence is an indication of an impending reversal. When the RSI then turns down and falls below its most recent trough, it is said to have completed a "failure swing." The failure swing is considered a confirmation of the impending reversal.

## Chart Patterns

Patterns often repeat themselves and can be exploited based on this similarity. Below are the most common of those patterns.

## Head-and-Shoulders

The Head-and-Shoulders price pattern gets its name from the resemblance of a head with two shoulders on either side. The reason this reversal pattern is so common is due to the manner in which trends typically reverse.

An up-trend forms as prices make higher-highs and higher-lows in a stair-step fashion. The trend is broken when this upward climb ends. The "left shoulder" and the "head" are the last two higher-highs. The right shoulder is created as the buyers try to push prices higher, but are unable to do so. This signifies the end of the up-trend. Confirmation of a new down-trend occurs when the "neckline" is broken.

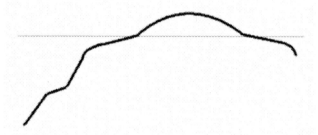

## Head and Shoulders pattern

During an up-trend, volume should increase during each rally. A sign that the trend is weakening occurs when the volume accompanying a rally is less than the volume accompanying the preceding rally. In a typical Head-and-Shoulders pattern, volume decreases on the head and is especially light on the right shoulder. You can see the similarity to tape reading principles once again.

Following the penetration of the neckline, it is very common for prices to return to the neckline in a last effort to continue the up-trend (as shown in the preceding chart). If prices are then unable to rise above the neckline, they usually decline rapidly on increased volume.

An inverse Head-and-Shoulders pattern often coincides with market bottoms. As with a normal Head-and-Shoulders pattern, volume usually decreases as the pattern forms and then increases as prices rise above the neckline.

## Cup and Handle

As its name implies, there are two parts to the pattern: the cup and the handle. The cup forms after an advance and looks like a bowl or rounding bottom. As the cup is completed, a trading range develops on the right hand side and the handle is formed. A subsequent breakout from the handle's trading range signals a continuation of the prior advance.

*Cup and Handle Pattern*

## Triangles

A triangle occurs as the range between peaks and troughs narrows. Triangles typically occur as prices encounter a support or resistance level which constricts the prices.

A "**symmetrical triangle**" occurs when prices are making both lower-highs and higher-lows.

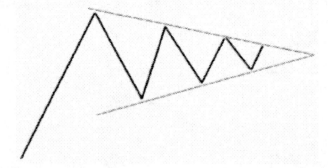

*Symmetrical Triangle*

An "**ascending triangle**" occurs when there are higher-lows (as with a symmetrical triangle), but the highs are occurring at the same price level due to resistance. The odds favor an upside breakout from an ascending triangle.

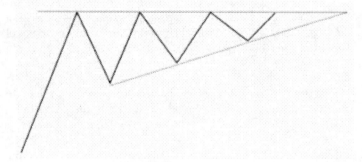

*Ascending Triangle*

A "**descending triangle**" occurs when there are lower-highs (as with a symmetrical triangle), but the lows are occurring at the same price level due to support. The odds favor a downside breakout from a descending triangle.

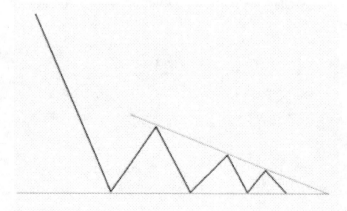

*Descending Triangle*

Breakouts are confirmed when they are accompanied by an increase in volume. The most reliable breakouts occur somewhere between half and three-quarters of the distance between the beginning and end (apex) of the triangle. There are seldom many clues as to the direction prices will break out of a symmetrical triangle. If prices move all the way through the triangle to the apex, a breakout is less likely. There are multiple variations to this theme, as Flags, Wedges and Pennants.

## Double Tops and Bottoms

A double top occurs when prices rise to a resistance level on significant volume, retreat, and subsequently return to the resistance level on decreased volume. Prices then decline marking the beginning of a new down-trend.

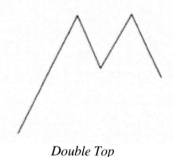

*Double Top*

## Double Bottom

A double bottom has the same characteristics as a double top except it is upside-down.

*Double Bottom*

## Japanese Candlesticks

Candlestick charting is a technique developed in the 1600s. This is a graphic way of representing of supply/demand shift patterns. The most popular patterns are:

## Bullish Patterns

| | | |
|---|---|---|
| | | **Long white (empty) line.** This is a bullish formation. It occurs when prices open near the low and close significantly higher near the period's high. |
| | | **Hammer.** This is a bullish line if it occurs after a significant downtrend. If the line occurs after a significant up-trend, it is called a Hanging Man. A Hammer is identified by a small real body (i.e., a small range between the open and closing prices) and a long lower shadow (i.e., the low is significantly lower than the open, high, and close). The body can be empty or filled-in. |
| | | **Piercing line.** This is a bullish pattern and the opposite of a dark cloud cover. The first line is a long black line and the second line is a long white line. The second line opens lower than the first line's low, but it closes more than halfway above the first line's real body. |
| | | **Bullish engulfing lines.** This pattern is strongly bullish if it occurs after a significant downtrend (i.e., it acts as a reversal pattern). It occurs when a small bearish (filled-in) line is engulfed by a large bullish (empty) line. |
| | | **Morning star.** This is a bullish pattern signifying a potential bottom. The "star" indicates a possible reversal and the bullish (empty) line confirms this. The star can be empty or filled-in. |

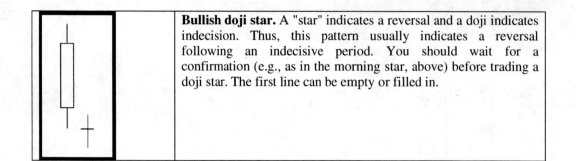

**Bullish doji star.** A "star" indicates a reversal and a doji indicates indecision. Thus, this pattern usually indicates a reversal following an indecisive period. You should wait for a confirmation (e.g., as in the morning star, above) before trading a doji star. The first line can be empty or filled in.

## Bearish Patterns

| | | |
|---|---|---|
| | | **Long black (filled-in) line.** This is a bearish formation. It occurs when prices open near the high and close significantly lower near the period's low. |
| | | **Hanging Man.** These lines are bearish if they occur after a significant uptrend. If this pattern occurs after a significant downtrend, it is called a Hammer. They are identified by small bodies (i.e., a small range between the open and closing prices) and a long lower shadow (i.e., the low was significantly lower than the open, high, and close). The bodies can be empty or filled-in. |
| | | **Dark cloud cover.** This is a bearish pattern. The pattern is more significant if the second line's body is below the center of the previous line's body (as illustrated). |
| | | **Bearish engulfing lines.** This pattern is strongly bearish if it occurs after a significant up-trend (i.e., it acts as a reversal pattern). It occurs when a small bullish (empty) body is engulfed by a large bearish (filled-in) body. |
| | | **Evening star.** This is a bearish pattern signifying a potential top. The "star" indicates a possible reversal and the bearish (filled-in) body confirms this. The star can be empty or filled-in. |

| | | |
|---|---|---|
| | | **Doji star.** A star indicates a reversal and a doji indicates indecision. Thus, this pattern usually indicates a reversal following an indecisive period. You should wait for a confirmation (e.g., as in the evening star illustration) before trading a doji star. |
| | | **Shooting star.** This pattern suggests a minor reversal when it appears after a rally. The star's body must appear near the low price and the line should have a long upper shadow. |

## Reversal Patterns

| | |
|---|---|
| | **Long-legged doji.** This line often signifies a turning point. It occurs when the open and close are the same, and the range between the high and low is relatively large. |
| | **Dragon-fly doji.** This line also signifies a turning point. It occurs when the open and close are the same, and the low is significantly lower than the open, high, and closing prices. |
| | **Gravestone doji.** This line also signifies a turning point. It occurs when the open, close, and low are the same, and the high is significantly higher than the open, low, and closing prices. |
| | **Star.** Stars indicate reversals. A star is a line with a small real body that occurs after a line with a much larger real body, where the real bodies do not overlap. The shadows may overlap. |
| | **Doji star.** A star indicates a reversal and a doji indicates indecision. Thus, this pattern usually indicates a reversal following an indecisive period. You should wait for a confirmation (e.g., as in the evening star illustration) before trading a doji star. |

## Neutral Patterns

| | |
|---|---|
| | **Spinning tops.** These are neutral formations. They occur when the distance between the high and low, and the distance between the open and close, are relatively small. |
| | Doji. This line implies indecision. The security opened and closed at the same price. These lines can appear in several different patterns.<br><br>Double doji lines (two adjacent doji lines) imply that a forceful move will follow a breakout from the current indecision. |
| | **Harami.** This pattern indicates a decrease in momentum. It occurs when a line with a small body falls within the area of a larger body.<br><br>In this example, a bullish (empty) line with a long body is followed by a weak bearish (filled-in) line. This implies a decrease in the bullish momentum. |
| | **Harami cross.** This pattern also indicates a decrease in momentum. The pattern is similar to a harami, except the second line is a doji (signifying indecision). |

We just scratched the surface of technical analysis. It can be overwhelming for a newer trader as there are hundreds of indicators and new ones are being created. Do not overcomplicate your approach by putting too many studies and indicators on your charts. They will contradict each other in some cases and create confusion, clouding general principles of price movement for an observer. Always keep in mind those major principles as a context for indicators; check any results obtained by technical indicators against those principles. A chart with 10 indicators on it will not do you much good.

No matter how sophisticated an indicator is, never rely on it as a "predictor" of price movement. It is just a certain way to look at price and volume movement. It is a tool and a tool is as good as your skills to apply it. It does not "work" by itself – it simply indicates what it is designed to indicate, and it is up to you how to build this indication in your trading system.

Some indicators are designed to measure the same conditions. You might like one over another, but it is not sensible to use them together. For instance, RSI and Stochastic both measure overbought and oversold conditions and momentum. Try to use indicators complementing each other.

## Classification of Patterns and Indicators

In the *Trading Philosophy* part you answered a question for your trading plan: what kind of movement you are going to trade. Before building your trading system, now you need to define what kind of indicators or price patterns you are going to use in accordance with that choice. We will look closer into it in the next section. At this point, we need to realize that indicators and patterns serve different purposes and are useful for different type of traders. Some of them are trend continuation tools and some are trend reversal. Let us list some of them by these categories.

### Trend Continuation

Chart patterns signalling trend continuation are:

- Cup with Handle
- Flag, Pennant
- Symmetrical Triangle
- Ascending Triangle
- Descending Triangle
- Price Channel

### Trend Reversal

- Double Top
- Double Bottom
- Head and Shoulders
- Wedge

You also saw the breakdown of candlestick patterns by this principle.

Another question in your trading plan concerned your **level of aggressiveness**. It is related to another aspect of technical analysis: leading indicators vs. lagging. **Leading** indicators are designed to lead price movements. Early signalling for entry and exit is the main benefit. With early signals comes the prospect of higher returns and with higher returns comes the reality of greater risk – exactly as we discussed before. **Lagging** indicators follow the price action. One of the main benefits of trend-following indicators is the ability to catch a move and remain in a move. They are not as useful in a ranging market and their signals tend to be late.

Examples of leading indicators are RSI, Stochastic. Examples of lagging ones are Moving Averages and MACD.

## You Asked

*Question:*

Do you believe chart patterns or technical indicators work "on their own" or they are a self-fulfilling prophecy, in the sense that they work simply because people react on them en masse, making them work?

*Answer:*

Both! See, they were not invented – they were discovered, by observing and summarizing. In this sense, they did exist "on their own" and reflected certain patterns of a player's psychology. After all, a chart is just that – a mirror of human reactions. A chart is created by actual trades, which are a result of people's actions that, in turn, are being caused by people's opinions and reactions. Therefore, graphical presentation of these opinions resulted in trades in a chart. If you believe that there are patterns in human behavior, you have to assume patterns in charts, too.

Now, on the other hand, when a pattern becomes widely known and many players start exploiting it, they do affect the pattern behavior on the merits of the pattern itself. It remains an open question whether they would act just the same if they did not know about the pattern – most likely they would, maybe in different numbers, maybe within a broader price area. Here we run into the next question...

*Question:*

Right! Do people who participate in a certain pattern overuse and kill it? I have heard about this, and it seems to be somewhat contradictory to the idea that they add fuel to the pattern.

*Answer:*

Sounds paradoxical, yes? In fact, there is no paradox. It is simply different stages of the pattern life cycle. At some point, when everyone and their brother starts using a pattern, it ceases working (it is not exactly the correct way to say it, but we will get back to it in a minute). It happens for one simple reason: the market works in a way that allows a handful of traders to take money from the majority. If everyone is using a pattern and the pattern works, then from whom is everybody taking money? A pattern has to stop working in order to restore the normal order of things and continue going in the direction of the least resistance. And, the path of the least resistance is AGAINST the majority.

Now, let us get back to that "ceases working". It is not exactly right because the pattern is still working – just differently. It may reverse, or it may add some new element to shake out the weak hands – and all this is possible to observe and exploit. That is why you never stop learning in the market – you are always on the lookout for changing patterns in order to exploit a trap instead of becoming trapped. Just do not consider these cycles of pattern life as someone's manipulation – it is simply the way the market works. And it just cannot be any different; if some pattern or indicator could work no matter how many people know and use it, then at some point everyone would be using it and everyone would win (don't ask me from whom), not leaving any money in the market. The markets close down, currencies and commodities do not trade anymore, economy crashes, world stops revolving... now you know why there is no Holy Grail in the market, why black box systems do not work, and why you should run when you hear advertising of another "sure to win system".

Now, there is one more thing left to say on this matter. Let us distinguish a real pattern and a trick. A real pattern, as we said, is based on players' behavior. A trick is exploiting some artificial inefficiency in the market that disappears as market mechanics improve (or worsen, from the point of view of those who made money from the inefficiency). Let me cite an example of such inefficiency. In 1999, there were opportunities of easy arbitrage between two market participants, one of which put a bid higher than the offer put by another one. It happened because of cumbersome, overcomplicated and fast changing systems of order routing. Things changed fast, taking this moneymaking opportunity away. That was a trick, not a strategy. It never restored itself. Tricks rarely, if ever, do.

*Question:*
Is there anything to help distinguish a pullback from a reversal?

*Answer:*
This is a very involved question. There is no surefire way to tell, that would be way too simple. You need to answer this question in one of two cases. Either you are trying to find an entry on a pullback – an aggressive entry for trend continuation; or you are thinking of closing your position and want to give it a chance to run while limiting your risk. I am not including considerations of short entry as a separate case here for simplicity's sake.

As with everything in trading, there is a way to put probabilities on your side. First, pay attention to volume. As a rule, if volume is drying up on a pullback while increasing on an advance, probabilities are on your side for trend continuation. Second, watch for the signal in terms of your trading system. If you are trading chart patterns, you have a support level that indicates more than just a pullback if broken. If this is the technical indicator that signals your entry with a certain reading, then you have defined criteria for failure too. The idea is, you are going with the trend using confirmations by your system, and as long as your read is right, probabilities are on your side. And, the cases when odds do not work are taken care of by stops.

So, returning to the two cases we listed earlier, if you are looking for entry on a pullback you will be on watch for the situation where volume shapes up right for the trend continuation, and your indicator or chart formation signals entry. Since your entry will be very close to the support level, your stop will be tight enough to take care of a wrong reading. If you are looking for an exit of a position established earlier, this is essentially going to be trailing stop, moved to the closest support. It will be triggered if the support does not hold, protecting your profits.

As you can see, this is the "fatalistic" approach we discussed earlier: you do the right thing and let the market do what it wants to do.

## Resources for Technical Analysis

http://www.hardrightedge.com/control.htm - big collection of resources for technical analysis; thorough glossary of technical terms and topics with explanations.

http://www.equis.com/Education/TAAZ/ - online reference book by Stephen B. Achelis.

http://stockcharts.com/education/ChartAnalysis/index.html

http://stockcharts.com/education/IndicatorAnalysis/index.html - Good introduction in the world of technical analysis.

## Recommended Reading for Technical Analysis

RR6; RR7; RR17;

## Trading Plan

Trading Plan Form: Trading System for Technical Trader

I apply the following set of chart patterns, candlestick formations, technical studies and indicators:

_____
_____
_____

My settings for each of them:

_____
_____
_____

# Designing Your Strategy

Now that you armed yourself with knowledge of the related tools and made your choice, you will need to design your system. At this point, everything we discussed earlier is going to fall into place and create a new entity: your trading system. If at the beginning of this book this task seemed enormously gigantic to you, at this stage your carefully thought through trading plan is going to make it quite natural as all the pieces click together.

Let us establish from the onset that the system you design is not going to be a "once and forever" decision. As with many other aspects of trading, it is going to evolve and change. You can try and design it from scratch or you, as we said before, can try to apply any existing system that appeals to you. In any case, your trading system should be tailored for you. It means that even using someone else's system you will most likely find certain tweaks that make it more comfortable for you. This is a process that is going to take a while, but do not let it slow you down. The fact is you are going to tweak it even when you are a seasoned trader with years of experience. It is a never-ending process accompanying a trader's development and caused by both this development and changes in the market.

One more thing needs to be said at this point. In terms of material to study this is the largest part of your trading approach. Take your time to design your system, but do not try to learn everything about all kinds of analysis. No trader uses them all; no trader knows them all. Find what appeals to you and go ahead with it. After all, you already know it is not a system that makes a trader, it is a trader that makes a trader. There is no objective system that will work similarly well for everyone anyway. Give the same system to ten traders and you will obtain ten different results. The edge only partially lies in the system; most of it lies in your particular tweaks and your discipline. The best system is YOURS.

## Elements of a Trading System

First and foremost, **align your strategy with your trading plan**. It means that you pick those elements that match your decisions regarding trading approach, timeframe and trading method. You are not likely to need fundamental research if you decided to be a scalper; and you do not need an intraday momentum indicator if you decided to base your trading on fundamental data. Let us try to narrow it down for some typical approaches.

### Example 1

*Let us say you defined your approach as swing trading with a holding time within a week, following the trend and reading it by chart patterns with certain indicators; you approach your trading aggressively.* You are going to trade only financially sound companies – mostly well-known names. Most likely, you will largely ignore fundamental research. You are going to get familiar with tape reading principles as a foundation of any price and volume reading. You will pick those chart patterns that read trend continuation. If you are fascinated by the Japanese technique, you study candlesticks; if traditional chart patterns appeal more to you, you study Cup and Handle, Triangles etc. You get familiar with reversal patterns in order to recognize them for your exits. You add one or two leading indicators. This mix allows you to define your entry signals. Probably you are going to carry 3-5 positions, maybe a bit more at the same time.

### Example 2

*Your chosen trading approach is conservative intraday trading based on chart reading; you are going to trade trend reversals.* In this case, you again are not too interested in fundamental research. Among chart and candlestick patterns you are going to pick those that aim for trend reversal; you are going to be interested in indicators that deal with overbought/oversold conditions. Applying a reversal pattern, for instance a double bottom, you are going to define your entry signal as a break of the resistance created by a top between two bottoms. This choice is dictated by your decision to trade conservatively; if you want to be aggressive, you will define your entry signal as second bottom itself. Tape reading principles will help you pick those that are supported by the right volume configuration. You are likely to devote your capital to one to three positions at a time.

### Example 3

*You decided to be a long term trader, managing your positions over months and years. You are interested in high growth companies yielding potentially big rewards.* Obviously fundamental analysis becomes a major study for you. You are hunting for companies that are undervalued, with interesting new products and creative management that accumulates a company's shares. You apply tape reading principles to a stock's chart to define the moment when the Smart Money starts accumulating shares. The role of indicators is not profound for you, although you might want to pick a couple for your purposes. Your trading system assumes many small positions spread across your targeted industries.

### Example 4

*You are an aggressive scalper with tight risk control; you are trading breakouts.* Fundamental analysis plays no role in your trading. You are going to study tape reading to distinguish false breakouts from true ones. You might be interested in trend continuation patterns and indicators. You will trade one position at a time.

Now, study the setups that you chose to find out their major parameters. This studying will give you insight into the steps from **second** to **fifth**.

The second step is to define your **entry signal**. This is where your chosen method of reading comes into practice, resulting in trade initiation. Let us say, you picked trading breakouts, reading them by chart patterns with a moving average as an added indicator, using a regular way of entry. Your patterns for breakout are Triangle, Cup and Handle, and consolidation near the high. You are trading stocks priced between $10 and $50. This gives you an entry signal as print at breakout price of these patterns. Pay attention to aligning your entry with your level of aggressiveness.

Third, define your exact **risk parameters**. You trade, for example, stocks with average daily volumes not lower than five million shares a day; spread not wider that .05 cents; float not lower than fifty million shares. Your loss is limited to $250 per trade. You are chasing stocks not higher than .05 cents above your ideal entry point. This narrows down the universe of stocks for your scanning and further elaborates your entry point: breakout level plus .05 cents.

Fourth, define your **stop level** and **position size**. Your stop is dictated by the pattern you are going to use. All the setups that you design include a stop level in their structure. A break of a supporting moving average included in your system in this example can be such a stop signal. If you trade a breakout of a Cup and Handle, this setup sets the bottom of the Handle as the stop level. Seeing the width of this stop on the chart, you are using your maximum allowed loss to define your position size. Again, align your stop with your level of aggressiveness. It means that if you decide to enter aggressively, your stop is very tight since an aggressive entry is near support level. If you place your stop much wider, you will get the worst of both worlds: less confidence in new highs and a wide stop, which is obviously not a good strategy. Revisit the definition of different levels of aggressiveness and reread their trade-offs to make sure that your strategy matches those trade-offs and does not include their worst sides.

Fifth, determine your **exit signal**. Your system includes a decision on profit taking. Let us say you are going to take half of your profits when a stock moves into a 1:1 risk/reward point (see Useful Tip below). At this point, you are moving the stop to your entry level. A move into 2:1

signals another exit point for you, and you sell half of the balance there. After that, you are trailing your stop for the remaining shares until your stop is hit. Keep in mind that your exit signal is not necessarily tied to the measurable movement in terms of your profit; those risk/reward ratios are just a guideline. It means that the market can produce an exit signal at the point not matching your monetary objectives. Thus, your exit is a flexible component that needs to be re-evaluated as the trade develops. Ultimately, it is the market action and not your objectives that define your exit point. That is what is meant by "listening to the market" in terms of our trading philosophy.

> Risk/reward ratio is simply the ratio of a stop size to profit size. If your initial stop is .25 cents, then at .25 cents of profit the ratio of 1:1 is reached; .50 cents give you 1:2 ratio.

Sixth, define your "**uncle point**" for the day. Three losses in a row is your signal that the market today is not cooperating with your system. Your mindset is not likely to be in the best shape after that, and you need to regroup.

Seventh, define your "**relax point**" for the day. It is the level of profit, after which you stop looking actively for a trade because you have achieved your profit objective. It does not necessarily mean that you have to stop trading as opportunities could still be there. However, you want to become picky at this point and protect your profits, so you lower your aggressiveness in seeking the trade and take only those that are literally screaming at you from the screen.

At this point, you have the foundation of your trading system. The next step is to try and **test** it, analyzing historical charts and watching how your trading signals, defined by patterns and indicators, would have worked out. You also need to determine the **maximum drawdown** that your system produces in order to see if you can sustain it. We will return to this testing process in the *Practical Trading* part.

> In order to illustrate the idea and purpose of the testing period I would like to show you the preliminary draft of a trading plan written by an acquaintance of mine who started looking into trading as a possible continuation or supplement to his business career. This is a very interesting draft with keen observations and a highly methodical approach.
>
> *Being a mathematically inclined person, I am trying to create my probability equation for trading.*
>
> *(Probability of a Gain  X  Average Gain)  -  (Probability of a Loss  X  Average Loss)  = Result*
>
> *Sample Equation:  60% x 200 – 40% x 100  =  80*
>
> If I successfully execute my trading system over and over again, the long term average will begin to approach the expected result.
>
> While the market and I share control over what the variables are in any given trade, there are things that I can do to achieve the target values in the sample equation. I only have these variables to work with and only partial control of them, so I have to be disciplined about using the control that I do have.
>
> I can achieve a long term target of 60% gains by:
>
> **Before Entry**
> * Waiting patiently for a high probability chart pattern (or whatever technique)

- Avoiding lower probability set ups

## After Entry

- Not sabotaging myself, by second guessing the system
- Working the chosen trading system until it is proved or disproved

## After a Series of Losing Trades

- Taking a day off
- Trading smaller or on paper, until I start establishing gains again

*I can achieve a 2 to 1 gain to loss ratio by:*

## Before Entry

- Placing a stop loss correctly on the chart
- Calibrating the size of my trade so that my predetermined 'threshold of fear/maximum allowable loss' is not exceeded
- Identifying a suitable reward target on the chart that will allow a gain that is twice the size of the potential loss

## After Entry

- Never moving my stop down
- Moving the stop up to new locations, when appropriate
- Letting the position do its work (i.e., bump into the stop or the target)
- Letting the targeted gain run if it wants to, but with a closely trailing stop

Note: My threshold of fear is the point at which the loss is so big that I cannot be sure that I will act rationally. Below the threshold, the losses are small enough that I can manage them emotionally and know they are just part of my system.

Everything I do is to try and achieve the target values in the probability equation.

### Observations

Sometimes the market will give me a gain and sometimes it will give me a loss. I cannot control which. I can let the market give me as much as it wants to give, and on some occasions, this will be quite large. On the downside, when the market wants to give me a loss I can control the size of the loss and keep it small, regardless of how much of a loss it wants to give me.

*My two biggest threats come from myself. I might:*

- Let the market give me a really big loss. I cannot ever let this happen.
- Change my mind in mid-trade, resulting in a series of small losses or gains that are too small to make my probability equation work (i.e. come to a positive result)

There will be lots of variations on the basic probability model as one adapts the trading system and learns the profession, but it is a good place to start.

## My Ideal Trade Log

Although the real world will intervene so that the ideal log cannot be achieved, it is still a useful target to have in my mind in my daily struggle with reality. It is what I am trying to achieve.

This is the trade log that I visualize. This is how the probability equation will look in my trade log. Regardless of how frequently I trade, I want the last 10 trades to look like this.

| Trade # | Result | Amount |
|---------|--------|--------|
| 1 | Gain | 200 |
| 2 | Gain | 200 |
| 3 | Loss | -100 |
| 4 | Gain | 200 |
| 5 | Gain | 200 |
| 6 | Loss | -100 |
| 7 | Loss | -100 |
| 8 | Gain | 200 |
| 9 | Gain | 200 |
| 10 | Loss | -100 |
| Total | | 800 |

**Observations**

I am expecting four losses. This is OK and it is part of the business.

This is the benchmark that I will measure my performance against and this is how I will know whether I should be in this business.

The real world will be much messier and will include many things that knock me off this ideal. I will still keep this pattern in mind as the goal I am trying to achieve.

Trades do not have to be big to add up.

Keep in mind that your system has to include various market conditions. For instance, if you intend to trade breakouts, what are you to do when the market is trending down? Should you switch to breakdowns or simply stay away? If the market is locked in a tight range, should you start fading false breakouts or wait until a trend defines itself again? These are the questions to be answered when you build your system. You might want to include several market conditions in your system or you might want to trade only when you see the market matching your favorite conditions.

If you see the percentage and size of winning trades that satisfies your requirements, you are ready to move to the next step. This step is choosing the right tools that match your trading system and approach. Let us finish this part with a mind map review, a trading plan and move on to picking your trading tools.

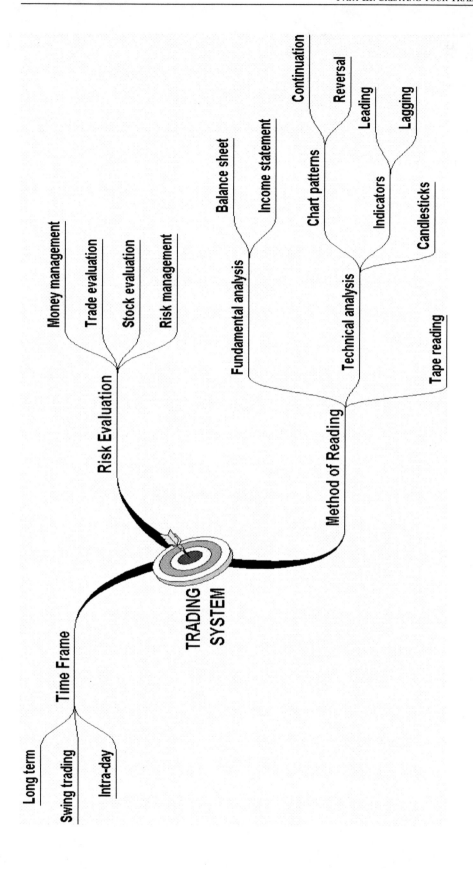

## Trading Plan

### Trading Plan Form: Trading System Design

My entry signal is generated when the following conditions are met:

_____

_____

_____

_____

My entry is initiated not farther than _____ from the point of signal.

My stop is triggered when the following criteria are met:

_____

_____

_____

_____

My exit signal is generated when the following happens:

_____

_____

_____

My daily (weekly, monthly) loss is limited to _____

When in profit, I am decreasing my activity when _____

# *Traders Talk - Daryl Guppy*

*Trades since 1991. Author of Share Trading, Chart Trading, Trading Tactics, Better Trading, Bear Trading, Trend Trading. Regular contributor to Technical Analysis of Stocks and Commodities magazine, Active Trader, the Sydney Futures Exchange magazine, Your Trading Edge, Australias' Shares magazine, TheEdge and Smart Investor in Singapore. Regular speaker on trading topics and techniques in Australia, Asia and the United States. Developer of the Guppy Multiple Moving Average Indicator which is included in Metastock, OmniTrader and other charting programs. Founder of www.guppytraders.com. Swing and position trader with timeframe from intraday to 30 days and longer, trading is a primary source of income. 50 years old, Darwin, Australia.*

I started trading by making all the classic mistakes. I started as an investor. I purchased my first stock within a few cents of its all time 14 year high. It's been going down ever since. I still hold it because it reminds me of why I am not an investor.

My next stock had more volatility. It ran up 70% and I felt very smart. Then it fell back and gave a small loss. I felt very silly. When it went up again I sold it and locked in a 70% return. Then I bought it back after it fell, and sold it again. This was the key that opened my eyes to the way trading is used to capitalize on volatility changes.

I was fortunate because I started trading in very remote and isolated conditions in the outback of Australia. I could not use news or fundamental information in my trading. Newspapers were delivered a week late. The area was too remote for TV reception. The result was that I had no choice but to try to understand what price activity was telling me. My focus was on chart analysis, and the technical analysis of prices. I started with simple Excel graphs, and then used trading profits to buy more sophisticated charting tools.

I believe there are inevitable mistakes that all traders make. How big they are, how disastrous they are, and at what stage we make them varies. But there is no escaping from these mistakes. This is one of the reasons I wrote my first book Share Trading. The objective was to show the mistakes so that others could recognize them early and take corrective action before they did too much damage.

It took me less than a year to achieve consistent trading results. It was partly luck in terms of selecting a stock that had consistent volatility ranges. However, it required judgment to recognize the opportunity offered by that type of volatility. Many people just hold on through the peaks and valleys and fail to realize that there are methods that capitalize on those price changes. I started with blue chip stocks and I now appreciate the damage these can do to your portfolio account. My real trading started with penny dreadful speculative stocks. (These are not pink sheets, or OTC stocks. They are listed stocks trading at around $0.10.) Like others I was attracted by the high returns. This is now considered to be a sort of disreputable approach to trading. It's made more respectable when we use leverage in futures and other derivatives to achieve the same objectives. I prefer to use price leverage offered by these lower priced fully listed stocks because there are aspects of risk management that are not available in derivative markets.

I haven't experienced devastating losses at early stages thanks to the early understanding that trading is first and last about risk management. However, cutting losses with discipline remains a constant everyday challenge in every trade. You are tested every time and you have to pass every time.

The real challenge is to use money management so that the high return high risk correlation is broken. This is achieved through better chart analysis and by better money management. Many people do not understand how the 2% risk rule operates. Of those that do, there are even fewer who understand the relationship between this financial stop loss, the use of support levels based on chart analysis, and the way this impacts on position sizing.

Understanding that this is where the trading solution rests is the most important step towards long term success.

The key understanding is that the trading methods and risk management methods used by large investors do not scale downwards. Small accounts need different risk management approaches. Risk management is scaleable upwards above one million. It is not readily scaleable downwards for those with small accounts of 50K or less. And for most people, this is the size that they start their trading with. They start trading with spare capital, not with their savings. We all start small, but few people talk about effective ways to manage the risks of trading at this size.

My timeframe depends on the market conditions. In some markets, I switch to short term 3 to 5 days trades, or intraday trades. In nervous markets, time becomes a significant risk factor. Most of my trades are open for an average of 30 days. This is position trading. I look for high probability trades based on a small selection of chart patterns. I also use longer term trend trades which may last for many weeks or months. Analysis of the strength of the underlying trend is the key factor in this type of trade.

What we plan to do, and what we actually do in response to market conditions are two different things. I may plan to be a position trader, but that does not mean that all my positions will remain open for a set amount of time.

I jot down a trade plan for every trade. It sets entry points, stop loss points and where appropriate, defined reward targets. Depending on the nature of the trade, these can be quite detailed and specific. Others are just as simple as 'ride the trend' and exit when these signals are generated. Trades change as they develop, so we need constantly revalue the priority of the indicators we are using for trade management.

This is something we try to demonstrate in our weekly newsletter where we aim to teach readers how these processes are applied to notional real time trades. Of course, most people don't want to learn this. They prefer to lose thousands of dollars themselves trying to understand the difference between how professionals approach the market and how they are approaching the market.

Planning is essential, but it does not have to be a laborious exercise. The simple trades with simple trade management are the most effective. Plans do not have to be complicated. Complexity aids confusion, and does not assist us in developing discipline. We are either in or out. A complex plan gives the trader too many opportunities to fudge the exit and that eats away at trading discipline.

I consider fundamentals an ongoing comedy show of the market. Enron is the best summary of the usefulness of fundamentals. Simple chart analysis revealed more than a legion of highly paid fundamental analysts could discover. If they looked at a chart they would have realized Enron was in a steady downtrend. Sellers in the market knew more than the financial industry.

I am primarily a chart reader. I rely on simple methods to understand price and crowd behavior. I do not use many technical indicators. I find they are simply too unreliable. When we look at an indicator display, we 'see' the correct signals and ignore the failed signals. It's easy on an historical chart, but much more difficult to make these decisions in real time.

I use classic chart patterns for many of my trading decisions. I use my own Guppy Multiple Moving Average indicator to better understand the nature and character of trends. This helps me to track the inferred behavior of traders and investors in the market. These are the two most powerful groups and I want to know how they relate to each other. This in turn helps me to select the most appropriate trading strategy. I manage developing trends using a count back line to set risk and stop loss points, and to confirm, the continuation of the trend. I also apply modern Darvas trading methods to manage long term trends. I did a lot of work modifying and adapting classic Darvas techniques so they were effective in dealing with modern markets which show increased volatility. All of these are covered in detail in Trend Trading. I just trade ordinary stocks from the long side. I don't trade short. I don't manage money, and I don't trade on the margin. I use trend lines, and parabolic trends to understand trending behavior. My objective is to locate just one or two opportunities. That's all I need. I do not have the time or the inclination to attempt to trade 100 stocks a year. I leave that to the industry professionals who have to trade every day when they go to work. I look for a reasonable return on my capital and a lifestyle that allows me to do the other things that I like doing. This includes writing and speaking about trading and teaching others some of the skills required.

Most times I do not trade intraday. I trade for lifestyle, and being stuck in front of a screen all day is not a desirable life style. I use a variety of trading methods, depending on market conditions. I am most comfortable using end of day data. The signal is delivered today after the close and I get to act on it tomorrow when the market opens. I apply this approach to several different national markets and it delivers consistent results. I trade Singapore, Malaysia and Australia. I also follow domestic China markets and Hong Kong for a number of clients.

I could summarize my trading philosophy in a following way. Trading is about the management of risk. It is an effective way to use capital and make it grow. The market is an emotional place. Prices are created by emotional behavior at both an individual and crowd level. I am trading the emotions of the crowd. I am not trading a company or company fundamentals. I understand that I am the least informed, person in the process. I cannot hope to match the skills of the research analysts, the stock researchers, the company accountants, the company managers, or those who are intimately concerned with developing business. Heck, if I had those skills I would be running the company. However, when these informed people make a decision about what they believe about the value of the company they buy and sell in the market. This action sets a price. This price reveals all of the research that these skilled people have done. They give this information away free to those who have the chart analysis skills to understand it. This is where the trading edge is developed. This is my understanding of the market and the role that price has to play.

The market provides an equal opportunity for us all to take a small amount of capital and turn it into larger amount of capital. We can do it and I reject the idea that there is a 'club of professionals' to whom we ought to defer to because they understand things that are beyond our ken. You might not want to trade yourself, but you should have the knowledge and the skills to understand whether your selected fund manager or advisor is actually doing a reasonable job. These philosophies run through all my books from Trading Tactics and Better Trading to Snapshot Trading and Trend Trading.

Consistent trading for me is about trend trading and trend continuation. Trend reversals are for the greedy. The failure rate is high, but it can be very successful if you have the discipline to act on stop loss points. Greed is what often prevents us from giving trend trading the attention it deserves. We believe we have missed out if we miss the trend turn. That's simply rubbish. Entering established trends lowers risk because the underlying trend is established and strong. Some of these trends can persist for months or even a year or more. Returns are in the order of 50% to 200%. How many of these trades do you need a year to make a reasonable return on capital?

I was more aggressive when I started trading because I believed the myth that the best returns came from catching the trend change or reversal. An objective analysis of the charts shows that trends deliver superior consistent returns, so why stress out trying to catch rebounds?

I am aggressive in trading high probability chart patterns. I aggressively seek flags, triangles, stirrups and a handful of other rigorously defined patterns. These offer high probability and high reward trades with well defined risk points.

Trading is about risk. If you are not comfortable with it, and do not understand it, then you cannot trade. Risk is controlled by better analysis and by money management. This brings together financial and chart based calculations in a logical fashion. Those who believe that high reward entails high risk do not understand the genuine risks in trading. Trading success rests on identifying high probability trade opportunities where the high reward is protected by methods which reduce the risk. Risk is not reduced by being right. It is reduced by using effective logical chart based stop loss points in conjunction with correct position sizing.

Prolonged periods of concentration can and do cause the stress. At times you simply lose touch with the market. Recognize this, and step back. Stop trading. It is an important advantage we have as private traders. We do not have to trade. It is the most significant advantage we have in terms of risk management and stress management. We can afford to wait until the absolutely best trades develop, and then we take them. That really reduces stress. To cope with stress, I cook. Cooking is an important relaxation. I also go fishing, and I travel. Much of my travel is associated with work, shopping trading methods and approaches, but this is also relaxing and enjoyable.

We all go through the same learning curves. I wrote about these in Trend Trading and in Stocks and Commodities magazine. The curve has plateaus where we reach a certain level and drift sideways. At each plateau we can fall of the edge and into financial oblivion. Or we can move to the next level. The plateaus are defined by basic mastery, then by mastery of the mechanics of analysis, i.e. understanding charts and indicators. The highest plateau is defined by understanding the impact and role of money management. The most successful traders move quickly from plateau to plateau. Most people never get to understand money management and this affects their ability to understand risk.

Here are eight things I have learned and believe about markets and trading. They have served me well and they may assist you.

- First, that simple approaches work effectively. You do not need complicated methods. If you cannot quickly explain what you are doing then you will fail.

- Second, keep greed for Christmas presents. It has no place in the market. The market is about the management of risk and return on capital. Look after these things and your money will grow.

- Third, understand you are trading the emotions of a crowd and they reveal their feelings through price. Emotional reactions are high probability reactions. This gives you the trading edge.

- Fourth, if you cannot accept responsibility for your own actions then the market will kill you.

- Fifth, the most dangerous myth of all is that you should only use the money you can afford to lose. Approach the market with this belief and the one thing that is certain is that you will lose your money.

- Sixth, we never master the market. It changes every day, and we have to adjust our methods and approaches to remain in tune with it. There are no universal answers. Each of us develops a unique solution. We can and should learn from others, but ultimately, the methods we use are entirely our own.

- Seven, the market is not about mathematics. It rewards those with well-developed analytical skills who can think independently. It is above all a mental challenge.

- Eight, the final understanding is that trading is not about being right. It is about being profitable.

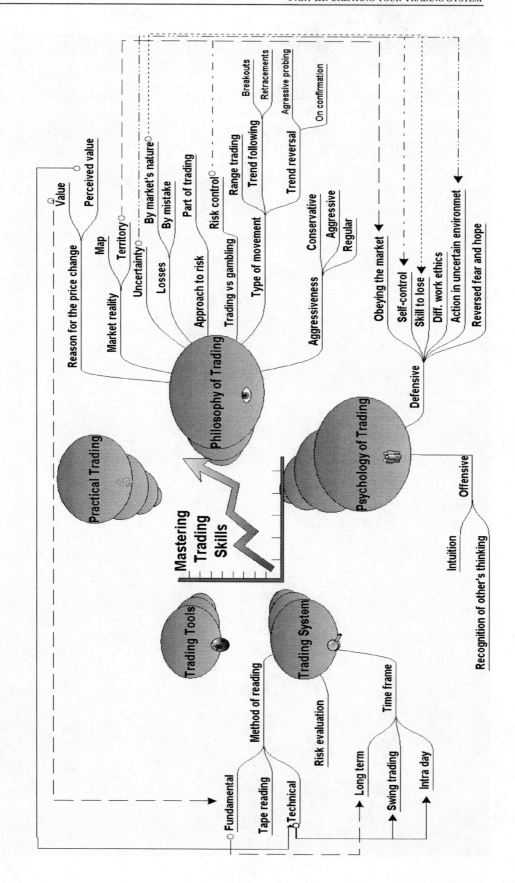

confirmation of its execution. It is easy to configure the software in such a way that default parameters of your order match your standard and it takes just a couple of clicks to adjust the parameters if you need.

## Control Over Routing

Your order can go to the marketplace in many different ways. It can be executed "in house" out of a broker's inventory when your broker acts as the principal. Alternatively, it can be sent directly to the market and executed against other market participants. There are many different ways to send your order and each of them has its advantages and shortcomings.

With traditional brokerages, you have practically no control over the way your orders are handled. You can instruct a broker of your requirements regarding price and other details, which can be a time-consuming process and will not allow an immediate reaction to market events.

With an online broker, you usually have somewhat greater control as you can observe what happens in the market and send your order at the appropriate time. Still, your choices of routes are limited.

With a direct access brokerage, everything is in your hands. You observe the market events and can send your order with a single click. You have total control over how and where your order is routed. You can hit a bid or an offer that you see on your screen with your order. You can bid or offer your shares, managing the way they display to other market participants. For instance, you can shape up your order in such a way that other players see only 300 shares on their screen while in fact you offer 2,000. You can send your order before the market opens or after it closes. There are many variables, which we are going to discuss in the Order Routing section.

## Commission Schedules

Traditional brokerages often have fees on the high end of the scale. Their full service might justify such prices for certain types of market players. Online brokers have fewer services and their commissions are accordingly lower. In both cases, commissions are fixed.

Direct access brokers usually offer a more flexible structure. You can find a choice between per trade fee and a per share fee. If you frequently break down your orders by many parts, building your position or scaling out of it, per share fee is usually preferable. The same is true for trading small shares. For big size orders sent at once, a per trade fee is preferable. In addition, direct access brokers often offer you a volume discount – a scale by which your commissions decrease if you execute a bigger number of trades.

## Services

This is the area where traditional brokerages shine – IF you need it. Traditional brokerages will help you with research, find necessary data, and alert you if certain events occur. Online brokers sometimes offer you access to research tools leaving it to you to utilize them. Direct access brokerages serve as an agent between you and the marketplace, providing you with the tools to access it and leaving the rest to you.

## Support

Phone support is something you might need very rarely, but it could be crucial when an urgent need arises. While most brokerages offer constant support, most direct access brokers distinguish themselves by responding immediately to urgent customer calls. They have a trading desk where you can call and get your order executed right away if your Internet connection goes down while you are in a trade. With traditional and online brokers it could be

---

# Part IV: Trading Tools

## Tool-Belt Contents

This part of a trader's preparation takes everything we have put together and takes it down to a practical level. This is the last step that defines what tools you are going to use in order to realize your trading goals. When you have your tools in place, you have everything you need to start implementing your trading plan. Elements of your tools are: **Brokerage**, **Quote/Charting software** and **Scanning software**. Depending on your previous choices, you will face several new ones, picking those tools that match your chosen trading style, providing you with everything necessary for your trading system.

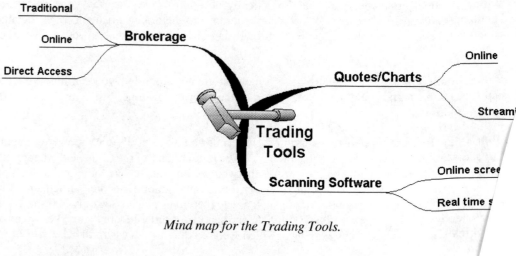

*Mind map for the Trading Tools.*

## Brokerage

The first element of tools is a **brokerage**. Your orders will be routed to the mar[ ] through a broker firm. It is extremely important to make sure the brokerage you us[ ] requirements of your trading approach. For self-governed trading, you have a choic[ ] three kinds of brokers: traditional, online and direct access. The table below shows[ ] compare. As with most of our choices, there is no better or worse choice that w[ ] You need to pick what suits your goals best. After going over different brokera[ ] strengths and weaknesses, we will make a summary that will help you make the ri[ ]

The main considerations for choosing your broker are:

1. Speed of order execution and confirmation
2. Control over routing
3. Commission schedule
4. Services offered
5. Support
6. Ease of use

### Speed of Order Execution and Confirmation

Traditional and online brokers usually use a browser form to fill in to co[ ] order. It is fast enough, especially in a case with online brokers for any a[ ] require precise to the cent and instant execution. If your timeframe i[ ] hours rather than hours, days and weeks, their speed will not satisfy yo[ ]

A direct access broker's software gives a trader immediate access to [ ] the fastest and the most efficient way to present your order. A singl[ ] your order to the market instantly. Providing that your order is m[ ]

somewhat cumbersome and a time-consuming process. Again, as with other choices it depends on your trading approach whether you need such immediate help or not. In any case, do your own research on a broker's reputation using internet search engines and sites that rank brokers and post customers' reviews.

## Ease of Use

The interface of online brokerages and those of traditional ones that offer online orders is usually very straightforward and intuitive. While it is still necessary to make sure to read their on-line help and get familiar with all of the details, it is a fairly easy process as you simply fill in an online form.

The interface of a direct broker's order entering software is much more sophisticated. While it is intuitive enough in most cases, it certainly requires considerable time to learn. A great array of options is available to you and you will be rewarded for the couple days spent learning how the software works. Direct access brokerage software help is extensive and thorough, often with video files helping you learn all of the features. Once you get a handle on this, it becomes very easy to configure your orders quickly. In the following section, we will show an example of such software.

| Type | Speed | Control over routing | Commissions | Services | Support | Ease of use |
|------|-------|----------------------|-------------|----------|---------|-------------|
| Online | Good | Average | Fixed, usually moderate | Less | Average | Good |
| Direct Access | Excellent | Excellent | Flexible, often the lowest possible | Less | Good | Requires studying |
| Traditional | Poor | Poor | Fixed, usually on high end | Most | Average | Good |

*Brokerage type comparison*

## Broker Type Selection

Now let us analyze your need for different variables, depending on your chosen trading approach.

As a long term trader, you do not intend to trade by minutes or seconds. You do not need lightning order execution and you do not really care how your order is routed. You are probably not going to trade very frequently and you are after significant profits on each given trade. This combination of factors renders the size of commissions as a less important factor to you as they are going to be a very small percentage of your profits. In order to do your research you might need a broker's help. Infrequent trading makes ease of use not a very important factor for you.

As a swing trader, speed of execution could be an important factor for you, although not as crucial as for a day trader or a scalper. You are not too concerned about how your orders are routed. Commissions become a more important factor for you. Most likely, you will not be relying on a broker in your research. Ease of use is more of a factor for you although still not crucial.

As a day trader or a scalper, your need for instant execution is absolutely crucial. Control over routing is an absolute must for a scalper and very important for a day trader. With frequent trading, relatively small gains and a high possible need to scale in and out of a position requires flexibility in commissions and the lowest fee structure possible. You do not care about the full range of brokerage services. You need your software to be intuitive and easy to use after your learning curve.

The table below reflects your needs in the different aspects of brokerage offerings.

| Type | Speed | Control over routing | Commissions | Services | Support | Ease of use |
|------|-------|---------------------|-------------|----------|---------|-------------|
| Long term trader | Non-issue | Non-issue | Limited | Probably | Limited | Not overly important |
| Swing Trader | Desirable | Not overly important | Important | Not overly important | Limited | Limited |
| Day trader, scalper | Crucial | Crucial | Crucial | Non-issue | Important | Important |

*Need in Brokerage Aspects*

It is easy to see which type of brokerage satisfies your needs best by depending on your trading approach. For a long term trader it is going to be a choice between traditional and online brokerage. Depending on your need for a full range of services, and on commissions offered, you will be able to make your pick.

For a swing trader it is going to be a choice between online and a direct access broker. Some direct access brokers offer scaled down versions of their software suitable for practically all of a swing trader's needs.

Finally, for a day trader and especially for a scalper, the choice is clear – a direct access broker is the only type that suits their needs.

If your trading is supposed to be of a mixed kind, including trades from two or more types, always choose a broker that satisfies your most crucial needs. It means that if you are going to have a mix of long term trades and swing trades, you are going to need an online broker. If you are going to have swing trades mixed with day trades, go with a direct access broker.

*Decision tree for choosing a broker*

```
                          ┌─────────────┐
                          │ Your        │
                          │ chosen      │
                          │ timeframe   │
                          └─────────────┘
              ┌──────────────────┼──────────────────┐
        ┌───────────┐      ┌──────────────┐   ┌──────────────┐
        │ Long term │      │ Swing trading│   │ Day trading &│
        │           │      │              │   │ scalping     │
        └───────────┘      └──────────────┘   └──────────────┘
              │           ┌────────┴────────┐          │
      ┌──────────────┐ ┌──────────────┐ ┌──────────────┐ ┌──────────────┐
      │ Mixed with   │ │ Mixed with long│ │ Mixed with  │ │ Mixed with   │
      │ swing trades?│ │ term trades?  │ │ day trades? │ │ swing trades?│
      └──────────────┘ └──────────────┘ └──────────────┘ └──────────────┘
        │        │      │         │      │         │      │         │
     ┌─────┐ ┌─────┐ ┌─────┐ ┌─────┐ ┌─────┐ ┌─────┐ ┌─────┐ ┌─────┐
     │ No  │ │ Yes │ │ No  │ │ Yes │ │ No  │ │ Yes │ │ No  │ │ Yes │
     └─────┘ └─────┘ └─────┘ └─────┘ └─────┘ └─────┘ └─────┘ └─────┘
        │        └────┐    │     │      │    └───┐      │    └───┐
   ┌──────────────┐ ┌──────────────┐        ┌──────────────┐
   │ Consider     │ │ Consider     │        │ Consider direct│
   │ traditional  │ │ online broker│        │ access broker │
   │ broker       │ │              │        │               │
   └──────────────┘ └──────────────┘        └──────────────┘
```

## Direct Access Software Example

Considering direct access is the only kind of brokerage whose software requires considerable effort to learn, we will go over some of the features of this type of software. This example shows Navigator by MB Trading. In Canada, this order entering technology is provided by TradeFreedom. Navigator can be used in integration with charting software or as stand-alone. We will show it as a stand-alone program.

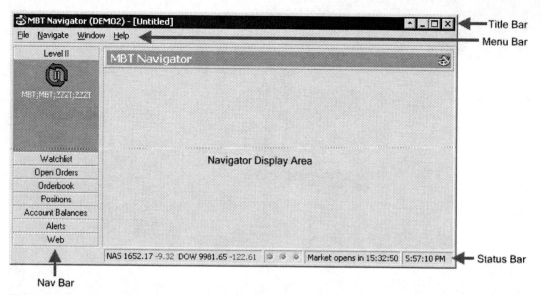

This is a screenshot of the Navigator menus. You can place in the display area or anywhere else on your monitor, any of the components you need for trading. Below is a screenshot with Level II.

This software allows you to drag and drop components, placing them where you need them, freeing up space for other components. By clicking on the price level on the Level II screen, you will place this price in your order entry bar (next screenshot), making it easy to adjust the price quickly. There is also streaming data on NASDAQ and NYSE indices in the status bar, and three lights that show connection status to quotes, orders and message servers.

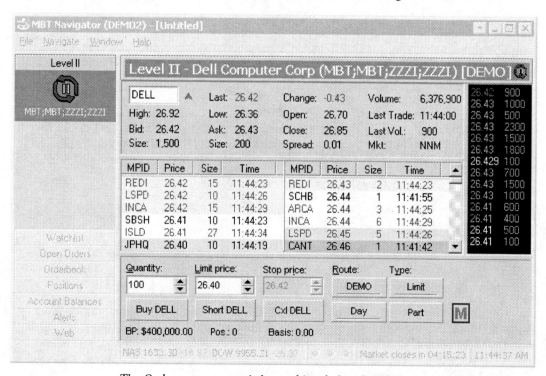

*The Order entry screen is located just below Level II.*

It has buttons sending orders to buy, sell, and cancel orders and to change order types. It is easy to adjust the shares amount and price by using little arrows near the related window. A click on Pos will adjust the amount of shares to your actual position. A click on BP will change the amount of shares to the maximum you can buy with your buying power – **be careful with this feature!** Right click on buttons and you will bring up a dropdown menu with options you have. You can see whether the stock you are watching is available for shorting. There are several templates for order entry screen for various styles of traders, from the simplest shown above and to more sophisticated below:

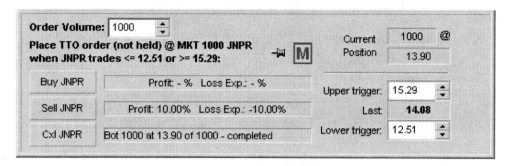

Using Order Entry Preferences, you can set default values for your order so that the most frequent combination of parameters would be always there as you switch from one stock to another.

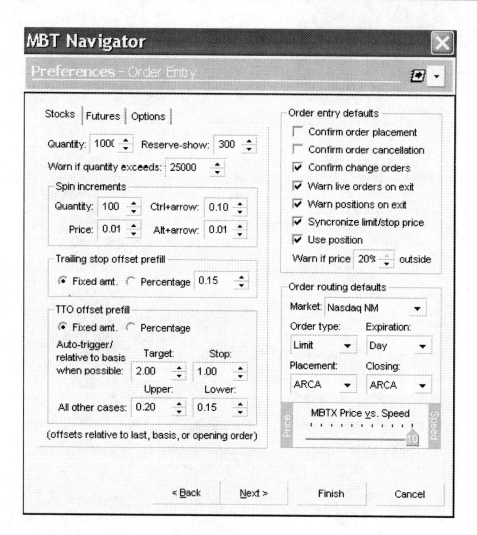

While you are not confident yet in your order configurations, you can set Navigator to ask you to confirm the order before sending it, giving you one more opportunity to review it:

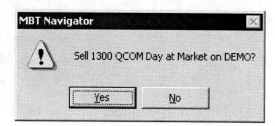

As soon as your order is sent, Orderbook comes up displaying the status of your order:

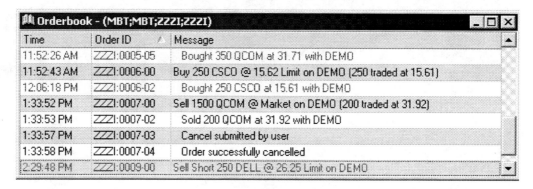

Your open positions are monitored in real time so you can see the status of them updated dynamically:

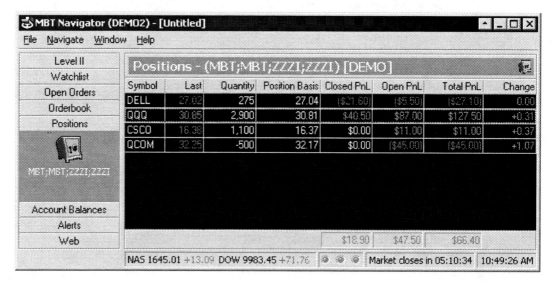

You can see the entire balance of your account updated dynamically:

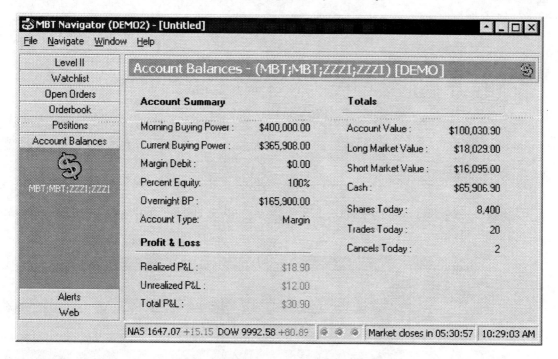

To monitor many stocks in your portfolio or stocks related to a certain sector you can create Watchlists:

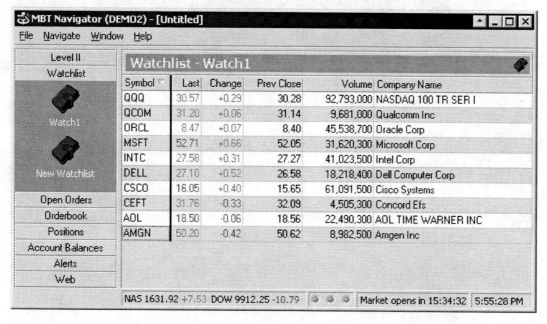

Navigator has integrated chat for help by one of their representatives for non-urgent questions and various reports with daily or monthly statements, trade summary etc.

As you can see, this is quite a powerful weapon enabling you to participate in the market activity with an extremely efficient tool.

<hr>

## You Asked

*Question:*
There are several order entering templates available. Do you prefer one over another and why?

*Answer:*
I prefer to use the simple template for simple trades, switching to advanced ones only when I need to set a more sophisticated order. If I do not need an advanced type of template for a particular trade, I prefer using the 'Alternate; one. The reason is simple: Buy and Short buttons are far from each other and I do not risk clicking the wrong one accidentally. It happens more often than you would imagine.

## Order Types

One more important aspect we need to go over at this point is order types. There are basic and advanced orders. Basic orders are usually sufficient for a beginning trader. Here is description of **basic order types** for Navigator:

### Limit

An order to buy or sell a security at a specific price. A buy limit order can only be executed at the limit price or lower, and a sell limit order can only be executed at the limit price or higher. Remember that your limit order may never be executed because the market price may quickly surpass your limit before your order can be filled. But, by using a limit order you also protect yourself from buying the stock at too high a price.

### Market

An order to buy or sell a stock at the current market price. The advantage of a market order is you are almost always guaranteed your order will be executed (as long as there are willing buyers and sellers). The disadvantage is the price you pay when your order is executed may not always be the price you obtained from a real-time quote service or were quoted by a broker. This may be especially true in fast-moving markets where stock prices are more volatile. When you place an order "at the market," particularly for a large number of shares, there is a greater chance you will receive different prices for parts of the order.

### Market-on-Open (MOO) for Nasdaq

A market order initiated at the Nasdaq market open (9:30 EST). Upon activation, MBTX uses its algorithm to find the best price in the marketplace, however, the price cannot be guaranteed.

### Market-on-Open (MOO) for NYSE

A market order initiated at the opening print of the NYSE or AMEX. The order is forwarded to the specialist and held until the open. Prices vary based on conditions that are not always reflected. The price at which your order is filled may be better or worse than you expected.

### Stop Loss Market

Buy or sell a stock at market once the price reaches or passes through a specified price. Used by traders who either own a position (long or short) and want to close the position if it moves against them OR by traders that wish to open a new position once the stock rises to a specific level. The stop price on a sell stop must be below the current bid. The stop price on a buy stop must be above the current offer. Stop orders in volatile issues will not guarantee you an execution at or near the stop price. Once triggered, the order competes with other incoming market orders.

## Stop Loss Limit

Works like a Stop Loss Market order with one major exception. Once the order is activated (by the stock trading at or through the stop price), it does not become a market order. Instead, it becomes a limit order with a specified price.

The advantage of this order is that you set a specified price at which your order can be filled. The disadvantage is that your order may not be filled. In this case, your exposure to loss will continue until the position is closed.

## Reserve

Only display a fraction of your actual trade size on Level II. Someone that trades larger sizes may find this very useful. It provides a terrific way to keep costs down because you are only charged one commission and you have the benefit and advantage of hiding your true order size.

## Trailing Stop

Ride a stock's price trend, profit from its movement, and limit your downside risk without constantly monitoring prices. Trailing stops move your stop price with the price of the stock and are server-sided, protecting you in the event you lose your internet connection.

**Advanced orders** are much more sophisticated and allow you to operate with great flexibility and in a highly automated manner. As your trading style evolves, you can find some of them quite useful. Here is description of those orders for Navigator:

## Discretionary (equities only)

Set a discretionary price range when placing an order. For example: Buy 100 CSCO at a limit price of 65 with a discretionary price of 65 1/2. Your order is displayed at your specified limit price, not your discretionary price. When a bid or offer appears at or within your discretionary price range, your order will be routed to the Nasdaq Market Participant(s) at their quoted price. Please note that stock can trade ahead of you because your discretionary price does not necessarily make you the best bid or offer.

## Discretionary Reserve (equities only)

Same as Discretionary order but also provides the option to show only a fraction of the total trade size. Someone that trades larger sizes may find this very useful. It provides a terrific way to keep costs down because you are only charged one commission and you have the benefit and advantage of hiding your true order size.

## Threshold Triggered Order (TTO)

Specify two prices, an upper and lower price threshold. Once the inside market trades at either threshold, a market order is sent to the marketplace. TTOs were designed to help limit potential losses and lock-in potential profits.

## Limit + Trailing Stop

Initially places a limit order on one side (either a buy or sell) and upon execution, places an opposite trailing stop on the other side (either a buy or sell).

### Limit + TTO

Initially places a limit order (either a buy or sell) and upon execution, places an opposite TTO (either a buy or sell).

### Market + TTO

Initially places a market order (either a buy or sell) and upon execution, places an opposite TTO (either a buy or sell).

### Stop + TTO

Initially places a stop order (either a buy or sell) and upon execution, places an opposite TTO (either a buy or sell).

### Reserve + TTO

Initially places a reserve order (either a buy or sell) and upon execution, places an opposite TTO (either a buy or sell).

### Price vs. Speed

Adjust how aggressively your orders seek liquidity. A proprietary algorithm uses the entered limit price "price vs. speed" setting to scan the market for liquidity. A high "speed" setting typically results in faster fills, while a "price" biased setting typically results in greater price improvements. This effectively provides a brake and accelerator for MBTX.

## Commission Plan

It is necessary to select the correct plan to match your trading style. Earlier you defined your trading strategy. Now it is time to use that decision to optimize your trading fees. Do not worry if your strategy changes down the road – it is easy to switch from one plan to another. Often brokers offering flexible commission structures provide a simple table which allows you to figure out which plan is most suitable for you. You will find it is easy to calculate your optimum commission structure by using the table. Using the broker's data and including all the factors broker indicates (ECN's fees for instance), fill in the table for each amount of shares and for both plans to find out at which point one plan gains an advantage over another. Then see what amount of shares you plan to trade and pick your plan. Also, consider how partialling in or out of a position impacts your decision. If this is part of your trading plan, most likely you will opt for per share fee. Keep in mind that, as you see from description of order types, TTO orders can be executed in parts even if partialling is not a part of your original plan.

| Shares per trade | Comm. Per share | Comm. Per Trade |
|---|---|---|
| 100 | | |
| 300 | | |
| 500 | | |
| 1,000 | | |
| 2,000 | | |
| 5,000 | | |

*Commission Plans Comparison*

Usually if you plan to trade 1,000 shares or less, the per share fee is preferable. With bigger lots, the per trade fee could be a better fit. It is generally a good idea to start with a per share fee in the first stages of your practical trading and switch later if you increase your shares.

## Resources for Choosing a Broker

www.mbtrading.com

www.tradefreedom.com

# Quote/Charting Software

Depending on your chosen timeframe, you are going to need either browser-based charting or a real time streaming application. If you are a long-term trader whose timeframe is weeks and months, you can use one of the websites that offer quite good interactive charting. Being a swing or intraday trader, you are going to need a real time, continuously updating application.

### Browser-based Charting.

This kind of charting offers many tools where you can change timeframes, apply different technical studies and indicators and with more sophisticated websites, even scan the markets to pick your trading candidates. The simplest example of such a service is http://finance.yahoo.com/. You have a choice of timeframes from intraday to multi-years; you can add moving averages and about ten different indicators, compare different charts in a single window and obtain some of the fundamental data on the company you are researching. Examples of sites that provide sophisticated charting with many capabilities are http://stockcharts.com, http://bigcharts.com.

### Real time Streaming Application

There are basically three ways for a trader to obtain and use real time quotes: charts provided by a broker, stand alone and a choice of several to integrate with your broker's software.

**The first way** involves finding a brokerage that offers such software along with order entering capabilities. This is the simplest way, as you get one stop shopping. There are, however, some disadvantages to this as well. One of them is you are locked in with this particular software even though there are others that could be more to your liking. Another important disadvantage is you do not have redundancy. If your broker's software lags for whatever reason, you do not really have a way to spot the troubles in time. If you execute a certain amount of trades each month, the cost of the software is often subsidized by a broker. While it is providing an advantage to an experienced trader, it could be a detrimental factor for a beginner as it provokes overtrading.

**The second way** involves using separate execution software provided by a broker and an independent quote feed by a third party. You have the luxury of many choices, having two independent sources of quotes and you have much higher reliability. The downsides to this choice are higher costs and a less convenient situation where you cannot send your order right from your quote software.

**The third** way requires a broker that offers you a choice of several packages with which order entering software can be integrated. This approach combines the advantages of the first two ways, effectively getting rid of their shortcomings. In discussing choosing a brokerage, we saw an example of such a solution provided by MBTrading and TradeFreedom (for Canadian residents).

As with other choices, it helps to read reviews. Additionally, most providers offer a free trial, giving you an opportunity to get familiar with their software and to make sure you are comfortable with it. During your trial, make sure that you go over all the features. Ensure everything you are going to need is included and you find it easy to memorize and use. Finally, make sure that you run and observe the quotes at the open of the market. That is when you will experience heavy loads, which make for a great test of reliability and helps reveal possible lags.

> Keep in mind that in the case with quote software, a free trial usually involves some small cost. The reason for the fee is that the market exchanges charge for their data and this non-refundable fee is passed by quote providers onto customers. During your free trial period do not order all the exchanges you might need in the future; it is enough to have only the vital ones.

Let us sum up the choices in a mind map.

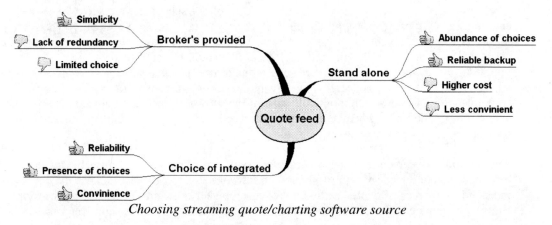

*Choosing streaming quote/charting software source*

## Main Features

When you subscribe for software, you are offered a choice of features from which to subscribe. At this point, you will need to apply the choices you made earlier. If you are a scalper, you will need Level II data. Being a swing trader, you most likely can do without it. If you are going to trade both futures and stocks, you will need to pick the appropriate exchanges. If you focus on just one of them, you can skip exchanges not related to your trading vehicle. It is easy to add them later on if you decide to broaden your approach. If you focus on stocks, your next question is whether you are going to trade the NASDAQ, NYSE and AMEX or just one of those markets. If your choice narrows to one of those, it will help cut down on exchange feeds and, accordingly, expenses.

> If you are not going to trade futures but want to have a chart of general market movement, there is a cash index that serves this purpose well and, unlike futures, it is included in the main application cost. For instance, instead of NASDAQ 100 e-minis you can use NDX, cutting down on cost.

A charting application allows you to create multiple windows with various streaming data. The most important among them is **chart**. You can customize it for your particular style of trading: change timeframes, create bar or candlesticks, put numerous studies and indicators on it, draw support and resistance lines. Spend a reasonable time configuring the windows and make it fully comfortable for you. Sometimes such simple thing as changing colors of the background and lines can make a big difference. Make sure you get familiar with the auto-scaling feature that allows a chart to fit the window as the trading range expands. One more important feature is making a chart snap to the window, so you can see the entire period within your chart without scrolling back and forth. In the process of paper trading you will have time to go over all the menus and get familiar with them.

Charting software has a window that allows you to create a **list of stocks** that you want to watch. Different software have different names for this window: watchlist, portfolio, marketminder etc. This list usually has limited data: close, open, high, low, and change from yesterday's close. It is intended to let you keep an eye on many stocks and/or indexes without overloading yourself with information.

**The Level II** window allows you to see the market depth for NASDAQ stocks. Quotes by market participants at different price levels with sizes of their orders help you see, to a certain degree, the liquidity of a stock. The significance of this tool is often exaggerated. While it is a great instrument for risk evaluation as discussed earlier, it is not really a tool that helps you determine the direction of movement beyond the nearest tick or two. Unless you are an intraday trader and scalper, opt out.

**The Times & Sales** window shows scrolling trades as they occur. This window, too, has significance for an intraday trader and scalper more than for any other timeframe trader. Prints are usually color-coded so you can get a visual perception of buying versus selling.

Windows can be linked to each other in such a way that when you put a certain symbol into one of them, it comes up on others linked to first one. This is a great feature to save time and reduce the margin for error.

I have listed the major windows only. There are more available, each software package offering different features and proprietary names. As you learn your software package, you will pick those features that match your purposes. Do not overload yourself with unnecessary information. Keep it simple. If you need a different sets of windows for different purposes when you combine timeframes, it is better to create several layouts and assign your names to them rather than putting everything on one single page. You will be able to switch between layouts easily, keeping each of them unclouded.

---

### You Asked

*Question:*
Help me understand the need for a Level II window. I hear traders saying it is a magic tool and I hear others saying it is totally useless. Who is correct?

*Answer:*
Level II is a tool that for some reason developed the most legends about it. Maybe it is the pretty colors flashing, or maybe it has the feel of a professional tool that became available for the public. Unfortunately, plenty of traders became fascinated by Level II to such a degree that it became their only tool. When quotes switched from fractions to decimals, Level II lost its significance as a directional tool (not too big a significance in the first place). Now, the role of this tool in your trading totally depends on your timeframe and trading style. It has no use for a long-term trader; some day traders find it useful, and scalpers do need it. Risk evaluation is the major use for Level II in a short timeframe; for a scalper it helps improve timing of entries and exits. Games played sometimes by market participants and to a certain degree readable by Level II are of interest mostly to a scalper. You know the saying... for a man with a hammer everything becomes a nail. This is exactly what happens here: focus on Level II solely and your trading almost inevitably becomes scalping. Maybe that is your original intention – then no problem. However, make a decision and pick the appropriate tool for implementing it, not the other way around.

---

## Resources for Charting Software

http://finance.yahoo.com/
http://stockcharts.com/
http://bigcharts.com/

# Scanning Software

Scanning software will help you find stocks that match your trading criteria. Again, as with everything mentioned previously, choices you have made up to this point lead to different options for you.

There are **online screeners** – fairly simple and free. If you are a **long-term trader**, they might satisfy your need for preliminary screening, giving you candidates for further research. Below is a screenshot of one such screener, located at:

http://markets.usatoday.com/custom/usatoday-com/screener/screener.asp.

You can set several parameters, technical and fundamental, to find the stocks matching those parameters.

**Screeners** (Step 1 of 2)                    MarketWatch.com

Intraday Stock Screener        Mutual Fund Finder        Market Screener

The Intraday Stock Screener is designed to screen for stocks using as many or as few parameters as you wish. All parameters default to "none."      [ Next > ]

**– Price**

☐ **Show stocks trading per share from $**          [        ] to [        ]

☐ **Whose price has moved at least:**          [        ] **%** [ up    ⌄ ]
          [ During today's session    ⌄ ]

☐ **And that are trading:**          ⦿ Above their 52 week high
          ○ Below their 52 week low

**– Volume**

☐ **Current share trading volume between:**          [        ] **and** [        ]

☐ **Producing block trades of:**          [        ] **in** [ Today' Sess ⌄ ]

**– Fundamentals**

☐ **Show stocks with a P/E ratio from:**          [        ] to [        ]

☐ **With a market capitalization from $**          [        ] to [        ]
          (numbers are in $ millions)

**– Technicals**

☐ **Show stocks that are:**          [ outperforming          ⌄ ]
     **this moving average:**          [ 50 day          ⌄ ]

☐ **Show stocks that are:**          [ outperfor ⌄ ] **by** [        ] **%**
          the market index chosen below:
          ○ DJIA          ○ NASDAQ
          ○ DJ Internet          ○ Russell
          Index          2000

**– Exchange & Industry**

☑ **Show stocks that are trading on:**          ⦿ All exchanges  ○ NYSE
          ○ NASDAQ          ○ AMEX

☐ **Classified in the following DJ groups:**          [ Advanced Industrial Equipmen ⌄ ]

[ Next > ]

One more of this type is located at http://screen.yahoo.com/stocks.html

---

**Screener Settings**

Search for stocks by selecting from the criteria below. Click on the "Find Stocks" button to view the results.

**Category**

| | |
|---|---|
| Industry: | Any / Advertising (Services) / Aerospace & Defense (Capital Goods) / Air Courier (Transportation) / Airline (Transportation) |
| Index Membership | Any |

**Share Data**

| | | | |
|---|---|---|---|
| Share Price: | Any Min | Any Max |
| Avg Share Volume: | Any Min | Any Max |
| Market Cap: | Any Min | Any Max |
| Dividend Yield: | Any Min | Any Max |

**Performance**

| | | |
|---|---|---|
| 1 Yr Stock Perf: | Any | |
| Beta (Volatility): | Any Min | Any Max |

**Sales and Profitability**

| | | |
|---|---|---|
| Sales Revenue: | Any Min | Any Max |
| Profit Margin | Any Min | Any Max |

**Valuation Ratios**

| | | |
|---|---|---|
| Price/Earnings Ratio: | Any Min | Any Max |
| Price/Book Ratio: | Any Min | Any Max |
| Price/Sales Ratio: | Any Min | Any Max |
| PEG Ratio: | Any Min | Any Max |

**Analyst Estimates**

| | |
|---|---|
| Est. 1 Yr EPS Growth: | Any |
| Est. 5 Yr EPS Growth: | Any |
| Avg Analyst Rec: (1=Buy, 5=Sell) | Any |

**Results Display Setting**

| | |
|---|---|
| Display info for: | Actively Screened Data |

Find Stocks

---

Screenshots of both are pretty much self-explanatory; there is practically no learning curve in using them.

If you are trading in a short timeframe, you are going to need real time scanning software. There is no shortage of those for all tastes and trading styles. Some of them are built into charting software as add-ons; some are stand-alone. There are quite sophisticated scanners capable of searching for the stocks matching almost any conceivable criteria. Real time scanners do not have fundamental data as the search criteria. Their strength is in searches by technical parameters. An example of a very flexible and highly customizable powerful scanner is IntelliScan at:

http://www.realitytrader.com/iscan.asp.

It allows you to use pre-configured alerts or create any amount of alerts by your favorite criteria, with filters selecting the stocks you could be interested in. This scanner has filters satisfying practically any timeframes and trading style possible. Below is a screenshot of IntelliScan configured for a busy day trading style. Alerts are color-coded so it is easy to see right away what kind of alert is generated without reading the description. Double click on a symbol and it sends data to a charting application or right to your trading software. You can set limitations on the volume, volatility, spread and plenty of other criteria so you are getting the alerts only for stocks matching your trading style.

Here is how a busy screen loaded with multiple scans looks:

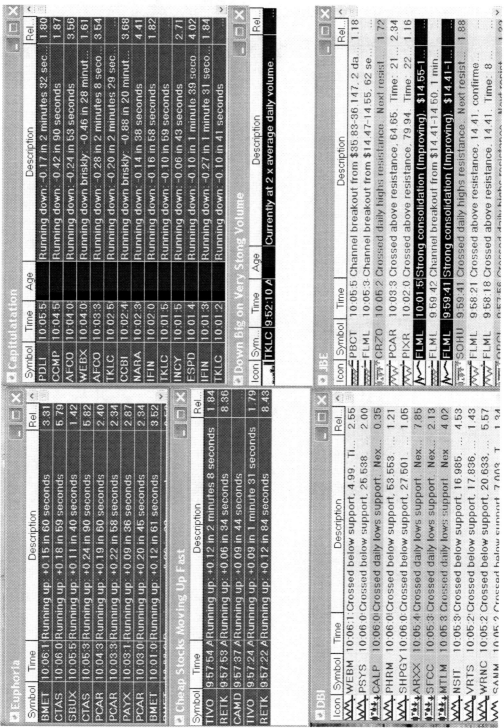

*Screen with multiple scans*

The next screenshot shows a scan designed for chart pattern recognition:

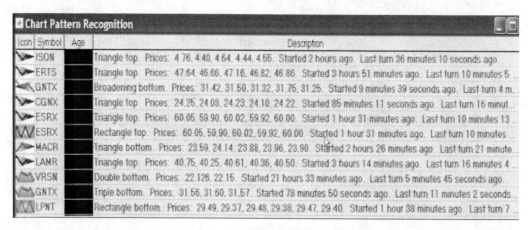

One more screenshot shows the scanning for a particular pattern, in this case: fast selling - Capitulation in terms of tape reading.

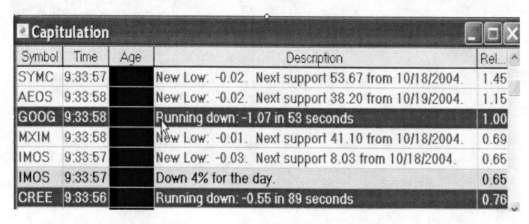

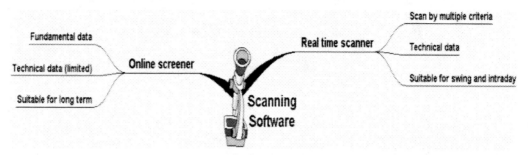

*Mind map for Scanning Software*

## You Asked

*Question:*

So, I am getting an alert from a scanner. Does it mean I enter on this alert and make money?

*Answer:*

THAT would be nice, wouldn't it? Nope, it will not work this way. That would be the Holy Grail – and we already know one does not exist. The scanner does what it is intended to do: it finds you stocks that match criteria that you set. Can you set criteria that ALWAYS provide a winning trade? You cannot and nobody can. Those criteria show you that a setup is forming. Get a chart, evaluate the situation and decide whether you like the trade. Any alert is an opportunity and it is up to you to take the opportunity or to skip it. Also, keep in mind that if you try to tighten your settings too much, you will be missing some of the alerts that do not match your criteria exactly but still could present an interesting trade under the right conditions. If on the other hand you make your settings too loose, you will get too many alerts. It is a process of fine-tuning. Playing with your settings, you adjust the scanner to your particular style.

*Question:*

Speaking of tools, could you tell me what hardware and software I need for trading, for example, the ideal computer configuration, layout of the screens, etc.?

*Answer:*

As any other selection of tools for the market, your decision on how to configure your hardware and what software to use is heavily influenced by your choice of trading style. If you are a long term trader, your requirements will be very moderate. Practically any modern computer will do, even with a dial-up connection. The shorter your timeframe, however, the more sophisticated your computer requirements. Day traders and scalpers will need fast machines with plenty of memory. Trading software vendors state their hardware requirements for trading. You will be safe, if at a minimum, you double the highest requirements. Make sure that your computer has room for an upgrade in the future because you will probably want to add memory at some point. Additionally, a stable broadband internet connection is necessary for day trading. A long term or swing trader can live with a single monitor. A day trader and a scalper will need several. I use three, which is average; however, there are traders that use more. Typically, a scanner is displayed on one of my monitors, charting software on another, with miscellaneous applications, like a chat room, news feed, etc. on the third monitor. Make sure you keep your computer protected with current anti-virus software and anti-spyware programs. If possible, try to have at least one computer dedicated just to trading with a minimum of non-trading related programs and network access.

## Resources for Scanning Software

http://markets.usatoday.com/custom/usatoday-com/screener/screener.asp

http://screen.yahoo.com/stocks.html

http://www.realitytrader.com/iscan.asp

# Trading Plan

### Trading Plan Form: My Trading Tools

For my charting needs I use

_____

_____

My settings are:

_____

_____

_____

_____

For trading I use: _____

For scanning I use: _____

My settings are: _____

_____

_____

_____

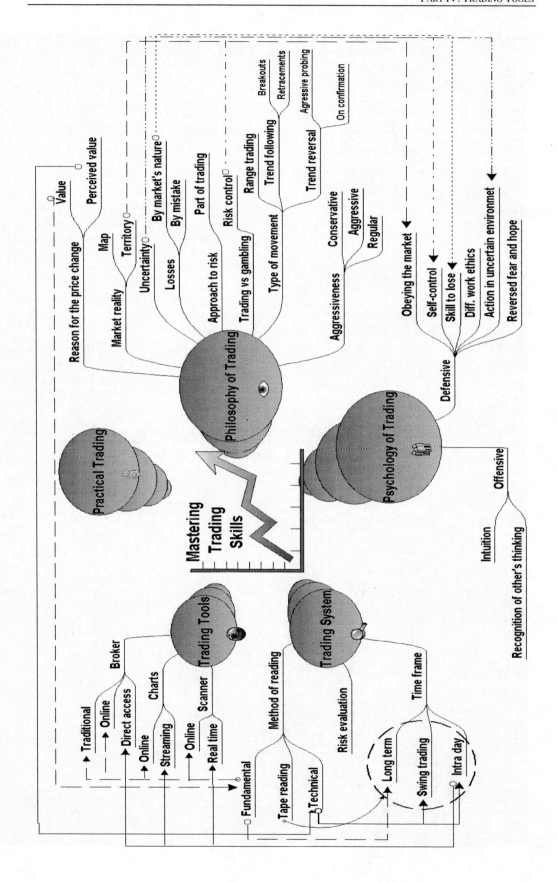

# Part V: Practical Trading

# When the Rubber Hits the Road

Now that all the theoretical preparations are done, it is time to start testing your methods in the real market. You have your general approach in place; your mindset is defined; you have chosen your method of reading the market and of risk control; your tools are ready and learned. A real life test will give you your first idea of the necessary corrections.

The major principle of beginning practical trading is capital preservation. You will go through many adjustments of all parts of your preparations before you arrive at your final trading approach. It is crucial to make sure this stage is not ruining your account. The excitement of live trading can cause recklessness; having powerful tools at your fingertips can be very tempting; the process is seemingly so easy that caution may be thrown out to the wind. In order to avoid this we will go step-by-step, slowly increasing your exposure to the market.

The first step of your practical trading is going to be **paper trading**. At this stage, you are going to test your market read and make sure the market acts as your system suggests in enough cases to satisfy your approach requirements. Only when you get satisfying results do you move to the next step.

The second step is **small size trading**. This is where you start participating in a real exchange between market participants for the first time. You are going to test and hone your tools, skills and mental preparedness. You move to the next stage only when you are fully comfortable with your tools, trading stress-free and making some money with small size trades.

The third step is **trading size increase**. This is the stage where you are moving ahead to take profits from the market.

An element that you master and apply at all these stages is your **trading diary**. This is your major tool for self-analysis and correction.

Let us draw our mind map at this point and proceed further into each of the stages listed.

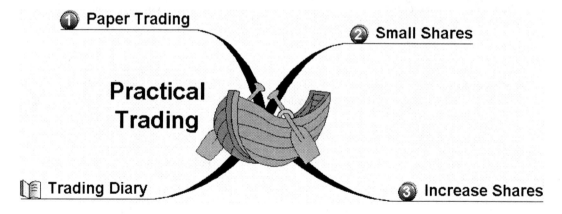

*Mind Map for Practical Trading*

# Paper Trading

The role of this stage of testing is often under-estimated by many and sometimes even scoffed at. The reason for this is the obvious limitations of paper trading. It does not allow you to estimate slippage during your execution and the probability of your order being executed at all; it keeps you in a relatively relaxed state of mind as there is no pressure of real money being on the line. Finally, it also does not allow you to master your order routing tools in full. All this being true, it still does not take away the value of paper trading. It allows you to ease into real trading and see if your approach works at all. It is a stage where you start measuring your method against market movements. You are going to have enough time to deal with elements listed above later on, adding them gradually as you start trading with small sizes. However, before your real money is actually used, the theory should be checked as an experiment, staged to be as painless for your trading account as possible. Even experienced traders return to paper trading to test new twists to their trading system or to sit out an unfavorable period of trading and see when it comes to its end.

Paper trading is conducted in a very simple way. It is an imitation of your actions without the actual sending of your order to the marketplace. You define your setup with all its components: trigger for entry, stop level, signs of exit, possibly with a partial exit and trailing stop. Then by observing the market action, you are imitating your responses by writing them down. This is going to be your first encounter with the market so take it seriously. Paper trading will teach you quite a bit about the market action without risking your money if you are watching carefully and acting responsibly.

Watch if your setups are working. Observe the market action and define if your response is reasonable. If you lose money on paper day-by-day, something is not right with your approach. Try to make corrections, find what factors are not considered. This is your troubleshooting stage – look for problems to solve. If you get negative results, do not get frustrated – take them as blessings in disguise. It is much better to find out about a problem before your actual money is committed to a flawed method.

Watch if your risk control is working. Do you lose within your defined limits on any given trade and on any given day? Maintain strict discipline at this stage as it is your future money that is going to suffer if disciplined behavior does not become second nature.

A crucially important purpose of paper trading is to find out the maximum drawdown that you can run into. This element might require a somewhat prolonged paper trading stage. The critical matter to consider is that losses and wins are not necessarily distributed evenly along the timeline of your trading. You can run into a cluster of losses. While the average of your losses might be affordable in terms of your trading capital, such a cluster may not. It is very important to make sure that a losing streak is not taking you out of the game. Methods of limiting such draw downs are going to be revisited in the Risk Control section closer to the end of this part.

In order to be as realistic as possible and to make paper trading effective as a learning tool, you need to keep several rules of paper trading:

1. **Make your decisions in real time only, not after the fact.** Looking at the chart and deciding where you would have entered and exited will not do you any good. Everything is easy in hindsight and looks very different when you are up against that Hard Right Edge, where the chart ends and you start reading the future. Write down your entry when it is on the chart and write down your exit when the chart hits your profit target or stop.

2. **Keep your trading rules exactly as if you were trading real money.** Any decision of "I'll do this, although with real money, I would do that" kind renders your paper trading worthless. If your stop level is hit, your paper trade is stopped and should be written down as such, even if the stock immediately bounced back up. If your profit target is not hit, do not write it down as less profit but still profit – it negates the very purpose of paper trading, which is to see if your targets are realistic and your stops are placed correctly.

3. **Take trades with the same degree of risk as if you were trading real money.** A decision to paper trade a risky setup that you do not intend to trade when doing live trading makes no sense. You paper trade to test your strategy, not to play around.

4. **Use the same set of tools as you intend for live trading.** If your trading strategy requires Level II for instance, then paper trading without it with the idea that with it, your trading will be even better, makes no sense. It will not be better because it will be different.

5. **Consider your entry and exit executed only if there are actual prints at the price you target.** Just seeing a bid or offer where you want them is not a guarantee that you could get your order filled at that price.

6. **Consider the amount of shares available at your price.** If you intend to trade 1,000 shares but there are only 100 shares offered, chances are in real trading you would not get your order filled in full.

7. **Do not use paper trading to project what kind of money you are going to make.** This is not the purpose of this stage. It can only make you unnecessarily impatient and eager to start trading live before you are ready. Simply write down the results to see if your planned strategy is working.

One more thing that is necessary to do at this stage – **get comfortable with your tools.** Configure the software you need for live trading. Move windows around your screens to have them placed as conveniently as possible. Start with your **charting software.** Play with the fonts to have all the information that you need on the screen so text is easy to read. Play with colors so that different windows are easy to distinguish. Learn to manipulate your charting software quickly. Change symbols, link windows, change timeframes – do everything that you will need to do in the course of trading. Draw necessary lines on the charts, add and delete studies and indicators that you are going to use. Practice long enough to make the process automatic.

When configuring your software, try to maintain uniformity of colors for critically important elements throughout all your tools. Use the green color, for instance, applying it to all of the components indicating upward movement, e.g. an up candle or bar, volume on upward movement, print at the offer, buy button on order entering screen and executed buying order. Assign the red color to downward movement: down candle, volume on downward movement, print on the bid side, sell button and executed short order. This will increase your ability to instantly recognize the type of action.

Learn your **order routing software.** Manipulate the controls changing quantity of shares, price of your order, type of order and route. Switch from limit order to market order and back, practice changing the price quickly. Play with the controls long enough to make the process automatic. See how to set advanced orders. If necessary, print out excerpts from your order routing instructions and place it within easy reach.

Finally, start routing orders in a way that keeps your money safe. Do it in the following way.

Set a small amount of shares – from ten to fifty. Set the price far enough from the market price so you are confident it will not be filled. If a stock is trading at $20, prepare your buy order at $10 and short order at $30. Send the order. Observe how confirmation appears. Now cancel the order and observe the confirmation. Make sure that all the messages you receive become familiar so you do not spend much time reading them later. Make sure that confirmation pop-ups do not get in the way of observing the action. Observe the reliability of your quote feed, especially in the most active periods – market opening produces fast conditions when the quotes are most likely to lag. Make sure that you have the trading desk phone number on speed dial to be able to reach help as fast as possible if something happens to your internet connection or quote feed – no technology is perfect.

Your trading software is usually configured to make you click once again to confirm an order you are going to send. Keep it this way at this stage. Only when you are fully comfortable with the software can you shut down this feature. While slowing you down a little bit, it gives you an opportunity to review your order for the last time. For longer timeframe traders, it is better to leave this feature on. When you gain more experience you can also look into using keystroke commands instead of mouse clicks, which allows you to speed up the process even more.

## You Asked

*Question:*
How long should I stay at the paper trading stage?

*Answer:*
I cannot give you a deadline because it is very individual. I know traders that breezed through it in two weeks and I know a trader that paper traded for a full year. It does not mean he was a slow learner. He just was perfecting his trading system until he was totally satisfied with it. Although I have to agree, a year is a bit on the extreme side, a week or two is not really what suits most people. This is usually not a matter of an exact period of time that is the same for everyone. Paper trading serves certain purposes, and you should move ahead when those purposes are achieved. Keeping all the rules of paper trading, do you show consistent profit? Have you observed how your setups work and gotten comfortable with them? Have you made sure that you know the drawdown your system can produce and that you can sustain it? Have you become comfortable with your charting and order entering software? If you can answer 'Yes' to all these questions, then paper trade for a couple weeks more. If not for any other reason, do it to practice one of crucial elements of your psychological makeover – patience. This skill to sit on the sidelines, will serve you well. It will also allow you to get into your first trading day with more feeling of self-control.

*Question:*
Do you think I should use help in the form of real time mentoring services? Does it negate the idea of being a self-responsible trader?

*Answer:*
I obviously consider such a service potentially a big help, since I am running one. Let us, however, look deeper into this issue. There are two kinds of such services. Some of them offer you stock picks only. This kind of services to a certain degree really negates the idea, as you said. I could accept the idea of an experienced trader using such a service as a source of trading ideas, "many eyes", you know… but for a beginner however, this is unacceptable. This approach will only slow down his learning process and make him fully dependable on someone's opinion. I have never heard of anyone who could make a decent income in trading by simply following someone else. Another kind of service is teaching. Commenting on market actions real time and educating its members, such a service can contribute greatly to your advance – providing that leaders know what they are doing. In my opinion, such a service must be tolerant to other styles of trading, not just push you into their own. Members have to be able to ask questions freely and offer their point of view. You can use such a service in the learning stage and "graduate" when you are able to trade on your own; or you can stay with it if you feel it contributes to your trading. Nevertheless, overall, a good mentor and helpful community can speed up the process greatly and save you considerable grief. There are plenty of mistakes you can make; keeping you from one of them already pays for your subscription.

*Question:*
Could you tell me more about quote delays? I observe them sometimes on busy mornings. How should I verify correct quotes and what source to trust?

*Answer:*
Unfortunately, technology is not perfect. It is much better and more stable than it used to be in 1990's but still, once in a while, you can find quotes lagging. First, look at quotes within a single source, in different windows. Sometimes you will see just one of them lagging. For instance, Level I quotes and chart go together while Level II lags – so you know you need to ignore Level II until it catches up. If a vital for your trading

window lags, simply do not trade until the situation is resolved. If you compare two different sources, look at volume to define which one is lagging. Obviously, you will see smaller volume on the lagging source's quotes.

# Small Size Trading

This is your final stage of learning before going full ahead. You are adding two very important elements at this point: testing of your execution skills and your emotional makeup. This is your first real interaction with the marketplace, and this is your first test of your inner strength.

Let us create a definition for 'small shares'. In trading stocks, it is usually 100 shares. Some prefer it to be 50 shares, some start with 200. One hundred shares seem to be commonly recognized as a good size to start with. This is exactly the stage where a smart choice of brokerage will pay off, as you do not want to pay full-blown commissions for such small lots.

Let us see how you transform your rules for this stage of trading.

1. **Keep your trading rules exactly as if you were trading a full lot.** Any decision of "I'll do this, although with bigger shares I would do that" kind renders your small size trading worthless. If your stop level is hit, your trade is stopped and should be written down as such, even if the monetary loss is well below your planned risk tolerance. If your profit target is hit as defined for a normal trading size, do not hold it longer just because you have small shares and you want a bigger payoff – it negates the very purpose of paper trading, which is to see if your targets are realistic and your stops are placed correctly.

2. **Take trades with the same degree of risk as if you were trading a full lot.** A decision to trade a risky setup that you do not intend to trade when doing bigger shares makes no sense. You trade small sizes to prepare yourself for trading bigger sizes, not to play around.

3. **Use the same set of tools as you intend for full lot trading.** If your trading strategy requires Level II, for instance, trading small shares without it with an idea that with it, your trading will be even better makes no sense. It will not be better because it will be different.

4. **Try to project the results of small shares trading on full size.** Now it makes sense as it validates your strategy or shows you the necessity to make last corrections before going full size. Remember that the purpose of this projecting is not to start counting future profits but to test your strategy.

5. **Use this stage to troubleshoot both, your strategy and your mindset.** If you feel nervous with 100 shares, you are going to be even more nervous with 1,000. Use this trading to get used to interaction with the market. Learn to become a calm, detached observer.

6. **Observe the amount of shares available for your orders to determine if there is enough stock that would satisfy your strategy from a liquidity point of view.** If you are trading 100 shares and get perfect fills on stocks where there are 100 shares available at your price level, your results will not be realistic for full lot trading.

---

When you project your results to bigger shares, apply a decreasing rate of about 70% to 80% of returns in order to be closer to reality. There will be factors impacting your results negatively when you increase your shares: liquidity, sudden price movements, mindset adjustments and others. Err on the side of caution.

---

If your order is not filled, never forget to cancel it to avoid being filled if a stock reverses back in price. It can happen when you are away from your computer, or in the middle of another trade. It happens more often than you would imagine.

# Increasing Trading Size

This is a transition period from small shares to full lot. It should be done gradually in increments: from 100 shares to 200-300 to 500 to 1,000 if 1,000 is what your trading approach requires. Let us leave the further increase to much later stages. It is only after gaining good experience and becoming a confident, consistently profitable trader that you can think of increasing the size of your trading positions beyond one lot, and this is beyond the framework of this book.

Here is the major principle of this stage: **if your performance worsens, go back to your previous trading size** to get back into a good state of mind. Move ahead only at the pace you are comfortable with. It could be two steps forward, one step back and that is totally fine. Experienced traders decrease their shares size when they hit a losing streak and there is no shame in doing that for you too.

Moving to 200 shares from 100 is not really making too much difference. Getting your orders executed is practically as easy as with 100 shares and your mindset is not getting impacted too much by this increase. The idea of this step is just to move slowly, without shocks. Such a slow transition helps you preserve the correct state of mind, not sending you into panic with each tick against your position. Control your state of mind carefully, making sure that you are not losing your cool, your ability to stay detached emotionally.

When you are at 500 shares, this is already a "working size", meaning it is quite possible to make decent profits with this lot. Use this size with respect. Stay at this level for a while, even when you feel you are ready to move further. The general idea of "err on the safe side" is a good idea here. If the jump from 500 to 1,000 feels a bit steep for you, add increments in between and trade 700-800 shares for a while. Keep in mind that moving past 500 shares you are already a player, not just a beginner. There are stocks where your 500 shares will make a difference at the bid or offer.

As you move from one trading size to another, change the default amount of shares in your order entering software. It will save you time when preparing your order.

Trading 500 shares and higher, start considering using reserve size on thinner stocks: show just 200-300 shares instead of a full lot. It will not matter much on thick stocks as described in the *Creating Your Trading System* part but can make a difference on thinner ones.

## You Asked

*Question:*
How do I know it is time to increase my shares to the next increment?

*Answer:*
When you are fully confident, make consistent profits and feel in full control. If you are not making money with smaller shares, you are not going to make it with a larger lot. If everything goes well from the very beginning, do not rush. Let your trading go through at least one setback, and better two, to make sure that you handle loss well and recover smoothly.

*Question:*
Trading starts before the official market open and continues after the close. Is it safe to trade at those time periods?

*Answer:*
It is a more risky period for trading. Not all of the market participants are in play and not all of the quotes that you see on Level II are firm. Less liquidity means more volatility. Instead of moving in cents, a stock could jump in tens of cents and more. Spread widens and getting your order filled can become tricky. Having said that, experienced traders do find times when pre- and post-market trading can be very profitable.

*Question:*
If I see news released before the market open, or earnings published after the market close, as it usually happens, how would you recommend I trade on it?

*Answer:*
Initiating a position on news released outside of regular market hours is something that should be done only at a certain level of experience, and if you start doing that – do it with small shares only. Remember that news releases can be, and often are tricky. For instance, earning announcements frequently come in parts, line by line: revenues, earnings per share (which is useful only when you know analysts' expectations), forward looking concerns, etc. Those numbers are not always straightforward, earnings can be before charges or after, revenue and earnings can contradict each other; often there is a conference call with analysts where even intonation of a company speaker can impact the stock action. In short, there is plenty going on and the information is not always easy to dissect in time. Try to paper trade this kind of movement for a while before going live; keep your bets small to compensate for increased risk.

*Question:*
Why do I see bids higher than offers before the market open? Can I make money on simple arbitrage, buying a low offer and selling to the high bid?

*Answer:*
Not really. As I said, pre-market quotes are not all firm. It means you can execute against some and cannot against others.

First, let us see whom you can trade with and whom you cannot. There are market makers and ECNs (electronic communication networks) on your Level II screen. Market makers can show yesterday's quotes or anything they wish since their bids and offers are not obligatory to fill matching orders outside of normal market hours. ECN quotes, on the other hand, are firm. It is easy to memorize them, and some trading software even mark them differently so you can distinguish them easily.

Second, let us see why this situation appears. When news or any other reason cause a stock to gap in the morning, market makers still have stalled quotes from the previous day displayed, while traders enter their new quotes via ECNs. This is when the overlap is created. To see real quotes you are going to look at ECNs only on both sides..

A market maker trying to set a trap can also create an overlap artificially. If he is trying to sell his shares and needs massive buying, he might try to encourage buyers by putting out a very high bid (which, remember, he does not have to honor) while offering his shares at a more reasonable price via ECN. This kind of trick was more popular in 1998 – 2000, although I still see it being done. Let me illustrate it by a couple of examples. The following screenshot is an example of such a fake out on a DCGN gap in the morning of October 19, 2004. The time is 8:23 AM.

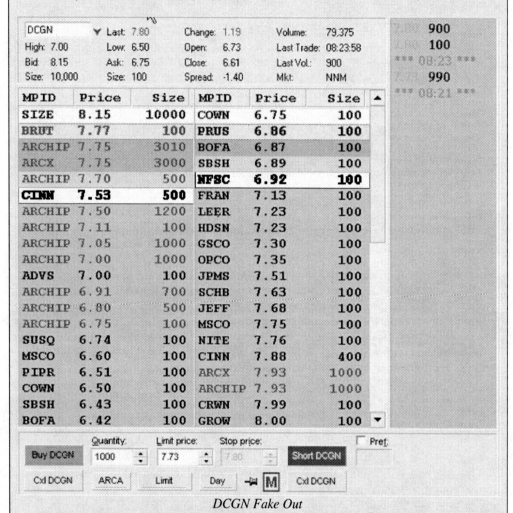

*DCGN Fake Out*

The stock closed at $6.61 on Oct 18 and gapped up on good news before the market open. As you can see on Level II, there is a fake bid at $8.15 for ten thousand shares; meanwhile trading occurs at $7.80. You can also see ECNs in red while market makers are in black.

The next example is a sequence of pre-market action on ISON, the same morning on October 19, 2004. The first screenshot simply shows the usual gap divergence between bid and offer quotes:

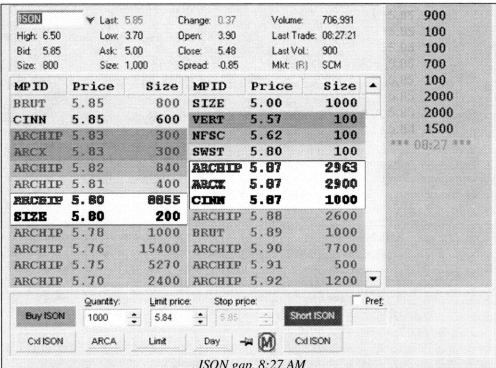

*ISON gap, 8:27 AM*

The stock closed at $5.48 and there is a gap to $5.85 where you can observe an overlap of quotes: an offer by a market maker is at $5. What happened next is rather dramatic.

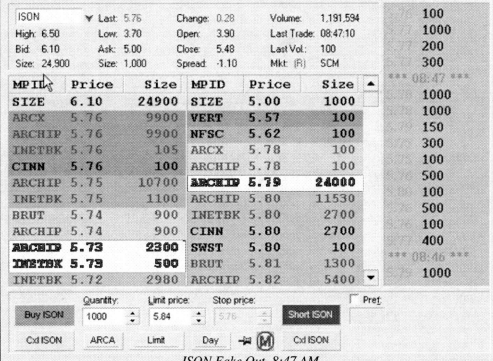

*ISON Fake Out, 8:47 AM*

There is a bid for an impressive 24,900 shares at $6.10 encouraging buyers. Notice this odd number, intended to create an impression of real shares ordered. Meanwhile the trades go off $5.70s. Let us see how events develop.

*ISON Fake Out, 9:02 AM*

Stock dropped over .30 cents, disappointing the trapped buyers. Notice that the "encouraging' bid disappeared - there is no need in it anymore, the fake buyer sold what he wanted. But the game is not over! That same player or different one (we will never know) wants to buy now, and look what he does:

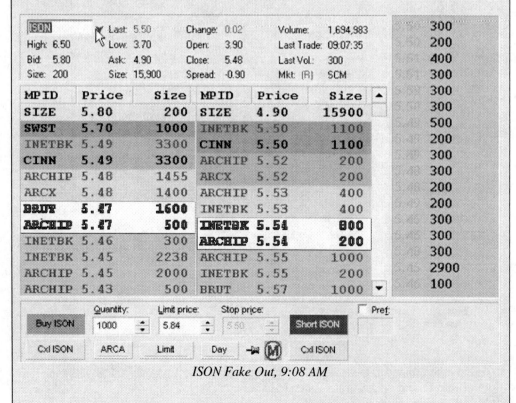

*ISON Fake Out, 9:08 AM*

That is right: he switched sides. He is showing a big offer at $4.90 now, scaring traders into selling and taking their offers.

<u>Masking intentions and faking intentions is the name of this game.</u>

*Question:*
I often miss my fill with limit orders and I do not want to use market orders. I would not mind to pay a little bit more but with market orders, it could be too much. Is there a compromise giving a stock a little room while still protecting me from too unfavorable a fill?

*Answer:*
Yes, there is. Simply set a limit order with the price a little bit beyond your exact trigger. For instance, if you want to buy a stock at $20 and are willing to give it 5 cent chase, simply send an order to buy at $20.05 when the stock is hitting $20. If there are shares for you at $20, $20.01 and up to $20.05, you will get them. If not – your order will not go higher than $20.05, combining the best of both, market and limit orders.

*Question:*
I have a problem with shorting. The very concept is not easy to grasp, I feel like I am doing something unnatural. It feels very intense and risky, even despite a tight stop loss that I apply.

*Answer:*
Let me skip all the theory about shares being borrowed etc. It does not really matter for practical purposes. Let us see what shorting is from the standpoint of a short term trader. I assume that you have all the reasons to believe the stock is going down in terms of your trading system, and the problem is just a practical execution. We are conditioned to think that money is made in upward markets and lost in downward markets. Shorting is considered to be a super-sophisticated concept available to professionals only. In fact, everything is much simpler.

When going long, you buy first, then sell – and in order to be profitable you have to sell at a higher price than you bought in. It is the same with shorting – if you sell at the price that is higher than you bought, you made a profit. The only difference is, you sell first and buy second. Going long, you open the trade by buying and close it by selling. Going short, you open the trade by selling and close it by buying. If buying low and selling high makes you money, then selling high and buying low does, too. Switch places of buying and selling, and for all practical purposes, the concept is grasped. If you feel uneasy about the conventional perception of moving up and down, imagine a stock moving left and right and see if it helps. As with all new concepts, start with paper trading, then small shares until you are comfortable with what you are doing.

*Question:*
Do you consider shorting more risky than going long? I heard reasoning about a stock capable of going upward indefinitely, thus making your loss indefinite, too. Also, there is some dreadful "short squeeze" – can you comment?

*Answer:*
A stock going upward indefinitely, while a downward movement is limited by zero, is a good scare for someone who has no idea about a stop loss concept or is not applying it. Why on earth would you, a trader controlling your risk, let a stock move to zero without cutting your losses? Or, in the case with shorting, why not apply a stop loss? Another matter is when a stock moves up with huge momentum, it often causes a strong desire to short it because "it cannot move any higher". That is a huge mistake. There should be a real reason for entry from both sides, long and short. The perception of a price being too low or too high is not a valid reason. You have your trading system, and your action has

to be defined by it. Amateurs, shorting any movement they consider "unreasonable", become burned and swear never to short again – and then all kinds of scary stories go around. It goes to the very roots of your trading philosophy. If you believe that the markets can remain irrational longer than you can remain solvent (and you better believe it), then you simply act on signals that your trading system generates and apply stops when the market proves you wrong.

Now, about short squeezes. This is a type of action where premature shorts have to cover their positions, adding the fuel to the upward momentum. The combined buying of new longs and covering shorts can create furious movement. There is just one thing to say about it: keep your stops.

*Question:*
What is short interest? Where could I find it and what use is it?

*Answer:*
This question is connected closely with the short squeeze idea. A short interest indicates the percentage of a stock's float that is shorted. It gives you an idea about the potential for a squeeze IF a stock gains upward momentum. It can be found at:

http://www.nasdaq.com/asp/quotes_full.asp?kind=shortint&symbol=

(There is plenty of other information concerning particular stocks, too). Keep in mind that this is not up-to-minute data though – it just gives you a rough idea. The data is updated monthly.

*Question:*
Do you consider time of day in your trading?

*Answer:*
I do. The first 10-15 minutes from the opening are the most volatile and risky. I am picky and very careful at this time. The period up to 11-11:30 AM is the normal trading time. After that, activity dies down and I retreat. Closer to the end of the trading day volume returns and activity picks up again. All this is not a hard and fast rule; it could be different for a particular day or a particular stock. These are only general guidelines.

# Trading Diary

This is a diary that you are going to keep updating for years to come. It will be your major tool for an objective look at your trading. Do not neglect it for even a single trading day.

The role of your trading diary is multi-fold.

First, it helps you **hone your trading strategy**. If you look at your trades and see that the majority of your profits are made between the open and noon, and you just lose money later in the day, it tells you how to correct your trading, time of the day-wise. If you make money consistently on breakouts and lose on trend reversals, it shows you where you are making incorrect decisions, so you can either stop trading those or look harder at how you trade them.

Second, it helps you **recognize the change in market conditions**. Certain setups can change the percentage of winning slowly, before you start noticing it in every day's fog of war. If there is an obvious trend in this change revealed from reviewing your diary, it can be your first clue to the market changing its ways.

Third, and probably the most important: this diary serves as your **window in your own mindset**. Analyzing the data objectively, you get a detached look into your reactions and you can spot the problem in the early stages of its development.

> Do not try to write down your perceived mental state. It will not help much as it is not going to be an objective evaluation – you will be writing it under the impact of the same mental state that you are trying to analyze. Let your trading diary become a reflection of your state of mind _through your trading decisions_ – these are the hard facts.

While many traders come up with their own forms of such a diary, we will offer you one to get you started. You can modify it as you see fit for your specific trading approach. Add elements that you feel useful; however, be careful not to overload it with too many unnecessary details. A trading diary should not become an end in itself; it is just a tool serving your needs, so keep your notes within it "necessary and sufficient". There could be a need for temporary additions to the journal which we will discuss in the **Form evolvement** section below.

There are two forms which form a trading diary. The first is reflecting the **details of each particular trade** and serves as a foundation for analysis of your strategy. The second is dealing with **your trading statistics** and reflecting your reactions. They intersect somewhat in their purposes as you will see from further explanations.

_Form 1_

| Trade # | Setup | Entry | | Stop | Target | Exit | | P/L |
|---------|-------|-------|------|------|--------|------|------|-----|
| | | Price | Time | | | Price | Time | |
| | | | | | | | | |
| | | | | | | | | |

_Analysis of Form 1_

From this form, you can see easily which setup works with what percentage. If you exit a trade before your stop or target is hit, it is going to be clear from this form. It will show you the need to make an adjustment in your mental state as you are clearly violating the idea we discussed in the *Trading Philosophy* part: Do not trade on noise, exit the trade when the reason for it is no longer valid or when an exit signal is generated.

If some setup shows random results, try to print out charts for each trade where you applied it. Study the charts to see if there is a pattern that distinguishes winning trades from losing ones. Maybe it is volume that did not play right in some cases; maybe the time of day was not right; maybe the stock's position in a daily range, etc. If you can spot such a pattern, you have your clue for your necessary adjustment. If there is no pattern at all, ask the next question: did this setup work well earlier and cease working recently? If yes, then you have to make a conclusion that the market is not right for it and you have to put it away for a while, paper trading it to see when it is back in play. Many setups go through this kind of cycle. If you just started trying this setup and it shows random results, it probably needs adjustments.

You can do the same kind of analysis if you want to try and optimize the setup for a higher percentage of winning trades, to locate and weed out factors leading to losses. Do not try to over-optimize it though; you cannot get rid of losing trades entirely.

## Form 1 Evolvement

You can use this form for a specific purpose in situations where you look for further optimization of your strategy.

To **maximize your profits**, you will need to add one more column to your form: High after your exit. If you see many trades where the stock moved significantly after you exited a trade, there clearly is a need to adjust your exit parameters. Go through the charts to see if there is a factor allowing you to tell the stocks proceeding higher from those that reversed after your exit. If you can locate such a pattern, you have a new parameter for your system. If there is no such pattern, try to paper trade longer holds on all setups of this kind and see if you get a real improvement. If yes, you have your adjustment.

To **optimize your stops**, add a column "direction/size of the move after stop". If stocks proceed lower in most cases, the first assumption is that your stop is placed correctly. If most of them bounced right back, it is a clue that your stop is too tight. Try to paper trade a bit wider of a stop to see if you get better results. If you see many of your stocks bouncing back into the profit zone, look through the charts to see if there is a pattern allowing you to recognize a stock bouncing back after your exit with a loss, from one that proceeds lower.

Now, returning to the case where most of the stocks proceed lower after stopping you out, try to model the situation with a tighter stop. Analyzing the charts, see how these statistics would change if your stop were tighter by a certain amount. Find the point where statistics change in favor of bouncing; if there is a gap between such a point and your stop, you can tighten your stop placement a bit, minimizing the loss on losing trades.

> Tightening your stop, be careful not to place it right at the level from which your stocks bounce. Always leave a little padding to factor in small random moves. In the case with intraday trading, padding by .05 cents is usually enough. In longer term trading, increase this amount, depending on timeframe and position size.

The adjustment and evolvement of this form is a creative process. As you see a need to optimize certain parameters of your trading approach, think of measurements for it and add an additional column to your form. Sort the form by this parameter and look for a pattern. It will be your hint as to what to correct.

**Form 2** is your trading statistics. I described it in detail in my book *Techniques of Tape Reading*. The following is an excerpt from it.

*I tracked my trading results in a journal, which helped me spot and prevent the problems in the early stages. This journal served me as a kind of mirror in which I could see where my trading mindset deviated from the right direction.*

*I tracked:*

- *Number of trades per day*
- *Number of winners*
- *Number of losers*
- *Winners/losers ratio*
- *Average winning trade size in terms of points*
- *Average losing trade size in terms of points*
- *Number of points per day*

### Number of Trades per Day

*Keeping track of the number of trades per day may seem simple and not too informative. However, look at it from this point of view. How many trades do you do in a winning day? In a losing day? The rule says to act more aggressively when you are on a winning streak and to decrease activity when you are on a losing streak. Many traders do exactly the opposite. When losing, they try to get it back, to take revenge. And, the result is usually not good. In this situation, our trades may depend on our wishes more than on real opportunities.*

### Winners/losers ratio

*If a trader experiences a winner/loser ratio below 50 percent, something is wrong, assuming that the reward-to-risk scenario does not allow for trading under 50 percent. My system will not allow the ratio to be under 50 percent. It tells me that I am probably overtrading, trying to squeeze something out of a juiceless trade. Also, my understanding of market dynamics and patterns is not quite right, and it is time to go back to paper trading. A ratio of 50 percent and higher seems fine, as long as winners are bigger than the losers.*

### Average Winner and Average Loser.

*The average winner and average loser show us whether we follow the basic rule of cut our losers quickly and let our profits run. Each trader has a level of comfort, with respect to stops, depending on his or her risk tolerance, the kind of stocks played, expectations and so on. When we look at our average loser for a month, we can see if we manage to keep our stops as small as we wanted. If an average winner is too small, it tells us that we do too many scalps or have problems with staying in a winning trade. Different combinations of these statistics give us different angles. For example, a large number of trades combined with low winners/losers ratio means that many low percentage trades were picked.*

*Here is an example of such a journal with analysis. This is taken from a real week of trading. I selected a volatile, losing week (after commissions), to show how I acted to spot the problem using the numbers shown.*

| | # of trades | # of winners | # of losers | W/L ratio | Average W | Average L | Total |
|---|---|---|---|---|---|---|---|
| Mon | 12 | 8 | (3) | 2.7 | .35 | (.173) | 2.28 |
| Tue | 15 | 8 | (6) | 1.3 | .25 | (.237) | 0.58 |
| Wed | 11 | 2 | (6) | (0.3) | .23 | (.273) | (2.10) |
| Thur | 18 | 8 | (8) | (1) | .156 | (.22) | (0.512) |
| Fri | 10 | 6 | (2) | 3 | .23 | (.156) | 1.068 |
| Total | 66 | 32 | (25) | 1.3 | | | 1.316 |

*Monday: As you can see, Monday was a very nice day. There was a good percentage of winners (67%), and a not bad winner/loser ratio (2.7/1, which is fairly decent for a scalper).*

*Tuesday was not that great. The percentage of winners dropped to 53% and the ratio went almost flat. After commissions, it was a slightly losing day, most likely resulting from overconfidence after a very nice start to the week. My number of trades went up, too – a possible sign of reckless picking.*

*Wednesday: Wednesday was a total disaster. Over 50% of my trades were losers; and the losing trades averaged more than winning ones. Apparently, I was trying to press hard to resume a winning streak interrupted by a sluggish Tuesday. Losses were not cut effectively – had I tried to hold despite the market telling me to get out?*

*Thursday: Whoa! Look at this sucker's reaction on a losing day! The number of trades is way up – revenge trading, pushing hard instead of becoming less aggressive while on a losing streak. There are an equal number of losers and winners – churning, trying to jump on everything that moves with fairly random results. Winners are small – did I get scared and started taking any profits, just to win? Losers are still bigger than winners – misplaced hope, "Maybe it is going back to my entry."*

*Friday: Friday was somewhat better. I evidently attempted to put myself together. I did not trade aggressively – my lowest amount of trades for the week. I was more selective with my plays, which could constitute a not bad day but could not save the week. I made 66 trades, 132 tickets plus some unavoidable partial fills, $20/ticket (usual commissions at that time), down almost $1,500 for the week.*

*As this kind of analysis built up, I was able to see the problem as it just appeared. Familiar patterns of my behavior became visible for me at early stages thanks to the tables I created. For instance, I already knew that I tended to overtrade after a losing day. I had to keep myself from doing that by effectively improving my reactions. I could track my reactions when I was on a winning streak and spot the moment when I was getting too reckless. All this monitoring was giving me a good look within myself. As a result, I became constantly aware of my inner state and could diagnose a problem just in time to prevent it from getting worse.*

As with Form 1, be creative with this form, too. For instance, adding a 'Time of Day' column and breaking down each day in three parts (morning, lunchtime, close) can show you clearly the percentage of your trades depending on this factor.

Your trading diary is going to be with you throughout your entire trading career. This is an ultimate tool of keeping yourself in check and for constant self-improvement.

---

## You Asked

*Question:*

I have made money consistently during the past three months and I have reached the maximum share size I intended to trade. Considering my risk tolerance, I do not plan increasing my lot size anytime soon. Should I take money from my trading account or let it increase?

*Answer:*

Assuming that you do not need this money as immediate income (if you do, then the question is answered automatically), it becomes more a psychological issue. It is certainly a good idea to reward yourself for a job well done and to get a taste of the money derived from trading. Another reason supporting the decision to take some amount out is to avoid possible recklessness caused by your "cushion". It is nice to have this cushion and feel safety but I have seen numerous examples of "when we become successful, we tend to stop doing what made us successful in the first place". Keep yourself in check and be alert to avoid reckless trading. It is always a good idea to take your profits off the line of fire, if you do not intend to use it for more aggressive growth of your account. If you hesitate with this, do the following: remove two-thirds of your winnings from your account and leave one third in; this way you do both, secure your profits and increase your cushion.

# Risk Control

Your method of trading was defined by you earlier. Risk control is one component of that method and arriving at practical trading, you have it thought through already. However, the importance of this element is such that I would like to devote the last section of this part to it.

We already went over stop placement on several occasions and we defined the main sign of a trade gone badly – the original reason for a trade not being there anymore. Let us establish your actions necessary for risk control in the course of a trade. We will track the entire development of the trade in order to see what you need to do at any given moment.

**Position sizing**, **stop placement**, **partial exits** and **stop trailing** are the major components of your risk control while managing the trade.

Risk control starts with **position sizing**. In order to find out the correct size of your position, you need to divide your maximum loss allowed for a given trade by the size of your stop loss, as dictated by the chart. An example of such an approach follows.

Your trading capital is $30,000. You want to keep your loss on any given trade under 1 percent. It gives you a maximum loss of $250, which keeps you just under 1 percent when you account for commissions. Looking at the chart, you see a stop level at .25 cents under your entry point. Dividing 250 by .25, you obtain 1,000 shares as your maximum trading lot for this particular trade.

You enter your position and now the **passive phase** of managing your trade starts: you do nothing until the market shows the next signal. If your stock moves within the "noise" range, you simply wait. Your **stop** is entered, and you are watching the action. If the stock hits your stop, there is nothing to think about – the stop is just executed without hesitation or rationalizing.

If a stock moves in your favor, you are watching for signs of exiting as defined by your trading system. If you are a scalper, you are going to look for your exit as a stock moves into 1:1 risk/reward, in our example approximately .25 cents of profit.

If you are a day trader, you are not likely to exit your position in full at this level. You either hold it in full for a bigger move or **exit part** of it to secure the profit. However, if the stock forms a new resistance level and new consolidation range, you have your reason to **trail your stop**. The reason is a new support is being formed. If a stock breaks this support, it is weaker than expected and you can exit the trade. Continuing with our example, if a stock moved up about .25 cents and stalled, you have a new support level – former resistance that your stock broke triggering your entry. Now your stop is going to be trailed just under this support, let us say by .05 cents of padding. Your risk is not .25 cents anymore – it is just .05 cents that you lose if a stock drops back. Additionally, if you exited half of your original position, the overall trade is going to show a profit even if your trailing stop is hit.

The process is repeated as a stock breaks new resistance and moves further in your favor. If the next exit signal is generated at a .50 cents level from your entry, you have the choice again: exit the reminder of your position, or part of the remainder, or continue holding it.

In all of the cases where you hold your shares, you are going to trail your stop again – just under your new support formed by this former resistance. You saw an example of such a stop trailing on the charts illustrating trend following in the *Trading Philosophy* part – review them again and they will make even more sense to you now.

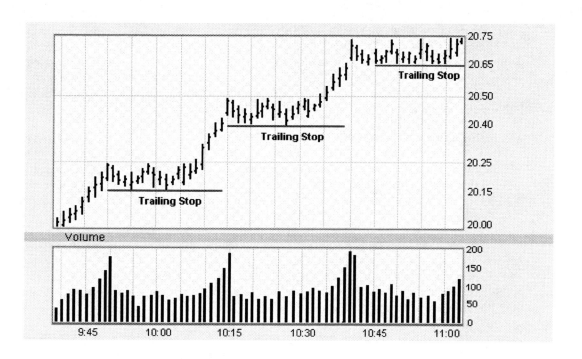

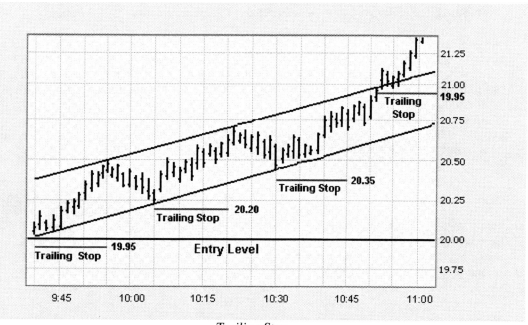

*Trailing Stop*

Your timeframe, signals for entry and exit, and exact size of the movement will vary from trader to trader, depending on your trading system and the choices you made for yourself. However, the main principles of risk control and this sequence of action will remain the same.

Finally, the last component that you need to align with your survival requirements is **maximum drawdown**. How big a losing streak can you sustain? If you defined your maximum loss allowed for any single trade as 1% of your trading capital and your uncle point for the day as three losing trades in a row, it means that, as a day trader, 30 losing days in a row will destroy your account. Indeed, this is an extreme turn of events and you should never let the situation go that far. Instead, you need to define an alert point where you obviously need to re-evaluate what you are doing. This is true for any stage of your training, from paper trading to full blown trading at any stage of your development as a trader. Let us say you defined such an alert point as 5 losing days in a row. There are two questions to be answered at this moment. The first question: is it the market that changed its behaviour so that your system stopped producing good results or is it your discipline in executing your system that failed you? The second question: what should you do about it?

The first question can be answered by analyzing the market action as a detached observer. Return to the paper trading stage where you tested your system. Find all the signals that your system generated during this period and analyze what happened after they were generated. If you see that your system still produced positive results, it is you who acted in disconnection with your system. If you see objective negative results, it is the market's behaviour that changed in a way that caused losses to your system.

Now, how do you react in both cases? The first rule in this situation is, **decrease your activity or stop trading altogether.** Pressing harder when in a losing streak is a major mistake that costs traders dearly. In fact, gradual decreasing of activity has to start even before you reach your alert point. If you defined it as 5 days in a row, you should cut down your trading size after the third day.

Now, if your diagnostics showed that the root of the problem is you, your action should be aimed at restoring your confidence. Keep your trading size small and decrease your timeframe. The theme of this period has to be to get as many wins as possible, however small they are. Faster profit taking serves this purpose well increasing your win/lose ratio while sacrificing your profit/loss ratio. There is nothing like winning to feel like a winner.

Deploy your Model Trader that you created when designing the basics of your trading psychology. Observe the Model Trader's action in a detached manner. Give yourself the chance to restore confidence that facilitates your "being a winner" feeling. Take it slow. Give yourself some time away from the market. Retreat to your favorite activities that make you feel good. Reread the part of your plan devoted to your psychology. Reread your favorite books on forming the winning mindset. Revisit interviews with traders that inspire you. Finally, start increasing your trading size only when you feel full confidence again (that wonderful feeling of "can do no wrong") and your trading results improve.

If your diagnostics showed that it is the market actions that impact your performance, you face two possible choices. If you feel that the change is long-term, for example – a big trend change or volatility change, then you need to redefine your trading system. If a change is temporary and short-lived – a pause in a trend for instance – your system should include such conditions as we discussed in the *Creating Your Trading System* part. How to tell the former case from the latter is a question that goes way beyond the scope of this book. This is something that causes huge, institutional trading firms big headaches. In fact, your entire trading career is going to revolve around finding major turning points of the market behavior. In any case, the ability to constantly adjust and re-adjust is what makes or breaks a trader.

There is just one thing remained to say about risk control: Never forget about it. EVER.

# You Asked

*Question:*

If I decrease my trading activity, will I make my recovery slower? If I lost 5 days in a row and cut my trading size in half, it is going to take 10 days to recover, providing that I got it right?

*Answer:*

Do not let yourself be fooled by what seems to be a natural reaction. This way of thinking is the exact cause of losses mounting up. You decrease your activity in order to nail the problem. It allows you to slow down, diminish your stress, restore your cool and to return to objective evaluation. The key words in your question are: Providing that I got it right. You need to get it right first and to recoup your losses based on a new understanding. Focus on this new understanding first. If your vehicle starts making strange sounds, you do not accelerate. You troubleshoot the malfunctioning equipment by shutting it down first, by taking it apart, diagnosing the problem, fixing it and testing it again.

*Question:*

What about trading halts? How risky are they, how big is the risk of running into them? Is there any way to minimize this risk?

*Answer:*

A trading halt is practically the only situation in which an intraday trader loses control over a stock's action. When some material news must be disseminated, or a huge trading imbalance appears, or some important information from the company is needed, the exchange can halt a stock for trading. If the news will impact a stock's valuation significantly, it can open after the halt with a gap. A trader that is stuck in such a halt can make a substantial profit if the news is positive, or be exposed to a substantial loss. In any case, it is better to avoid halts. Even though it is a rare occurrence, the outcome can be catastrophic. Do not play a stock ahead of significant news coming – an FDA decision or earnings announcement for instance. Do not try to enter a stock on a sharp sell off when there is no known news causing it – it is the most probable candidate to be halted.

## Trading Plan

### Trading Plan Form: Practical Trading

I am going to start with paper trading. At this stage, I am testing and fine-tuning my system. I am learning my trading tools. I am going to stay with paper trading until the following conditions are met:

_____

_____

_____

I start trading _____ shares. At this stage, I check my executions skills and my ability to stay emotionally detached. I am going to stay with this trading size until the following conditions are met:

_____

_____

_____

I increase my trading size to _____ shares. If I see no negative impact on performance, I stay with this size for two weeks and move to _____ shares.

I move to _____ and _____ shares under the same condition.

I keep my trading journal. I fill it out after each trading day (after each trade for longer term traders) and analyze the results. I evaluate market conditions and my own state of mind using this journal.

If I experience _____ losing days in a row, I stop trading and evaluate what is going on. If I see changing market conditions I _____

If I see myself as the culprit, I

_____

_____

_____

When I am fully confident and trade consistently for a _____, I am going to analyze my trading in order to see what I can do to improve my trading results. I do it in the following manner: _____

_____

_____

_____

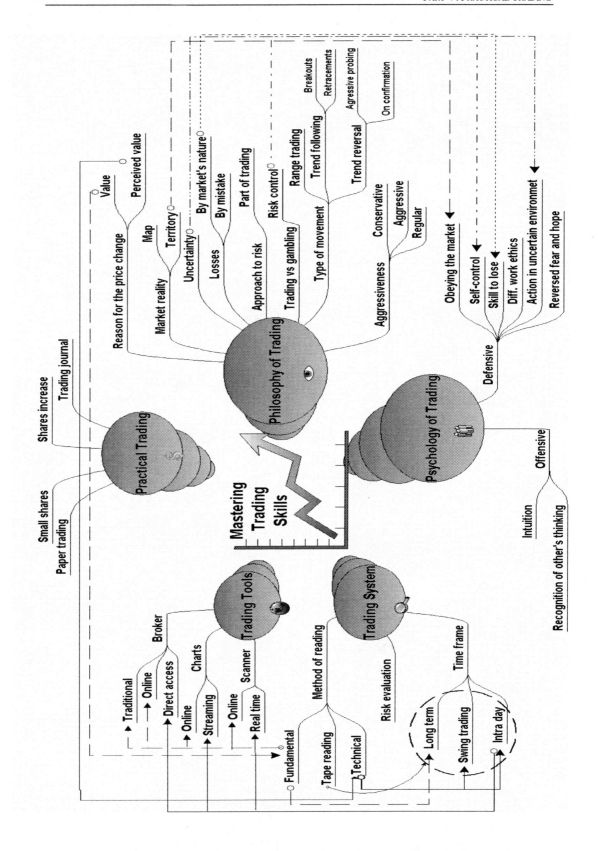

# Trading Plan Samples

The following are five samples of trading plans. They are taken from real plans kindly provided to me by the traders with whom I am in contact. Reading them, please keep in mind that four of them are experienced traders with established trading approaches. It results in their plans being shorter since there is no part devoted to the learning stage. In order to keep certain uniformity I took the liberty to move some parts around. There are also some elements excluded as authors wanted to keep them private. Nonetheless, these samples will provide you with a clear idea how different traders create their plans.

# Beginner

## My Vision Statement

I am going to become a day trader trading for a living. I am inspired by the free lifestyle and a perspective of being my own boss.

## My Financial Commitments and Objectives

My trading capital is going to be $40,000.

My goal is to make $70,000 a year eventually. I plan to achieve this goal within 1 year.

My planned expenses:

- charting software $150/month
- scanning software $45/month
- books $300 one time
- subscription to services: $250/month

## My Trading Philosophy

In my approach, the market's action is dictated by human reactions; this is all I am trying to read.

The ultimate market reality for me is the price action. I never consider the market wrong.

I do not expect the market to act with certainty. I expect it to hand me losses now and then, even when I am doing everything right. I am going to analyze my losses in order to find repetitive patterns and to fine-tune my strategy.

I appreciate that risk is a necessary part of trading. Risk is opportunity in disguise.

I apply tight risk control. This is what guarantees my survival and profitability.

In my approach, a reason for taking a trade is a valid setup.

A setup failure is a sign to me to terminate my trade.

The type of movement that I am going to trade is trend continuation.

My level of aggressiveness is conservative at first, with ongoing evaluation and possible switch to another type, if observations show me better results with regular or aggressive entries.

## My Trading Psychology

The market is my boss. I am not arguing with it.

I am totally responsible for results of my trading. It is my decision that determines the results of my trades. I maintain strict discipline.

When my stop loss is hit, I am out. No exceptions.

I do not expect to know an outcome of my trades. I let the market decide.

I fear losses so I limit them with stops. I want my profits to grow so I protect them with trailing stops but I am not rushing to take them.

My correct mindset is:

1. Emotional detachment,
2. Focus on market action and not on money,
3. Every day is a fresh day: hard feelings or excitement over yesterday's performance is not carried into my new day.

My method to achieve a correct mindset is constant re-checking of my trading journal in order to see whether I trade outside of my intended strategy. I write down two parallel journals: one is factual and another is an extract from it, for losing trades only. I analyze losing trades to see whether I did everything in accordance with my strategy. If I deviate from it, I punish myself with two days detention to paper trading only. I love trading; thus my desire to avoid this detention keeps me in line.

When I am looking for a trade, I am waiting for a trade to come to me. I am not forcing my view on the market and not twisting my setup to coincide with the market.

When my entry signal is generated, I hit the button. No thinking involved.

When I am in a trade, I wait for its outcome not adjusting my stop until my trading system requires it.

When a trade is going against me, I will be stopped out with no thinking involved.

When a trade is going in my favor, I watch for my exit signal, not observing my profit/loss.

## My Trading System

My planned timeframe is intraday.

I limit my losses to $200/trade.

I control my risk by stop losses.

At one time, I am trading not more than two positions.

In relation to margin, I am using full margin if needed, on an intraday basis. Since I am not holding positions overnight, margin risk is not an issue.

I set the following criteria to limit the risk of each particular trade:

- Volume: 5 million shares and more
- Spread: up to .05 cents
- Float: over 10 million shares
- Maximum length of bar or candle: .05 cents
- Order sizes on Level II: 1,000 shares and higher

I am not taking a trade if possible slippage is evaluated as more than .05 cents.

I apply technical analysis as my method of reading the market.

## Trading System Design

I apply the following set of chart patterns:

- Open Break
- Cup & Handle
- Triangle
- JBE consolidation

My settings for each of them:

- Open Break: not earlier than 15 minutes after the open; range is not wider than .20 cents
- Cup & Handle: Cup is not less than 90 minutes and not deeper than $1; Handle is between 10 and 30 minutes and not deeper than .30 cents
- Triangle is not longer than 2 hours at apex, break should occur between 2/3 and ¾ of base length
- JBE consolidating for no longer than 2 hours, range not wider than .20 cents, J phase is not shorter than .60 cents.

My entry signal is generated when the following conditions are met:

1. Break occurs
2. initial spike is not higher than .15 cents
3. pullback takes the price back to new support (just broken resistance)
4. new support is holding
5. I can buy a stock within .05 cents of new support.

My entry price is not farther than .05 cents from the point of signal.

My stop is triggered when the following criteria are met: <u>the price is breaking down through the new support by more than .15 -.20 cents from my entry.</u>

My exit signal is generated when the following happens: 1:1 risk/reward for first partial out; 2:1 is for exiting of ¼ of position. Trailing stop .20 cents after that.

My daily loss is limited to $600.

When in profit, I am decreasing my activity when I am up $600.

## My Trading Tools

For my charting tool, I use:

- 3 minute chart, intraday,
- 30 min chart, 30 days,
- 365 days, daily,
- Level II for risk evaluation.

For trading I use: <u>MB Trading with a TTO order panel to minimize the impact of my emotions.</u>

For scanning, I use: IntelliScan with settings for:

- JBE
- chart pattern recognition
- 52-week high
- 5 days consolidation

## Practical Trading

I am going to start with paper trading. At this stage, I am testing and fine-tuning my system. I am also learning my trading tools. I am going to stay with paper trading until I am fully comfortable with my trading system and tools. I plan to stay with paper trading for two months at least.

I start trading with 100 shares. At this stage, I check my executions skills and my ability to stay emotionally detached. I am going to stay with this trading size until I am fully comfortable and start to break even in my trading.

I increase my trading size to 200 shares. If I see no negative impact on performance, I stay with this size for a month and move to 500 shares.

I move to 700 and 1,000 shares under the same condition.

I keep my trading journal. I fill it out after each trading day and analyze the results. I evaluate market conditions and my own state of mind using this journal.

If I experience 3 losing days in a row, I stop trading and evaluate what is going on. If I see changing market conditions, I go back to paper trading.

If I see myself as the culprit, I cut my size to 100 shares until I get breakeven again; then I increase my shares gradually, every 3 days if the results are good.

When I am fully confident and trade consistently for 2 years, I am going to analyze my trading in order to see what I can do to improve my trading results. I will determine the exact steps when I am there.

# Swing Trader

Swing Trader, Full Time, Primary Income. 4 years experience

## My Vision Statement

As a full time trader, I am fully committed to derive sufficient income from trading. I appreciate a lifestyle with no bosses and deadlines.

## My Financial Commitments and Objectives

My trading capital is $70,000.

My goal is to make $120,000 a year minimum after expenses and commissions. I will accept $70,000 as a minimum.

My expenses come to $250 a month. They include:

- charting software          $150
- scanning software          $50
- subscription to a newsletter:   $50

## My Trading Philosophy

The force behind market movements for me is people. I read charts to read people. Charts do not lie. It is up to me to read them accurately.

Now and then, I can be wrong. I accept it and move on. Now and then I can do everything right and still lose. I accept it and move on.

When I am wrong, I will analyze and correct my actions.

Risk control is my safety net. This is the first element of any trade that I am looking at.

A chart signal is my reason for putting on a trade.

A chart signal is my reason for exiting a trade on any side.

I am a reversal trader. I am interested in trend changes.

I am highly aggressive. I put on a trade when my system generates an extreme reading and I keep tight stops. I will re-enter a trade again if the first attempt fails.

## My Trading Psychology

The market is my guide. I am not going to impose my opinions on it. I am going to listen to it and obey it.

Self-control is my major weapon in trading. The market provides the guidance; I control myself and follow it.

I am comfortable with taking responsibility for my actions. This is what gives me strength and makes me self-reliant.

I never trade what my system defines as noise. It is a stop or profit target for me. I do not change my plan in the middle of a trade. My profit taking plan can be changed if the market action changes – my stop plan cannot.

I do not get emotional about trades. This is my profession. I just do what my job description requires me to do as a trader. That is, I exist and enter according to my system signals.

If I lose, I do not take it personally. The market is not after me; a loss is not making me a fool. A loss is simply a trade gone bad or my mistake. If it is my mistake, it means I got a hint from the market and I better take it to avoid a similar mistake in the future.

Scanning for a trade, I remain inactive. I do not press actively. I do not accept mediocre setups. I want all my parameters to align. When everything is right for an entry, I take a position automatically. Being very selective when scanning, I am decisive when a scan produces the right result. I never chase a stock – it is my price or no trade.

After entry, I set my hard stop immediately and from this moment on my stop is not a matter I think about again. I monitor my trade only to see if I get an exit signal at a different point than planned.

## My Trading System

My timeframe is from 1 to 15 days; I close my position within one day only when a stop or target is hit. If a trade moves in my favor without generating a clear sell signal, I might stretch my holding time. If a trade hovers near its stop without hitting it, I will close it on day 15. I trade the NYSE, NASDAQ and e-mini DOW, NASDAQ 100 and S&P.

I limit my losses to $1,000 per trade, or 1.5% of my trading capital with commissions included. I control my risk by diversification between several positions using small sizes and by applying tight stop losses.

At any given time, I am trading 5-7 positions.

The portion of my capital devoted to any single trade is 15 – 20%.

I do not use margin.

I am not trading stocks with daily volume under 5 million shares.

I apply the following set of chart patterns and indicators:

- Double bottom and top; Head and Shoulder; Triangle Failure; Cup and Handle Failure; Gravestone Doji.
- I use MACD divergence and MACD moving average crossover with custom filters.
- I apply volume confirmations to all my patterns listed below in accordance with tape reading principles.

Being an aggressive trader, I enter:

- on the second bottom or top for reversal, not waiting for price confirmation, with a volume decrease toward the second top;
- on Head and Shoulder as soon as the neckline is touched with increasing volume;
- on Triangle Failure when the price stays within its lines up to an apex and beyond;
- on Cup and Handle when a price stays at the bottom of the handle for more than 3 candles with increasing volume.

In a strongly trending market, I apply the same set of entry criteria with the addition by comparing my trading candidate to the overall market. I do not trade reversals on stocks that move with the market until the market itself generates a turning point in terms of my patterns. Instead, I am looking at the stocks that under-perform and align my entries with market retreats.

I am willing to chase my entry within .20 cents.

My stop is triggered when the stock shows a sign of trend continuation instead of reversal. A new high(low) with volume increase is a sign of trade gone wrong.

I aim for my first partial out when the risk/reward ratio is 1:2. I sell half of my position at that point and trail my stop to a breakeven level.

My trading journal tracks each trade. I use it to follow my trading statistics and diagnose possible problems at the early stages.

Five losing trades in a row is my signal to stop trading. I take two days off, never looking at the market and completely relaxing. After that break, I gain a more objective state of mind and start analyzing what is happening. My next 5 trades will be paper trades. I get back in the market when my paper trades show my usual profits.

# Retiree

Swing Trader, Scalper, Supplementary Income, 7 years experience.

## My Vision Statement

Trading for me is a hobby that brings me supplementary income. Fun and money are a necessary combination in order to make me satisfied with my trading results.

## My Financial Commitments and Objectives

My trading capital is $40,000.

My goal is to make an average $200 a day. However, I am happy with any income derived from trading. I exceed this target routinely but I keep it as a measurement for my performance.

My expenses:

- charting software       $180 a month
- scanning software       $45 a month
- subscription to trading room:       $250 a month

             **Total:**       **$475 a month**

## My Trading Philosophy

My general trading approach is very simple. I pay attention to clear market action only and take the safest opportunities leading to fast and easy profits.

Any sign suggesting that a trade could be a struggle puts it in an "avoid" category for me.

Risk is a necessary part of trading for there would be no reward if there were no risk. I embrace risk and appreciate the fact that it provides me with opportunity.

Risk control is turning trading into a planned activity. When a reason for a trade is not there anymore, a trade must be closed.

I am interested in small stocks with increasing volume. As they get more attention, I am trying to take the easiest part of their movement.

I am not too aggressive and not overly conservative. I am not trying to be the first to buy, nor am I waiting for too much confirmation. A rising interest in a stock gets my interest. A sign of a trade being wrong for me is stalled price with dying volume.

## My Trading Psychology

I am in full self-control. My major objective is to maintain a relaxed state of mind. Trading must remain fun for me. I enjoy it.

I never regret my premature exits as I am not trying to take all the money a stock can offer. Slow nice easy movements or quick and easy to read scalps offer me both fun and money.

I hate losses. I cut them as quickly as possible. My intolerance for losses is my weak spot. Knowing it, I aim for the safest trades only. Once the trade shows no promise, I am out with no regret.

I do not feel obliged to trade all the time. I trade when I want to. I never make myself trade if I am not in an appropriate mood.

I stay with slow moving positions as long as the movement matches my perception of trend continuation.

I am not too eager to find a trade. My best trades come to me naturally. I am looking at what the scanner and trading room offer, picking those trades that feel best to me.

## My Trading System

My timeframe is scalping and swing trading up to three days.

I limit my losses to $150 a trade.

I control my risk by a tight stop loss.

At any given time, I am trading one scalping position and up to three swing positions.

My trading capital is divided into two parts. I use $20,000 for intraday scalping and $20,000 for swing trading. I use full buying power for intraday scalping positions and I spread $20,000 for swing trades between up to three positions.

I use margin intraday; I use cash only for swing trades.

My risk limiting criteria:

- Volume: on a rise, not less than 1 million a day for swing trades, not less than 500,000 shares for scalps.
- Spread: up to .10 cents.
- Order sizes on Level II: not less than 1,000 shares.


I apply tape reading as my primary method, with several chart patterns.

## Trading System

I trade the long side only. I trade trend continuation only, never the reversals. I am interested in stocks up to $5.

I use intraday breakout patterns to find my entries: Ascending Triangles, Cup and Handle, JBE setup. I do not use any technical indicators – only chart patterns and volume. I start every trade as a scalp. If a stock is just starting its move on its daily chart, I watch it closely toward the end of the day. If I observe volume is rising and a stock holding near the high, I take a swing position.

I use a regular type of entry at a breakout level. I am not chasing a stock higher than .05 cents.

I monitor small stock's activity closely. When they cycle, my activity increases. When they are dead, I just wait for sporadic activity and mostly limit my trading to scalps.

When scalping, I take profits of between $200-300 per trade with risk about $150.

My daily loss is never higher than $300. I stop trading when I am down that much.

I stop looking for new trades when I have $400 profit for the day. I leave my computer and return 1 hour before close, to see if I can find a safe scalp or swing trade candidate. If I have previously established swing positions when I leave my computer, I set an automatic stop and sell.

## My Trading Tools

My settings for the charting software are: two sets for three chart windows each, daily for 180 days, hourly for two weeks and intraday 1 minute. I have three Level II windows.

For trading I use MBTrading Navigator integrated with charting software.

For scanning, I use IntelliScan with four customized windows. I scan for JBE, Chart formations and Small stock activity. My settings are limiting a stock price to $5.

## Practical Trading

I am trading 1,000 to 5,000 shares. My swing trades are never more than 1,000 shares. If I trade bigger lots, I either take small profits (.05 - .15 cents) or sell half when I see a first spike after the breakout occurs. I trade big lots only in cases when I can set 2-5 cent stops.

I do not keep a trading journal. I always feel whether I want to trade or I do not feel good about trading on a particular day.

# Fundamental Trader

Position Trader who is a Day Trader when opportunities appear; supplementary income, 20 years experience.

## My Financial Commitments and Objectives

My position trading capital is going to be a minimum of $100,000.

My goal is to make a minimum of $50,000 a year, or 50 % of my position trading capital. I will go into more detail below about my position trading approach.

My day trading capital will be a minimum of $50,000. In my day trading account, I would like to make $25,000 per year or 50% of my day trading capital. When I day trade I try to follow the basic rules used by most successful day traders. I look for recognizable set-ups, enter the trade, use a tight stop loss and close all trades at the end of the session. My primary focus is not on day trading and I am often not very active. It requires a lot of focus and is not particularly rewarding for me when the market is choppy and unpredictable. When there are many players in the market (both public and institutional), I tend to get quite active. That is when the low hanging fruit is easy to pluck. Day trading does tend to alleviate the boredom if one is a constant participant in the market throughout the day.

I limit my expenses to $400 a month. Those are:

- Data feeds:                              $ 125
- Charting software:                  $ 60
- Books, Magazines, Newspapers:     $125
- Subscriptions to services:         $ 25
- ISP fees:                              $ 65

## My Trading Approach

With my approach, I take a position in a stock when the fundamentals of the company are strong and the price is compelling with a sound risk-reward opportunity. I must also see the potential for growth in earnings as some extraordinary event may raise the price of the stock. Extraordinary events might include a new product introduction, a pending FDA drug approval, or the potential for a merger.

I am comfortable with my ability to analyze the fundamentals of a company. I can dissect a balance sheet and income statement. I have a working knowledge of accounting. This is what gives me confidence and makes me self-reliant and serves to limit my risk exposure.

The reason for abandoning a position is that there has been a material change in the company fundamentals or in the outlook for the company. For me, a drop in the stock price is not the sole reason to liquidate a position.

In establishing a position, I do consider the price action and use technical analysis to aid me in timing my purchases. I do not chase price rallies. I tend to wait until the price has settled into a trading range and preferably toward the lower end of that range. I like to buy when nobody is interested. I will frequently scale into a position by buying a partial position and adding to it if the price moves lower.

My planned timeframe is one to two years for a position trade. Obviously, this may be interrupted by sudden price movements in either direction. If the price drops for no particular reason, I will not sell and may add to the position. If the price drops because of a change in fundamentals and/or outlook, I will probably sell.

I control my risk by understanding the fundamentals of the company and by avoiding companies with weak balance sheets. I stay away from hyped stocks and tend to concentrate on a population of companies that I am familiar with and whose fortunes I have observed for several years. I watch sector performance and try to avoid taking positions after major sector moves have occurred. Similarly, I watch the major indices and am very careful when the market as a whole becomes overbought or oversold.

At any given time, I may have as many as 20 trading positions.

That portion of my capital devoted to any single trade is usually confined to a maximum of 5% but many positions are smaller than 5%.

I use margin sparingly and only when I see an opportunity and do not wish to liquidate another position to take advantage of that opportunity. Normally I am not fully invested and have cash available in the account and do not use margin at all.

I am interested in owning stocks that match the following criteria:

## Sectors

I primarily concentrate on technology stocks for position trading. I gravitate toward Semiconductor, Semiconductor Equipment, Nanotech, Software, Telecommunications and Biotech companies.

## Stock Price

I have a preference for lower priced stocks although the price is not a primary consideration. (Yes, I know all of the advice that stipulates never to buy a stock under $5 … or $10 … or whatever. Advice is cheap and often wrong.)

## My criteria for entry

I consider fundamentals first to determine whether or not I want to own a stock. I prefer cash rich companies with little or no debt. I look at earnings and earnings growth (or potential earnings growth) to determine if I want to be involved. I try to gain a basic knowledge of the company's business model and obviously look for drivers of growth. Lastly, I consider the technical situation of the stock before establishing a position. I will average down in price (yes, I know all of the advice against that strategy) because the market often misprices stocks for a period of time and that mispricing can present a great buying opportunity. Mispricing is often a function of emotion when players are in a state of fear and capitulatory selling occurs.

## My criteria for exit

My exit strategy is usually based upon the stock reaching a pre-determined price objective based on earnings or potential earnings. As long as the company appears able to deliver earnings, I will not exit unless the price gets overextended. Technology stocks unfortunately tend to get extremely volatile on the upside and downside and I often use a price chart to determine when the price has become overblown in either direction. I generally look at the trading channel that the stock follows and will often sell if the price jumps above the upper channel band. I will often repurchase the position when it sinks back down toward the middle of the channel.

## My criteria for selling at a loss

I do not sell a position unless there is a fundamental reason not to own *that particular* stock or unless I see a fundamental reason not to own *any* stock. I will get out of the market completely if I feel that it is necessary.

## My Trading Tools

For my charting needs I use:

- AIQ Systems Trading Expert
- E-Signal
- MetaStock Professional

For a trading platform I use:

- Real Tick

# Scalper

Scalper, Full time, Primary income, 6 years experience.

## My Vision Statement

I am a hard-core scalper. The market produces a lot on noise in terms of any other timeframe and I use this noise to make money.

## My Financial Commitments and Objectives

My trading capital is $35,000.

My goal is to make an average of $500 a day.

My expenses for charting software, scanning software and trading room come to $525 a month.

## My Trading Philosophy

The market is my milking cow. It moves in order to give me my bread and butter. The only thing I care about is to find stock movements.

I understand the probabilities of trading. I have chosen the smallest timeframe because that is where the odds of moves in my favor are the highest.

Loss is an inherent part of trading. I do not hesitate a second to take it.

I do not see my trading as an overly risky activity. My trading is controlled very tightly thanks to small timeframes.

In my approach, a reason for taking a trade is momentum. I do not sit in the stocks that do not move. I hunt for fast movers.

The types of movement that I am trading are breakouts and reversals.

My trading is highly aggressive on breakouts and conservative on reversals.

## My Trading Psychology

I do not care about anything but an immediate move that I see and can read. I do not have problems with entry and exit. I take stops and profits with equal ease. Stops are easy to take for me because with my trading activity I will find another stock to trade very soon. Taking profits is even easier because I love booking profits. My self-control is absolute.

My ideal mindset is total disregard for everything but the movement that is right in front of my eyes. My trading is highly intuitive; I can literally feel the next several ticks when I look at a Level II screen. I have setups but it is intuition that a trade has to pass as a last test, before I pull the trigger.

My method to achieve a correct mindset is to use my model trader. Cheap Eddie is my model trader. It is Eddie who does all the trading. He is a cool, sarcastic and an arrogant guy. Eddie laughs at others when he wins and at himself when he loses. When a stock moves in his favor and buyers take his shares, he says "Look at this crowd". When a stock moves against him and he takes a stop, he says "Look at this idiot", pointing to himself. He never loses his cool. He is the first to admit his mistakes. He always, however, points out that he is right more frequently and at the end of the day, he makes money. His arrogance gives him strength to keep up with active trading. Eddie's attitude allows me to remove myself from trading my emotions. I just observe him trading.

## My Trading System

I rarely hold a stock for longer than 10-15 minutes. I trade NASDAQ stocks and e-minis. I trade stocks in a price range from $5 to $100.

I limit my losses to $100 per trade. I control my risk by tight stop losses. I trade one position at a time. I can apply full buying power to one position. I use margin to its full extent.

I set the following criteria to limit the risk of each particular trade:

- Volume: not less than 1 million shares per day.
- Spread: not more than .02-.03 cents; if wider, I will decrease my position size.
- Maximum length of candle: .10 cents. If longer, I will decrease my position size.
- Order sizes on Level II: 1,000 shares and higher; if less, I will decrease my position size.

I will not take a trade if possible slippage is more than 3 cents.

I apply chart patterns, tape reading and a 20 period Moving Average indicator on a one minute chart.

I use trend continuation chart patterns for breakouts; I use double bottom, triple bottom and reversed Head and Shoulders for reversals.

For breakouts, my entry signal is a pullback to support in a breakout pattern. I prefer 20 period MA to meet the price at that point, too. It is not necessary but a desirable condition. I trade breakouts at an intraday high only. I enter my trade just near support and set a stop just below support. This method allows me to keep my stops very tight. Most often, I sell my position when it bounces back to a resistance level. Sometimes when a stop size allows, I take a double position; then I sell the first lot near resistance and see whether I can get a breakout for the second lot. If I can, I sell it on a first spike above resistance.

For reversals, my entry signal is a conservative entry on price confirmation. I always take fast scalps on reversal trades, and never go for a double lot.

I never chase my entries. My profit targets are too small to afford chasing a stock.

As a trader utilizing momentum, I exit my trades with a loss as soon as they turn against me and lose support. I can scratch the trade and sell near breakeven if a trade takes too long to work. I prefer to go and look for another opportunity than to sit and wait.

I slow down my trading if I lose 3 trades in row. If after a break I lose on the fourth trade, I stop trading for the day.

When trading on the profitable side I press harder. I stop trading only when I feel tired and start losing concentration.

# Trader Taxation

*The issues relating to taxation of traders are very complex, and it is a specialized area of taxation. I recommend you consult with a tax professional regarding taxation issues. The following chapter is contributed by Meany & Dedek, LLC, who have operated www.edaytradertax.com for several years. Bob Meany, CPA, and Simona Dedek, CGA, CPA run a professional CPA firm that caters exclusively to active traders that are required to file returns with the U.S. IRS. I would like to thank them for the following introduction to the issues surrounding the beginning trader and taxation.*

To determine how you should be taxed as a trader can be a tricky issue. You first must determine what tax classification you are. The basic options open to the trader are:

- Investor
- Trader in Securities
- Mark to Market Trader

Traders can also employ more sophisticated strategies that involve creation of partnerships, LLCs, and Corporations (S-Corps). We will not get into those in this book intended for the trader just becoming oriented in the trading world.

## Investor

The IRS defines an investor as: "An investor is looking for capital appreciation in the value of his investments, or for income from dividends on such investments. He buys and holds his investments for longer periods of time." (*) Generally speaking, by default, everyone is an investor, unless additional steps are taken by the taxpayer. All security transactions would be recorded on a Schedule D. If the trades are too numerous, they can be summarized, but the IRS does require that you submit all the trades as an attachment to your tax return. Investor is also required to comply with the "wash sale" rules that are especially complicated and cumbersome for the active investor, and can negatively affect the ability to deduct losses. The capital gain (or loss), would then be transferred to your 1040 form. An investor is limited to a $3,000 net loss per year, any additional loss over this amount must be carried over to future years. Carryover of more than $3,000 is applied against future gains first. Investor expenses are included on Schedule A (itemized deductions), and by definition you can only deduct the portion of the expenses over 2% of your adjusted gross income. This Schedule A limitation can drastically affect your ability to deduct expenses, especially if you can't qualify for the itemized deduction.

## Trader in Securities

A trader is in the business of trading, to the point where his trading is clearly at a level where it constitutes "carrying on a business or a trade". Case law must be relied upon to determine if one qualifies as a trader, the IRS has not issued any black and white guidelines. Some questions you may ask yourself to determine if you fall into the trader classification would be:

- Do you spend a lot of time researching and executing your trades?
  "A lot of time" could be pegged at, say, 20 hrs a week. There are no official IRS guidelines.
- Can you show a regular and continuous pattern of averaging several trades during the hours the market is open? You can take vacations and breaks.

- Are you strictly in short-term positions?
  Getting in and out of all your positions on the same day proves you intend only to profit from short-term market swings, as is appropriate for trader.

- Do you hold longer term positions? Then make sure they are in a separate (investment) account if you wish to be considered a trader for the rest.

- Do your "yes" answers to the above questions apply to a continuous period of at least six months?

- Did you net profits after all your deductible expenses?
  All businesses have bad years, but the IRS says that a "real" business is generally profitable at least three out of each five years.

- Can you say you do not have another full time profession or job besides trading? IRS takes a skeptical view of part-time traders.

- Will you likely be claiming trader status in the tax year following this one? As you are in the business of trading stocks, a one year only commitment where you do not follow up with same status the following year would appear more along the lines of a hobby or an aborted investment effort.

- How many trading transactions do you execute in a given time period? The number of trades that qualifies and individual to claim trader status as opposed to an investor is conspicuously absent from the IRS guidelines and regulations. Rather, it is left up to the individual's discretion to make such a claim, and the burden of proof is upon the taxpayer in the case of a subsequent audit to prove his trading activities.

What are the benefits of claiming trader status for tax purposes? A trader continues to report his trading transactions on a schedule D like an investor, as capital gains and losses. He is subject to the same $3,000 net loss deduction like an investor, and needs to consider wash sale rules calculations just like an investor.

The main difference is that he can utilize Schedule C (Income or loss from a business) to report expenses associated with his trading (or the applicable form if he is a partnership or corporation).

Therefore, he:

1. eliminates the 2% of Adjusted Gross Income threshold that an investor is subject to
2. widens the list of allowable deductions because he is in the business of trading

It is important to note that a Schedule C trader in investments is NOT subject to self employment taxes.

## Mark to Market Trader

Now that you have determined that you may in fact, qualify for trader status, someone may ask you: Have you filed the Mark to Market (MTM) election? What is this election, and what does it mean to you?

Mark to Market is an accounting method. All taxpayers, generally speaking, are cash method taxpayers by default, meaning you report your income and expenses as received and paid in cash. A trader with an MTM election has irrevocably elected to forgo the cash method, and instead chooses to use the "Mark to Market" accounting method. A trader (or an investment dealer) will have an "inventory" of securities at year end, and MTM means he will mark them to market at that time as if they were sold on that date. Note, that for a true active trader, this may not really have a dollar impact at all in its purest application, because a trader would most likely be all in cash on the last day of his tax year and would not have any inventory to mark to market. This trader's cash net gain or loss would be exactly equal to the cash method trader's (please keep in mind that we assume that trader's investment accounts are properly segregated and he is not applying MTM to these).

The MTM trader however, will definitely appreciate the other benefits of MTM election. With the MTM election, the trader now reports all his trading activities and expenses on Schedule C (or applicable form if partnership or corporation), as income or loss from business. The trading transactions are reported on Form 4797. He might still use Schedule D for his investment account transactions. Also, the MTM trader can just forget about those pesky wash sale calculations – he is now exempt from them. He is also able to deduct cumulative losses in excess of the $3,000 that a trader or investor are limited to.

The catch is, that the trader has to determine by April 15 of the current year that he will want to change to the MTM accounting method for that tax year, and file the necessary paperwork with his timely tax return (or properly filed extension request, complete with required estimated payments) at that time for the year still in progress. No retroactive elections are permitted, no exceptions. In addition, the Form 3115 must be filed (change of accounting method) with the first MTM year's tax return. This is outlined in section 475 of the IRS regulations (*).

Section 475(b)(1) provides that the mark-to-market rules do not apply to any security held for investment. If you also invest for long term appreciation, this point is rather significant to you. You most likely would not want to apply MTM accounting to your long term investments, especially in appreciating markets. We advise our clients that the best way to avoid this is to ensure that their trading account(s) are segregated in completely separate accounts from their investment accounts. When you file the MTM election, ensure that you have specified the trading account in your application and the accompanying letter. That way, you will get the benefit of MTM treatment for your active trading, and benefit of long term tax shelter for your investments.

Important words of caution about the MTM election

The MTM election is not to be "jumped into" lightly. The IRS essentially treats this election as "permanent". In order to stop using this accounting method in the future, a trader has to file a request to revoke the election with the Commissioner. The only official ruling is that the Commissioner grants the revocation "under special circumstances".

Also, before considering the MTM method of accounting, the trader (or his accountant) needs to review his previous year's tax returns for existing carry forward capital losses. The MTM election turns the trader's profits into regular income from a business (they are capital gains and losses for the trader and investor), and as such, he will not be able to deduct carry forward capital losses against regular income.

## Tax Deductions for Investors and Traders

Investor – expenses deductible on a Schedule A:

| | |
|---|---|
| Investment Interest | If you borrow money and use it to buy property you hold for investment, the interest you pay is investment interest |
| Interest on margin accounts | If you are a cash method taxpayer, you can deduct interest on margin accounts to buy taxable securities as investment interest in the year you paid it. You are considered to have paid interest on these accounts only when you actually pay the broker or when payment becomes available to the broker through your account. Payment may become available to the broker through your account when the broker collects dividends or interest for your account, or sells securities held for you or received from you. |
| Limitation on Deduction of Investment Interest | Investment interest that exceeds net investment income is not deductible. Interest for which deduction is disallowed is treated as incurred in next tax year for which deduction is allowed |
| Expenses of Producing Income | Deduct investment expenses (other than interest expenses) as miscellaneous itemized deductions on Schedule A (Form 1040). To be deductible, these expenses must be ordinary and necessary expenses paid or incurred: 1) To produce or collect income, or 2) To manage property held for producing income. The expenses must be directly related to the income or income-producing property, and the income must be taxable to you. The deduction for most income-producing expenses is subject to a 2% limit that also applies to certain other miscellaneous itemized deductions. The amount deductible is limited to the total of these miscellaneous deductions that is more than 2% of your adjusted gross income |
| Attorney or accounting fees | You can deduct attorney or accounting fees that are necessary to produce or collect taxable income |
| Clerical help and office rent | You can deduct office expenses, such as rent and clerical help that you pay in connection with your investments and collecting the taxable income on them. |
| Fees to collect income | You can deduct fees you pay to a broker, bank, trustee, or similar agent to collect investment income, such as your taxable bond or mortgage interest, or your dividends on shares of stock. You cannot deduct any broker's fees, commissions, or option premiums you pay (or that were netted out) in connection with the sale of investment property. They can be used only to figure gain or loss from the sale |
| Investment counsel and | You can deduct fees you pay for counsel and advice about |

| advice | investments that produce taxable income. This includes amounts you pay for investment advisory services |
|---|---|
| Trading Rooms | You may deduct costs for trading chat rooms, research rooms etc |
| Safe deposit box rent | You can deduct rent you pay for a safe deposit box if you use the box to store taxable income-producing stocks, bonds, or other investment-related papers and documents |
| Subscriptions | You can deduct costs for financial magazines and newspapers such as IBD and WSJ, Active Trader Magazine |
| Telephone | You may deduct specific telephone long distance charges, cell phone charges, as long as you segregate investment and personal usage |
| Books | If you purchase books or guides for investment you may deduct these |
| ISP | You may deduct ISP fees and on line service costs, also you could include portions of satellite feeds, and cable costs. |
| Equipment/furnishings cost | You may deduct depreciation on computers, equipment, printers, software |
| Supplies | You may deduct postage, supplies such as paper, toner, etc |
| Record Keeping | Any costs you have for record keeping, clerical costs, filing, etc |
| Fees for Quote services | You may deduct fees for real time quote services, or fees for services such as Windows on Wall street, Worden Brothers, etc |

## Non-deductible Expenses

Some expenses that you incur as an investor are SPECIFICALLY NON DEDUCTIBLE.

| | |
|---|---|
| Stockholders' meetings | You cannot deduct transportation and other expenses that you pay to attend stockholders' meetings of companies in which you have no interest other than owning stock. This is true even if your purpose in attending is to get information that would be useful in making further investments. However if the meeting is to protect the value of the investment, you may be able to deduct some costs |
| Investment-related seminars | You cannot deduct expenses for attending a convention, seminar, or similar meeting for investment purposes |
| Tax-exempt income | You cannot deduct expenses you incur to produce tax-exempt income. Nor can you deduct interest on money you borrow to buy tax-exempt securities or shares in a regulated investment company (mutual fund) that distributes only exempt-interest dividends |

## Trader – Expenses Deductible on a Schedule C

All the expenses of trading are included on Schedule C, and therefore there is no 2% threshold, as applies to Schedule A for an investor. All of the investor deductions listed above are available to the trader, as well as a few more. They are as follows:

| | |
|---|---|
| Office in the Home | Since this is now classified as a business, home office expenses may also be deducted, up to the income produced, additional expenses can be deferred to future years. Specific limitations apply. |
| Seminars/Trading | You may deduct the cost of trading seminars, or educational conferences relating to trading. Again there are some limitations for deducting hotel, etc, when your spouse travels with you |
| Wages | Costs paid to family members or others you may employ for trading related work |
| Interest Costs | These are fully deductible as business expenses, and can even be credit card interest costs. Interest is classified now as business interest expense, not investment interest. You must segregate these interest costs on your credit card |
| Retirement Plans | If you are set up as a corporation, LLC, etc, you may be able to set up a retirement plan if you pay yourself a salary – you can use an IRA, or another vehicle |
| Auto and Travel | These expenses are deductible when they apply to any trader related activities |

Depending on your situation, many other expenses may be deductible, check with a qualified tax professional.

## Is There a Downside to Filing as a Trader?

Your tax return will end up looking rather strange – capital gains (or losses) on a Schedule D, and a negative Schedule C (all your expenses, no income). So, there is obviously an increased audit risk. It is a good idea to work with a tax professional well versed in the trader taxation area, to ensure that all your ducks are in a row and the audit risk is minimized. A properly filed trader return will stand up to IRS scrutiny. Your accountant will ask you many questions and will carefully research your individual situation before you suggesting this status.

## Mark to Market Election – What is the Attraction?

Mark to Market (MTM) traders also report their expenses on a Schedule C just like traders. And, as we discussed earlier, short term traders will generally have no inventory to Mark to Market. So, why bother going through with it?

First, your capital gains/losses are now considered ordinary business income and losses, and are not reported on Schedule D, but rather Part II of Form 4797. This is significant: if you have a loss, it can carried forward to future years, or even carried back. The entire loss may be claimed in one year against other income – the $3,000 capital loss limitation does not apply.

Second, you no longer have to be concerned with the cumbersome wash sale reporting rules, as required by law. These can get very complicated, and most of the time are either reported incorrectly by traders, or ignored altogether. The dollar impact of wash sale rule also cannot be discounted. We often see traders with cash losses who end up with taxable income, because of the application of wash sale rule.

So why don't more traders elect mark to market accounting? There are several reasons.

First, the election itself is very tricky. You must make the election when you file your previous year's tax return, or, basically, in advance. To have MTM accounting method applied to the tax year 2004, you would have to have elected it when you filed your timely 2003 tax return, by April 15, 2004. The IRS will not accept any late elections. The election itself, in addition to being filed with your return, must also be copied to the commissioner of the IRS. So, at this point, if you are thinking about MTM for 2005, you have to be ready to file this with your 2004 taxes (or properly filed request for extension) by April 15, 2005. Also, the election cannot be revoked without the approval of the commissioner of the IRS – it is virtually irrevocable.

Second, if you had a significant trading loss the previous year(s), and have capital loss carryover, you are still limited to $3k carry forward loss per year – you can't apply this loss against your MTM trader gains, because the will be ordinary income, rather than capital gains. if this is your case, carefully consider the MTM election and seek professional help – you may want to forego it, especially if you believe you will have a significant gain in the current year to offset previous years' losses.

There may be cases where you successfully segregate investment accounts to remain outside of the MTM election, and these could work to offset the carry forward capital losses, but this is not the appropriate place to go into the fine nuances of this and other sophisticated techniques. Again, please work with your tax professional, they can help you sort out what's best for you.

Third, in addition to the mark to market election, made with your previous years return, you must also submit a Form 3115 (Change in accounting procedure), with the current year (the first year where MTM is used). This form is confusing at best, and must be attached to your return, as well as a copy to the commissioner of the IRS.

## A Few Words in Parting

Information contained in this chapter is just that, information. It does not constitute specific taxation advice. Please seek help from your qualified tax professional before implementing any of the strategies touched upon here. This chapter was written for the target audience of traders in securities, not in futures or commodities, additional rules apply when trading in these.

### Resources for Trader Taxation

All the necessary definitions and forms referenced in this chapter can be found at www.edaytradertax.com/realitytrader.htm for your reference.

# Recommended Reading

**RR1** Edwin Lefevre, Reminiscences of a Stock Operator, John Wiley & Sons; 1994
All-time classic. Inspiring story of a great trader, generously sprinkled with astute observations on the market's inner workings and a trader's psychology.

**RR2** Justin Mamis, The Nature of Risk, Fraser Publishing Co.; 1999
Deep and thought-provoking analysis of the paradoxical nature of the market and relation between risk and profits.

**RR3** Humphrey B. Neill, Tape Reading & Market Tactics, Fraser Publishing Co.; September 1997
Classic book on tape reading principles. One of the early books written in 1930s that laid foundation of this method.

**RR4** Vadym Graifer, Christopher Schumacher, Techniques of Tape Reading, McGraw Hill; 2003
Tape reading principles revived and applied to today's markets. Analysis of a trader's development, beliefs and practical psychology.

**RR5** Vadym Graifer, How to Scalp Any Market and Profit Consistently; 2004
Description of scalping as a trading approach. Scalping techniques for NASDAQ stocks.

**RR6** Bo Yoder, Mastering Futures Trading, McGraw Hill; 2004
No-nonsense book that provides you with the tools you need to spot futures market trends, identify pending rallies or pullbacks. Bridging the gap between trading concepts and theory to practical application, this valuable guide shows traders the best futures strategies, concepts, and methods to master futures trading.

**RR7** Alan S. Farley, Master Swing Trader, McGraw-Hill Trade; 2000
The hidden world of the master patterns and powerful trading strategies that respond quickly to changing market conditions. Complete, practical guide to modern swing trading including over 180 illustrations and dozens of proprietary setups that illustrate both classic and original short-term tactics.

**RR8** Mark Douglas, Trading in the Zone, Prentice Hall Press; 2001
Trading psychology in depth. Powerful book with great insights into inner world of a trader.

**RR9** Richard McCall, The Way of the Warrior-Trader, McGraw-Hill Trade; 1997.
Trading psychology, practical and to the point.

**RR10** Stephen R. Covey, 7 Habits Of Highly Effective People, Free Press; 1990
Classic book on self-development. Not devoted specifically to trading, this book is extremely important for a trader, too.

**RR11** Robert Koppel, The Tao of Trading, Dearborn Trade Publishing; 1998
Market philosophy and trader's psychology.

**RR12**  Robert Koppel, The Intuitive Trader, John Wiley & Sons; 1996
Window into the world of trader's intuition.

**RR13**  Edward Allen Toppel, Zen in the Markets, Warner Books; 1992. Market philosophy. Simply written, brief and powerful.

**RR14**  John A. Tracy, How to Read a Financial Report: Wringing Vital Signs Out of the Numbers, Wiley; 1999

**RR15**  John A. Tracy, Accounting for Dummies, Hungry Minds Inc; 1997

**RR16**  Michael J. Gelb, Thinking for a Change: Discovering Power to Create, Communicate and Lead, Aurum Press; 1996. If you became interested in Mind Mapping techniques and applications, this book will be a great help in this regard.

**RR17**  Robert Edwards and John Magee, Technical Analysis of Stock Trends, Prentice Hall Art; 1991. The textbook for technical traders, this historic book will help the beginning trader build a good foundation of the principles of technical analysis. This is the "common knowledge" of T/A that the crowd uses, and therefore a firm grasp of these concepts is essential to successful trading.

**RR18** Rollo Tape, Studies in Tape Reading, Fraser Publishing; reprint 1982
Another classic in tape reading from 1910.by Richard Wyckoff.

**RR19**  H.J. Wolf, Studies in Stock Speculation, Fraser Publishing; reprint 1966. Yet another classic book on market philosophy and tape reading from 1924.

# Conclusion

In the course of reading this book, you went over the process of a trading plan. Create your trading plan with the outlined forms provided here and you will have a solid foundation for successful trading.

This is an exciting journey, with many peaks and valleys. In the course of it, you will learn considerable insight about yourself. This undertaking is also likely to change you as a person. Becoming a successful trader, you will also become more disciplined and responsible, more confident, self-reliant and decisive. You will learn a lot about risk and about your ability to handle it, to calculate and manage it.

Trading is both hard work and fun. It is going to provide you with endless stories to remember. It will be a source of pride and, becoming a successful trader, you will have a very good reason to be proud. Overcoming of one's flaws and bringing up the new person in oneself is an amazing achievement – and this is exactly what you are going to go through as you follow the course of this plan.

Have an interesting and rewarding journey!

Vadym Graifer

# Glossary

**Above the Market**
An order to buy or sell at a price set higher than the current market price of the security.

**Advance/Decline Line (A/D)**
A technical analysis tool representing the total of differences between advances and declines of security prices. The advance/decline line is considered the best indicator of market movement as a whole. Stock indexes such as the DJIA only tell us the strength of 30 stocks where as the A/D line provides much more insight.

**After Hours Trading (AHT)**
Trading after regular trading hours on the major exchanges.

**American Depository Receipt (ADR)**
A stock representing a specified number of shares in a foreign corporation

**American Depository Share (ADS)**
A share issued under deposit agreement that represents and underlying security in the issuer's home country

**Amex**
Abbreviation for American Stock Exchange, Inc.

**Arbitrage**
Attempting to profit by simultaneously purchasing and selling the same or equal securities in a manner which takes advantage of price differences prevailing in different markets.

**Ask (Price)**
The price a seller is willing to accept for a security, also known as the offer price.

**At the Market**
An order to buy or sell at the best available price.

**Bear**
A trader who acts on the belief that a security of the market is moving downward.

**Best Ask**
The lowest quoted ask price for a particular stock among those offered from competing market participants.

**Best Bid**
The highest quoted bid for a particular stock among all those offered by competing market participants.

**Bid**
An offer made by an investor, trader, or dealer to buy a security.

**Bid Ask Spread**
The amount by which the ask price exceeds the bid, also known as Spread

**Bid Price**
The price a buyer is willing to pay for a security

*Big Board*
Nickname for the New York Stock Exchange (NYSE).

*Blow-Off Top*
A steep and rapid increase in price followed by a steep and rapid drop in the price.

*Blue Chip Stock*
Stock of a well-established and financially-sound company that has demonstrated its ability to pay dividends in both good and bad times.

*Bollinger Band*
A band plotted two standard deviations away from a simple moving average.

*Bottom Fishing*
Buying stocks whose prices have dropped dramatically, based on the belief that the stock has reached bottom and will now rebound.

*Breadth Indicator*
A specific type of indicator that uses advancing and declining issues to determine the amount of participation in the movement of the stock market.

*Breakout*
A chart pattern used to indicate a rise in a stock's price above it's resistance level (such as it's previous high price) or a drop below it's support level (commonly the last lowest price).

*Bull*
A trader who acts on the belief that the market is going to move upward.

*Buy Stop Order*
An order to buy a security which is entered in at a price above the current offering price. It is triggered when the market price touches or goes through the buy stop price.

*Candlestick chart*
A price chart that displays the high, low, open, and close for a security for each period of time in a form of candles.

*CBOE*
Abbreviation for Chicago Board of Options Exchange.

*CBOT*
Abbreviation for Chicago Board of Trade

*Circuit Breaker*
Halt to trading implemented by a major stock or commodity exchange when an index falls beyond a predetermined amount in a session. This is done to prevent further losses.

*Clearing House*
A firm that guarantees the obligation of the parties in an exchange traded security or derivative transaction.

*Close*
The end of a trading session. The closing price is what is quoted in the newspaper.

*CME*
Abbreviation for Chicago Mercantile Exchange.

*Consolidation*
A term used mainly by technical analysts to refer to the movement of a stock's price within a well-defined pattern or barrier of trading levels.

*Consumer Price Index*
An inflationary indicator that measures the change in the cost of goods and service that the average consumer purchases.

*Cup and Handle*
A pattern on charts that resemble a cup with a handle. The cup is in the shape of a "U" and the handle as a slight downward drift. The right hand side of the pattern has low trading volume. It can be as short as seven weeks and as long as 65 weeks.

*Day Order*
Any order to buy or sell a security that automatically expires if not executed on the day the order is placed.

*Dead Cat Bounce*
A quick, moderate rise in the price of stock following a major decline.

*Depth*
A term describing the ability of security to absorb buy and sell orders. Related to *liquidity*. Securities can be thin or thick depending on their relative depth.

*Discretionary Order*
An order giving a broker the ability to decide when to buy/sell securities at the best possible price for the customer. Some discretionary orders place restrictive terms to limit the amount of discretion that broker has.

*Double Bottom*
A charting pattern used in technical analysis. It describes the drop of a stock (or index), a rebound, another drop to the same (or similar) level as the original drop, and finally another rebound.

*Double Top*
A term used in technical analysis to describe the rise of a stock, a drop, another rise to the same level as the original rise, and finally another drop.

*Double Witching*
The third Friday of months during which both options and futures expire.

*Dow Jones Average*
The most widely used Averages to track overall market conditions. There are four Dow Jones Averages: Industrial, Transportation, Utilities, and Composite. The Composite is simply the previous three combined.

*Dow Jones Industrial Average*
The single most widely used average. It is a price-weighted average of 30 actively traded blue chip NYSE stocks. It is thought to give one of the best overall indications of stock market conditions.

**Downtick**
A transaction where the stock price is lower than the previous transaction.

**Dow Theory**
A theory which is based on the belief that the fluctuations in the stock market are both a reflection of current business trends as well as a predictor of future business trends.

**Earnings per Share**
Total earnings divided by the number of shares outstanding.

**Electronic Communication Network (ECN)**
An electronic system that attempts to eliminate third parties orders entered by an exchange market maker or an over-the-counter-OTC market maker, and permits such orders to be executed either in whole or in part.

**Exponential Moving Average(EMA)**
A type of moving average that is similar to a Simple Moving Average, except that more weight is given to the latest data.

**Fibonacci Numbers**
A sequence of numbers where the next number in the sequence is equal to the sum of the previous two numbers. For example, 5, 10, 15, 25, 40, 65.

**Fighting the Tape**
A trader's action contradicting the trend.

**Flag**
A technical charting pattern that looks like a flag with a mast on either side. Flags result from price fluctuations within a narrow range, they mark a consolidation before the previous move resumes.

**Float**
The total number of shares publicly owned and available for trading. The Float is calculated by subtracting restricted shares from outstanding shares.

**Fundamental Analysis**
A method of determining a securities value based on the analysis of several factors, such as a company's earnings, sales, assets and growth potential.

**Futures**
A financial contract that encompasses the sale of financial instruments or physical commodities for future delivery, usually on a commodity will be at some date in the future.

**Futures Contract**
An exchange traded agreement to buy or sell a particular type and grade of commodity for delivery at an agreed upon place and time in the future. Futures contracts are transferable between parties.

**Gap**
Situation where the range of a stock price on two successive days does not overlap; open of the second day is higher (gap up) or lower (gap down) than the close of the previous day.

**Gap and Trap**
Situation where a price reverses after a gap, trapping traders that entered at the open.

### Good till Cancelled Order
An order which remains valid until executed or cancelled by the customer.


### Head and Shoulders Pattern
A technical analysis term used to describe a chart formation in which a stock's price:

1.) Rises to a peak and subsequently declines,
2.) Then, the prices rise above the former peak and again decline,
3.) And finally, rises again, but not to the second peak, and declines once more.

The first and third peaks are shoulders, and the second peak forms the head.

### Hedge
Taking an investment position in which some investments are designed to offset the risk of others.

### Index
A select sampling of stocks used to reflect the basic trends of the market.

### Index Futures
A futures contract on a stock or financial index, such as the S&P 500. Each index can have a different multiple for determining the price of the future.

### Indicator
Statistics which provide an indication of the trends of the particular security or the economy in general.

### Initial Public Offering (IPO)
The first sale of stock by a private company to the public. IPO's are often smaller, younger companies seeking capital to expand their business.

### Insider
Any person who has or has accessed to valuable non-public information about a corporation.

### Intrinsic Value
The value of a company or an asset based on an underlying perception of the value.

### Inverse Saucer
A technical chart formation that indicates the stock's price has reached its high and that the upward trend has come to an end.

### Large Cap
Companies having a market capitalization between $10 billion and $200 billion.

### Level I
An informational screen which shows current bid and ask price.

### Level 2 (Level II)
An informational screen which shows, in addition to the current bid and ask price, all market makers and ECN's at different price levels on the bid and ask.

### Limit-on-Close (LOC)
A Limit-on-Close Order that is placed prior to the market's close. If the closing price is not at or better than the submitted price, the order is cancelled, else the order will be executed at the closing price.

### Limit-on-Open (LOO)

A Limit-on-Open Order that is placed prior to the market's open. This type of order will work at the exchange the next morning at the market's opening. If the order does not execute at the limit price or better, the order is cancelled.

### Limit Order

An order in which the customer sets a maximum price he is willing to pay as the buyer or a minimum price he is willing to accept as the seller.

### Listed Stock

A stock that is traded on a NYSE or Amex.

### Liquidity

The degree to which an asset or security can be brought or sold in the market without affecting the asset's price significantly. Liquidity is characterized by a high level of trading activity and *depth*.

### Locked Market

A highly competitive market in which the bids and prices are the same.

### Maintenance Call

A call from the brokerage to the customer requesting that the customer deposit additional funds into their account in order to return the balance to its required level.

### Maintenance Margin

The amount of equity that must be maintained in a margin account.

### Margin

The use of borrowed money to purchase securities, referred to as "buying on margin".

### Margin Call

A call from the brokerage firm to the customer requesting that the customer deposit additional funds into their account in order to return the balance to its required level.

### Market-on-Close (MOC)

A Market-on-Close Order that is placed prior to the market's close. This type of order will act like a typical Market Order and be executed prior to the market's close.

### Market Makers

A brokerage or bank that maintains a bid and ask price in a given common stock by always being available to buy or sell at publicly quoted prices.

### Market-on-Open (MOO)

A Market-on-Open is a Market Order that is placed prior to a market's open. This type of order will act like a typical Market Order and be executed at the market's opening.

### Market Order

An order to buy or sell a stock immediately at the best available current price. A marker order guarantees execution.

### Mid Cap Stock

Short for "Middle Cap," mid cap refers to stocks with a market capitalization of between $2 billion to $10B billion.

**Momentum**
The rate or acceleration of a security's price or volume.

**Moving Average**
Frequently used in technical analysis, a Moving Average is an indicator that shows the average value of a security's price over a period of time. When calculating, you need to specify the time span, i.e. 200 days and so forth.

**NASD**
Abbreviation for National Association of Securities Dealers.

**NASDAQ**
Abbreviation for National Association of Securities Dealers Automated Quotations.

**National Best Bid and Offer (NBBO)**
A term applying to the SEC requirement that brokers must guarantee customers the best available ask price when they buy securities and the best available bid price when they sell securities.

**New York Stock Exchange**
The largest and oldest securities exchange in the United States.

**Odd Lot**
An amount of a security that is less than the normal unit of trading for that particular security.

**Option**
A privilege sold by one party to another that offers the buyer the right, but not the obligation, to buy (call) or sell (put) a security at an agreed-upon price during a certain period of time or on a specified date.

**Option Chain**
A way of quoting options prices through a list of all the options for a given security.

**Options Contract**
One options contract represents one hundred shares in the underlying stock. The quoting price of an option is per share.

**Order**
The instruction, by a customer to a brokerage, for the purchase or sale of a security with specific conditions.

**Overbought**
In technical analysis, it is a market in which the volume of buying that has occurred is greater than the fundamentals justify.

**Over-the-Counter Bulletin Board (OTCBB)**
An electronic trading service offered by NASD. Traditionally home to many small and micro cap companies, it is considered very high risk.

**Oversold**
In technical analysis, it is a market in which the volume of selling that has occurred is greater than the fundamentals justify.

**Outstanding Shares**
Total shares issued by a company

**P/E Ratio**
Abbreviation for Price/Earnings Ratio

**Painting the Tape**
A person or group making numerous trades without any real change in ownership occurring. This is done to create the impression that there is heavy activity related to the stock, thus encouraging others to trade in the stock. Practice is illegal.

**Point**
A Point is a common notion for one U.S. dollar in equity trading.

**Position Trader**
A trader who holds a long position for the long-term.

**Post-Market Trading**
Trading done after the regular market close

**Pre-Market Trading**
Trading done before the regular market opens.

**Print**
Actual trade posted with indication of price and amount of shares.

**Program Trading**
Computerized trading used primarily by institutional investors, typically for large volume trades. Orders from the trader's computer are entered directly into the market's computer system and executed automatically.

**Rally**
A substantial rise in the price level of the overall market, following a decline.

**Relative Strength**
A measure of price trend that indicates how stock is performing relative to other stocks in its industry.

**Resistance**
The price a stock or market can trade at, but cannot exceed, for a certain period of time. Often referred to as resistance level.

**Retracement**
A reversal in the movement of a stock's price, countering the prevailing trend.

**Reversal**
A sudden change in the price direction of stock or index.

**Reverse Split**
A reduction in the number of a corporation's shares outstanding that increase the par value of its stock or its earnings per share. The market value of the total number of shares (market capitalization) remains the same.

**Ripple**
A metaphor for a short-term market trend.

**Round Lot**
The normal unit of trading for a security, which is generally 100 shares of stock.

*Russell 3000*
An index that covers over 3000 common stocks. Considered an excellent indicator of how the overall market is doing.

*Saucer*
A technical charting formation that indicated that a stock's price has reached its low and that the downward trend has come to a close.

*Share Repurchase*
A company's plan to buy its own shares from the marketplace, reducing the number of outstanding shares. Typically, this is an indication that the company's management thinks the shares are undervalue.

*Short Sale*
A market transaction in which a trader sells borrowed securities in anticipation of a price decline.

*Short Selling*
The selling of a security that the seller does not own, or any sale that is completed by the delivery of a security borrowed by the seller. Short sellers assume that they will be able to buy the stock at a lower amount than the price at which they sold short.

*SIPC*
Abbreviation for Securities Investors Protection Corporation.

*Specialist*
A stock exchange member who specializes in particular securities. The specialist must maintain an inventory of those securities and be available to buy and sell shares as necessary to equalize trends and provide an orderly market for those securities.

*Spread*
The difference between the bid and the ask prices of the security or asset.

*Stock Split*
The division of a company's existing stock into more shares. In a 2-for-1 split, each stockholder would receive an additional share for each share formally held.

*Stop-Market Order*
A stop order becomes a market order to buy or sell securities or commodities once the specified stop price is attained or penetrated. A Stop order is not guaranteed a specific execution price, and may execute significantly away from its stop price. It is typically used to limit a loss or protect a profit.

*Stop-Limit Order*
An order placed with a broker to buy or sell at a specified price (or better) after a given stop price has been reached or passed.

*Stop Order*
An order to sell a stock when its price falls to a particular point, thus limiting an investor's loss (or locking in a profit). Also referred to as a *stop-loss order.*

*Support*
A tendency for a stock not to fall below a certain price. This is generally due to the stock being in short supply at that price.

### Swing Trading
A style of trading that attempts to capture gains in a stock in a course of several days.

### Technical Analysis
A method of evaluating securities by analyzing statistics generated by market activity, such as past prices and volume. Technical analysts do not attempt to measure a security's intrinsic value but rather use charts to identify patterns that can suggest future activity.

### 10-K
A report at the end of a company's fiscal year that must be filed with the SEC. The report contains in depth statistics on finance as well as operations.

### Tick
The minimum upward (up-tick) or downward (downtick) movement in the price of a security.

### Trailing Stops
A stop loss order that is to be executed when a stock is followed up dips down below a specified amount or when a stock is followed down, goes up above a specified amount.

### Trend
The general direction of the price of an asset or market in general.

### Trend Analysis
A type of technical analysis used to determine or locate significant trends in a security.

### Trendline
A line on the price or value chart of a security depicting the general direction the security is headed, either up or down.

### Triangle
A technical analysis pattern created by drawing trendlines along a price range that gets narrower over time because of lower tops and higher bottoms. Variations of a triangle include *'ascending'* and *'descending'* triangles. Triangles are very similar to wedges and pennants.

### TRIN
Short for TRader INdex. A technical analysis indicator calculated by taking the advances to declines spread and dividing that by the volume of advances to declines.

### Triple Bottom
A chart pattern which shows that a stock has attempted to penetrate a lower price level on three different occasions.

### Triple Witching
The third Friday of March, June, September and December, when option contracts and futures contracts expire on stock indexes. This often results in a chaotic trading on those contracts as well as the underlying securities.

### Volume
The number of shares or contracts traded in a security or an entire market during a given point.

### Warrant
A derivative security that gives the holder the right to purchase securities (usually equity) from the issuer at a specific price within a certain timeframe.

***Wedge***
A technical chart pattern composed of two converging lines connecting a series of peaks and troughs.

# Index

# Mail Order Form

**Special offer!**

Get $5.00 off for each copy ordered with an order for 3 or more.

If you don't see the *Master Profit Plan*, ask your bookstore to visit us at:

www.realitytrader.com/masterplan/

Meanwhile, we offer a mail order service for your convenience.

Just indicate the books you would like below. Then complete the section below and send your order with payment to us.

Buying a gift? Enclose a personal note or card and we will be pleased to send it with your order.

Please send us the following Vadym Graifer's books:

_____ copies of  The Master Profit Plan at $ _____ each.

$_____ + $3.50 shipping = $_____ each

Total books _____ = Total Price _____

_____ copies of How to Scalp any Market & Profit Consistently at $___ each.

$_____ + $3.50 shipping = $_____ each

Total books _____ = Total Price _____

_____ copies of Techniques of Tape Reading

$_____ + $3.50 shipping = $_____ each

Total books _____ = Total Price _____

Please see www.realitytrader.com/masterplan for current pricing.

## Method of Payment:

Enclosed is my international bank draft or money order payable to:

RealityTrading Investment Services
11089 168St.
Surrey, BC, Canada
V4N 5G6

Charge to:      Visa    Mastercard   Discover   Amex

Card no: _____ Expiry date _____

Exact Name on Credit Card _____

Exact Address of Credit Card Statement:

_____

_____

Signature: _____

Phone: _____ (In case we have a question about your order)

Sold to: _____

Name: _____

Shipping Address: _____

Street: _____

City: _____

Province/State: _____

Postal code/zip code: _____

Visit us at: www.realitytrader.com and join us for a 2 FREE week trial. Please contact us at: orders@realitytrader.com and we would be happy to respond to you.

ISBN 1-41204332-8